Yearbook of Phraseology 2
2011

Yearbook of Phraseology 2
2011

Managing Editor

Koenraad Kuiper

Editors

Harald Burger
Jean-Pierre Colson
Jarmo Korhonen
Annette Sabban

De Gruyter Mouton

ISBN 978-3-11-023619-4
e-ISBN 978-3-11-023620-0
ISSN 1868-632X
ISSN online 1868-6338

Bibliographic information published by the Deutsche Nationalbibliothek

The Deutsche Nationalbibliothek lists this publication in the Deutsche Nationalbibliografie; detailed bibliographic data are available in the Internet at http://dnb.d-nb.de.

© 2011 Walter de Gruyter GmbH & Co. KG, Berlin/Boston

Typesetting: Apex CoVantage, LLC, Madison, WI, USA
Printing: Hubert & Co. GmbH & Co. KG, Göttingen
∞ Printed on acid-free paper

Printed in Germany

www.degruyter.com

Managing Editor

Koenraad Kuiper
Department of Linguistics
University of Canterbury
Private Bag 4800
Christchurch 8020
New Zealand
E-mail:
kon.kuiper@canterbury.ac.nz

Editors

Harald Burger
Universität Zürich, Switzerland

Jean-Pierre Colson
Université catholique de Louvain, Belgium

Jarmo Korhonen
University of Helsinki, Finland

Annette Sabban
Universität Hildesheim, Germany

Review Editor

Andreas Langlotz, Université de Lausanne, Switzerland

Editorial Board

František Čermak
Univerzita Karlova v Praze,
Prague, Czech Republic

Dmitrij Dobrovol'skij
Russian Academy of Sciences,
Russian Language Institute, Moscow

Christiane Fellbaum
Princeton University, USA

Natalia Filatkina
Universität Trier, Germany

Csaba Földes
Pannonische Universität,
Veszprém, Hungary

Sylviane Granger
Université catholique de Louvain,
Belgium

Annelies Häcki Buhofer
Universität Basel, Switzerland

Erla Hallsteinsdóttir
Syddansk Universitet, Denmark

Salah Mejri
Paris XIII, France

Wolfgang Mieder
University of Vermont, USA

Antonio Pamies-Bertrán
Universidad de Granada, Spain

Andrew Pawley
Australian National University, Australia

Elizabeth Piirainen
Steinfurt, Germany

Kathrin Steyer
Institut für deutsche Sprache,
Mannheim, Germany

Diana van Lancker-Sidtis
New York University, USA

Alison Wray
Cardiff University, UK

Contents

Koenraad Kuiper
   Editorial ix

Articles

Sieb Nooteboom
   Self-monitoring for speech errors in novel phrases and phrasal
   lexical items 1

Mathilde Pinson
   The paradoxical success of *can (-ed) not help but V*: When the
   extragrammatical meets the non-compositional 17

Jeanette King and Caroline Syddall
   Changes in the phrasal lexicon of Māori: *mauri* and *moe* 45

Britta Juska-Bacher
   Helvetismen: Nationale und areale Varianten? Kodifizierung
   und sprachliche Realität 71

Gerald Delahunty
   Contextually determined fixity and flexibility in 'thing'
   sentence matrixes 109

Maria Freddi
   A phraseological approach to film dialogue: Film
   stylistics revisited 137

Laure Gardelle
Whoop her up, hit it, go it alone: The role of the personal
pronoun in the fossilization process   163

Book reviews

Hrisztalina Hrisztova-Gotthard: *Vom gedruckten Sprichwörterbuch
zur interaktiven Sprichwortdatenbank*. (Britta Juska-Bacher)   179

Harald Burger: *Phraseologie. Eine Einführung am Beispiel des
Deutschen*, 4., neu bearbeitete Auflage. (Sylvia Jaki)   182

Meng Ji: *Phraseology in corpus-based translation studies.*
(Łucja Biel)   186

Christine Fourcaud: *Phraseologie und Sprachtransfer
bei Arte-Info*. (Tamás Kispál)   191

Editorial

Data and theory in phraseology

KOENRAAD KUIPER

This second volume of the *Yearbook of Phraseology* again contains an international and intercontinental community of authors showing that phraseology is of interest the world over. The range of approaches and leading questions in this year's *Yearbook* also shows how various are the data and theories which the domain of phraseological phenomena can give rise to.

This raises the issue of the place of linguistic theory in an account of phraseological phenomena. The issue receives some clarification if we consider phraseological units as lexical units, units stored and retrieved from the mental lexica of native speakers. As such they share properties with other lexical units, namely words, both simple and compound. Here the place of theory specifically in morphology is just as vexed because the human mental lexicon is not uniform in its nature, thus unlike the physical universe. It is, as Edwin Williams and Anna-Maria Di Sciullo pointed out in a memorable but not entirely satisfactory metaphor, like a prison in having as its inhabitants those who have broken a law. Lexical items are, to put it less memorably, idiosyncratic but not totally. Not all their properties are unpredictable. Chaos and anarchy do not reign in the prison house of the mental lexicon.

Wouldn't it be sensible if the lexicon contained words which were formed in a consistent manner? Let's say that those who produced works of art were all < action to create a work of art – er > s on the model of *painter*. But that is not the case. We have poets, novelists, playwrights and short story writers in the literary domain. What a number of this year's studies show is how much careful work there has to be to understand the idiosyncrasies of even one small family of phrasal lexical items. Do the local generalizations that apply to this little family of phrasal lexical items generalize to others? Usually not. But that is also the case in morphology. Many of the generalizations in morphology hold over quite limited domains and there are often exceptions. It is the case that most English compound nouns have primary stress on the first word rather than the second. But not all.

So should we give up trying to theorize about the phrasal lexicon? Not at all. We can only begin to understand the richness of human lexical knowledge if we both collect and analyse coherent data sets, and then try to understand how these are represented in the mental lexicon by proposing theories that explain this knowledge. Such theories then need to be tested.

I am grateful to the following for special help. First my fellow editors and the reviewers without whom this volume would not have come into existence. Everyone was efficient, punctual and helpful. The reviews are an important function for the *Yearbook* even when submissions are rejected since authors receive the views of their peers and can learn from them. A special thanks goes to Olivier Simonin who acted as an intermediary in having papers from the phraseology conference he organised in Perpignan submitted to the *Yearbook*.

Self-monitoring for speech errors in novel phrases and phrasal lexical items

SIEB NOOTEBOOM

Abstract

The preparation and production of phrasal lexical items (PLIs), e.g. proverbs, sayings, idiomatic expressions, collocations, clichés etc. is hypothesized to be more automatic than the preparation and production of novel phrases. Automatic processes are known to be less error prone and for that reason also less closely monitored for errors than are novel processes. Therefore it is predicted that speech errors occurring during the production of phrasal lexical items, although less frequent, will be less often detected and repaired than speech errors arising during the production of novel phrases. This prediction is tested against a corpus of speech errors and their repairs in spontaneous Dutch. Phrases containing speech errors with or without repairs were changed back into their intended equivalents, and the resulting phrases were subjectively classified as PLIs or novel phrases by three non-naive linguistic experts. The classification was checked against frequency of usage of these phrases, on the presumption that PLIs will, in general, be more frequent in corpora than novel phrases. The repair rate of speech errors was found to be significantly lower in PLIs than in novel phrases.

Keywords: speech production; phonology; speech errors; self-monitoring; phrasal lexical items.

1. Introduction

This paper concerns self-monitoring for phonological speech errors during the production of novel phrases and phrasal lexical items (PLIs). Novel phrases are assumed to be prepared by the speaker in the act of speaking, not part of what is stored in the speaker's mental lexicon. PLIs are assumed to be known as components of what a native speaker knows as part of his/her knowledge of the native language. The difference between novel phrases and PLIs is significant for language use. As is well known to foreign-language teachers, native-like fluency in a language is dependent on the number of PLIs known by the language user (e.g. Ketko 2000). It has been observed that English, for a large part, is *formulaic* (Bolinger 1975; Pawley and Syder 1983; Van Lancker-Sidtis 2004; Kuiper 2009), meaning that many utterances contain PLIs. Pawley and Syder estimate that there are hundreds of thousands of such PLIs in the lexicon of English. Jackendoff (1995) estimates 10,000–15,000 different English idiomatic phrases as having been used as stimulus items during 10 years in the TV-show "Wheel of Fortune" alone (idiomatic phrases or idioms are semantically non-compositional PLIs, Fraser (1970). There is no reason to think that the dependence on PLIs in linguistic performance will be different in other comparable languages.

Unfortunately for those who like clearly delimited classes, the distinction between novel phrases and PLIs is far from clear-cut. We may think of PLIs as *phrasal chunks* that are stored in the mental lexicon, whereas novel phrases are not so stored. But it is not always easy to know what precisely is stored in the mental lexicon and in what form. Proverbs provide more or less canonical examples of PLIs, being complete sentences that seem to be mentally stored as units, just as words are. But obviously proverbs retain their syntactic structure to the extent that speakers can make variations on them, as in *a new broom sweeps clean*, *new brooms sweep clean*, a *new broom sweeps cleaner than you will like* etc. Most idioms have explicitly open places to be filled by the speaker in the act of speaking: *He / she / John / my mother-in-law / etc. is pushing up daisies*. Also in restricted collocations like *dry wine, white coffee, white noise* the meaning of the adjective is restricted by the noun, and in this sense lexically determined. But this non-compositionality of meaning is not always complete: in idioms the literal meanings of the words may contribute to the idiomatic meaning of the phrase (Nunberg, Sag & Wasow 1994). Also non-compositionality is not a defining property of PLIs. There are PLIs such as *take note of, offer hospitality* that seem to have compositional readings, but nonetheless definitely are PLIs in the sense that native speakers know that this is how one says such things.

How are PLIs represented in the mental lexicon and how are they activated during speech production? Swinney & Cutler (1979) proposed that idiomatic expressions, the most studied variety of PLIs, are stored in the mental lexicon as long ambiguous words. This implies that idioms perhaps might have word-like morphological properties but not sentence-like syntactic and semantic properties. In contrast, later theories assume that idiomatic expressions and presumably other PLIs are not only themselves lexical units, but also consist of constituent lexical units, and more importantly have sentence-like syntactic and semantic properties (Cacciari and Tabossi 1988; Cutting and Bock 1997; Levelt and Meyer 2000). According to those theories one would predict that idiomatic expressions and other PLIs can not only be themselves units involved in lexical speech errors, but also that their constituent words can be involved in speech errors as they can in novel phrases. Levelt and Meyer (2000) coined the term *superlemmas* for internalized syntactic representations of PLIs, and supposed that a superlemma, once activated from its associated lexical concept, activates the constituent word lemmas of the PLI. Kuiper et al. (2007) analyzed collections of speech errors involving *Multi-word Lexical Items* or MLIs, MLIs comprising both PLIs and compounds. Importantly they found that all the speech error types known to occur in novel phrases also occur in MLIs. They found a number of error types characteristic of MLIs such as blends of MLIs and several types of errors where MLIs interact with semantically related single words. These error types and their distribution are predicted by Levelt and Meyer's superlemma theory, thus lending further support for this theory.

Assuming then that this theory is valid, one learns from it that the preparation in production of PLIs is, apart from the additional step required by the activation of the superlemma, quite similar to the preparation in production of novel phrases, with one additional important difference. The syntactic structure and word lemmas of a PLI are activated by its superlemma. This extra step in the generation process presumably takes time, and therefore one would predict that, other things being equal, production of a PLI takes more time than production of a novel expression. This is indeed suggested by research reported by Sprenger, Levelt & Kempen (2006). However, their results also show that, although idiomatic expression may take somewhat longer time to be prepared for production than novel expressions when expressions are not primed by context, idiomatic expressions are prepared for production significantly faster than novel expressions when one of the words in the expression is primed by identity priming. This is accounted for by assuming that priming of idiomatic expressions impinges not only on the word concerned but also on the expression as a whole, thus boosting all words in the expression. This has the consequence that less mental computation is needed in preparing PLIs than in preparing novel phrases. In everyday speech most often PLIs will be related to their preceding context or situation. We may assume then that in normal speech communication preparing a PLI is more routine, more automatic, than preparing a novel phrase. Automatic mental processes are more efficient, require less conscious guidance and monitoring than novel processes, and therefore use fewer attentional resources (Wheatley and Wegner 2001). An important reason that automatic processes require less monitoring than novel processes is that automatic mental processes are less error prone than novel ones. From these considerations one would expect that the probability of a speech error occurring in a phrase would be less for PLIs than for novel phrases. Whether this is the case is as yet unknown. There does not seem to be an easy way to test this prediction on collections of speech errors in spontaneous speech, because in most collections of speech errors there is no easy way to quantify this probability. There is, however, another related prediction one can derive. If PLIs are more automatic than novel phrases, and automatic processes require less monitoring because they are less error prone, then it is to be expected that speech errors made in PLIs will be less often detected and repaired by self-monitoring than speech errors in novel phrases. Below, this prediction is tested against a corpus of speech errors in spontaneous spoken Dutch.

2. Are speech errors less often repaired in PLIs than in novel phrases?

2.1. *The corpus*

The corpus of Dutch speech errors used here contains 2,455 errors in Dutch spontaneous speech, collected some twenty-five to thirty years ago in the Phonetics Department of Utrecht University (Schelvis 1985). For current purposes it is important to note that the collectors, all staff members of the Phonetics Department, were instructed to write down each error with its repair, if it was repaired. Note that the collecting of speech errors is potentially error prone (cf. Cutler 1982). Some errors may more easily escape detection by the observers than others. More specifically, it seems likely that unrepaired speech errors are more often missed than repaired speech errors, because the repairs are conspicuous and therefore easily observed interruptions of normal fluent speech. Thus the observers' bias would probably cause an overestimation of the relative number of repaired speech errors, and an underestimation of the relative number of unrepaired speech errors. It is also possible that there is an observer bias in the sense that speech errors in novel phrases are more easily observed than speech errors in PLIs. Thus potentially both unrepaired speech errors and speech errors in PLIs would be underrepresented in a corpus of speech errors. However, the relevant question here is whether or not these two biases are mutually dependent. I see no reason why the potential effect on error detectability of lexicalizedness on the one hand and of being unrepaired on the other would be mutually dependent. If they are independent, our specific hypothesis remains testable despite potential observers' biases underestimating the proportion of unrepaired errors and of errors in PLIs.

2.2. Paradigmatic and syntagmatic speech errors

Speech errors can be classified as paradigmatic and syntagmatic speech errors (Rossi & Defare 1998). An example of a paradigmatic error is when someone says a *verbal outfit* instead of *a verbal output*, where the substitution of one word by another cannot be traced to another element in the speaker's message. Examples of syntagmatic errors are exchanges like *teep a cape* instead of *keep a tape*, where two elements in the same message are interchanged, anticipations like *alsho share* instead of *also share*, where an element comes earlier than it should, often replacing another element, and perseverations like *John gave the boy* being spoken as *John gave the goy*, where an element is mistakenly repeated (all examples taken from Fromkin 1973). In syntagmatic speech errors one can distinguish between the *source* of the speech error, i.e. the position where a particular element should have been, and the *target*, i.e. the position where a misplaced element ends up. Here I will concentrate on syntagmatic errors, because paradigmatic speech errors generally involve only a single word. There is thus no way of knowing how much of the context should be taken into account when assessing whether this error occurred in a PLI. In syntagmatic errors at least one can examine the sequence of words including both source and target. Of the 2,455 errors in the corpus, there were 1,085 syntagmatic errors.

Of the 1,085 syntagmatic errors there were 163 lexical errors, all others were phonological speech errors. To keep the data set as homogeneous as possible, the lexical errors were removed. The remaining set of 922 phonological errors contained a number of errors in other languages than Dutch, mostly English. These were also removed, leaving 901 errors.

2.3. Length: the distance between source and target

Of these 901 remaining phonological errors 214 errors had the phonological source and target within the same word. Very often in the corpus only this single word containing source and target of the speech error, and, where applicable, the repair of the speech error, were noted down, making it impossible to find out whether or not this word was part of a PLI in the original context. For this reason all these cases were removed from the data set. This left 687 speech errors.

In many, if not in most cases, the complete expression, novel or lexicalized, within which a speech error occurs, is longer than the sequence of words including source and target of the error. It would be reasonable to assess the novelty or lexical nature of the complete expressions. Unfortunately, in many cases in the corpus of speech errors the complete expression is unknown, simply because the observer left out everything before and/or after the sequence of words including source and target. In order to follow the same procedure for all expressions, in all remaining cases everything before and after the sequence of words including source and target was removed. The error-containing sequences of words resulting from this procedure show considerable variation in length, from two to nine words.

2.4. *Novel and lexicalized: first impression*

In all remaining word sequences containing a speech error, the speech error and its repair, if it was repaired, were removed by changing the phrase back to its intended form. Most of the resulting word sequences did not form complete sentences and very many did not even have a finite verb form. But a first inspection showed that there are at least four different classes of such word sequences that probably should not be collapsed in further analysis.

One class is formed by those word sequences that are in themselves almost certainly PLIs, mostly collocations, comparable to English *knife and fork, black and blue, head of lettuce, world wide, one day a week* or *Barack Obama*.

A second class is formed by word sequences that might well be PLIs but probably not for all users of the language. Examples in English might be *decimal value* or *gross national product*. A particular class of uncertain cases consists of combinations of given and family name, or combinations like *John and Mary*. There is no way of knowing whether such combinations were or were not so familiar to the speaker at the time in order for them to be considered PLIs. For this reason all 28 such name combinations were removed from the data set, leaving 659 word sequences for further analysis.

A third class consists of those word sequences for which there is no reason to believe that they are PLIs or parts of PLIs. Examples in English would be *may lengthen a vowel, rapidly empty John, corner at Jacobs,* or *brake with my left foot.*

Finally, a somewhat special fourth class consists of combinations of function words, English examples being *in the, you at, they are on, from it, in on that.* It seems unlikely that these sequences constitute themselves as PLIs. They may or may not have been part of longer PLIs, but they equally likely may have been part of novel phrases. In this respect they form a source of uncertainty in the data.

2.5. Assessing novelty and lexicality of word sequences

The data set of 659 word sequences, from which the speech errors and their repairs were removed by changing these word sequences back into the correct intended word sequences, was presented to three linguistically non-naive judges, not including the current author. These linguists were native speakers of Dutch and familiar with the notions of novel phrases and PLIs as used here. Each judge was asked to assign one of four possible codes to each word sequence, defined as follows:

1. This word sequence is itself a PLI, or very likely part of a PLI.
2. This word sequence might well be a PLI or part of a PLI, but I am not certain of it.
3. This word sequence is not a PLI or part of a PLI.
4. This word sequence is a combination of function words that very likely does not in itself form a PLI.

The resulting judgments were further reduced in the following way. In 24 cases at least one of the three judges had assigned code 4 (combination of function words) to the word sequence, but the others had not. Where the judges differed this was mostly because of a difference of opinion as to whether certain auxiliary or modal verbs and certain adverbs are or are not function words. To be on the safe side, all these 24 cases were given the code 4 in order to keep them separate in further analysis.

In all 635 remaining cases agreement among judges was as follows: 386 cases where all three judges agreed, 215 cases where 2 of the 3 judges agreed, and 34 cases in which all three judges had a different judgment. In these 34 cases assignments of necessity were 1, 2, and 3, reflecting the degree of (un)certainty about the lexicalizedness of the word sequence. Therefore these were assigned the code 2. In all remaining cases the majority of the three judges was followed, giving 92 cases with code 1 (PLI),

75 cases with code 2 (perhaps a PLI), and 468 cases with code 3 (novel phrase).

In order to find support for this intersubjective approach, and on the assumption that PLIs have a higher than chance frequency in text corpora, the Yahoo frequency of all 659 word sequences was assessed, with Yahoo counting limited to Dutch and to the exact word sequence, using quotation marks. It should be noted that frequency of usage of multi-word sequences cannot reliably be assessed from existing linguistic corpora such as the Corpus of Spoken Dutch (Oostdijk and Broeder 2004), because even a corpus of 10,000,000 words is simply not big enough for determining reliable frequencies of multiword sequences. Admittedly, frequency counts by web browsers provide, at best, a rough measure, first because they are based solely on documents accessible to these browsers which have not been selected with a view to creating a balanced corpus, second because in the counting many documents may be accessed multiple times, and third because the web browsers, in estimating the reported frequencies, extrapolate from the actual counts employing rules unknown to us (for pros and cons of using web browsers in assessing frequency estimates see Janetzko 2008). Nevertheless the Yahoo frequency often appears to provide intuitively plausible outcomes, and may thus be used as circumstantial evidence. A similar exercise with Google frequencies basically gave the same results, and will not be reported here. The Yahoo frequencies found were transformed by taking the ^{10}log. In all those cases where the actual Yahoo count was 0, this 0 was set to 1 so that the ^{10}log was 0.

The data set for further analysis thus consists of 659 word sequences, each word sequence being the intended form of a word sequence in which a phonological speech error had occurred. Of each word sequence it is known whether it is (part of) a PLI, perhaps (part of) a PLI, or (part of) a novel phrase, or a combination of function words. Also the ^{10}log Yahoo frequency is known. Further it is known whether the original phonological speech error made in that sequence was an anticipation, a perseveration, or an exchange, and what the number of words in the word sequence is. These data are the basis of all further analysis, seeking an answer to the question if speech errors in PLIs are less often repaired than speech errors in novel phrases.

2.6. *Analysis of the data*

Before any further analysis, the classification following from our three judges was checked against the ^{10}log frequency obtained from Yahoo. Figure 1 gives the basic breakdown of the data, where *lexic* stands for (part of)

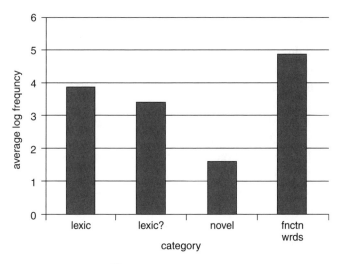

Figure 1. *Average ^{10}log frequency obtained from Yahoo for four classes of word sequences, definitely lexicalized (lexic; N = 92), perhaps lexicalized (lexic?; N = 75), novel (novel; N = 468), and combinations of function words (fnctn wrds; N = 24).*

a PLI, *lexic?* for perhaps (part of) a PLI, *novel* for (part of) a novel phrase, and *fnctn wrds* for combinations of function words.

The data were analyzed with a simple Univariate one-way Analysis of Variance, giving a significant effect of category on log frequency (df = 3; F = 97; p < 0.001). A post hoc analysis using Tukey's showed that *lexic* and *lexic?* were not significantly different, whereas all other contrasts were. The very high average log frequency of combinations of function words suggests that log Yahoo frequency in itself is not a good criterion for deciding whether or not a particular word sequence is (part of) a PLI. Whereas one may expect that many PLIs (not being proverbs) have a relatively high frequency of usage, individual highly frequent word sequences are not necessarily PLIs. There is no way of knowing whether a particular combination of function words stems from a novel phrase or from a PLI. This category is therefore excluded from further analysis. Thus the number of word sequences is reduced from 659 to 635. To this set of data, excluding the anomalous combinations of function words, a new Univariate one-way Analysis of Variance was applied, followed by a post hoc analysis using Tukey's, with estimated lexical category as fixed effect and log Yahoo frequency as dependent measure. The effect of estimated lexical category is highly significant (df = 2; F = 110; p < 0.001). There is no significant difference between *lexic* and *lexic?* and both categories differ significantly from *novel*. The big and significant difference between *lexic* and *lexic?* on the one hand and *novel* on the other, supports the intersubjective classification following from our three judges. The fact that *lexic* and *lexic?* do not differ much and not significantly in their log frequency suggests that these two categories may be collapsed in our further analysis.

An initial analysis of the repair data is presented in Figure 2. Here the actual fractions repaired as found in the corpus are presented for *lexic+* (collapsing *lexic* and *lexic?* from Figure 1) and *novel* phrases, separately for anticipations (*antic*), perseverations (*persev*) and exchanges *(exchan)*.

The data in Figure 2 at first sight are somewhat mysterious. Apart from a tendency that, as predicted, the fraction repaired is higher in novel phrases than in PLIs, there is a much greater effect on fractions repaired of the speech error class, viz. anticipations versus perseverations versus exchanges. Notably the *fraction repaired* is very low in the exchanges, and here also higher in PLIs than in novel phrases. This is worrying because the difference in *fraction repaired* and the difference in effect of lexicalizedness on *fraction repaired* between error categories may cause trouble for our further statistical analysis. The difference in *fraction repaired* is also unexpected because, where anticipations and perseverations contain a single speech error, an exchange contains two speech errors, viz. an anticipation and a perseveration. This gives not one but two chances that the error is detected and repaired. One thus would expect *fraction repaired* to be considerably higher for exchanges than for anticipations and perseverations. The

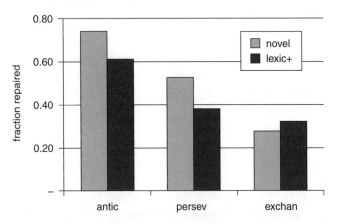

Figure 2. *Fractions repaired as found in the corpus for novel and lexic+ phrases, separately for phonological anticipations (antic; N = 391), perseverations (persev; N = 164) and exchanges (exchan; N = 80).*

following argument, provided by Nooteboom (2005), makes clear why in a corpus of speech errors repaired exchanges are more frequent and repaired anticipations less frequent than one would expect.

When a speaker, in mentally preparing an utterance for speaking, makes a phonological exchange such as *Yew Nork* for *New York*, this exchange exists in his or her internal speech for a short while before it is spoken. The speaker has now several chances to detect the error. First he or she may detect and repair the error in internal speech even before the first word *New* is spoken. If so, the chances are that the error is detected and repaired before it is realized, and the external world will never know that an error has been made and repaired in internal speech. Secondly, the speaker may detect an error after the first element has been spoken and before the second element has been spoken. Note that in this situation, the speaker may either detect the anticipation already made or the perseveration that is yet to come in overt speech but already present in the speaker's internal speech. Therefore the probability for error detection should be considerably higher for exchanges than for single anticipations and perseverations. However, we cannot see this in the corpus of speech errors because all such cases of repaired exchanges are classified as repaired anticipations. Thirdly, the speaker may detect that an error has been made after the second error (in our example *Nork)* has begun to be spoken. These latter cases are the ones that are classified as repaired exchanges in the corpus. The very low fraction of repaired exchanges can now be explained by assuming that most exchanges in internal speech that are repaired at all, are detected and repaired after the first element and before the second element of the exchange is realized in speech. All these cases end up in the corpus as repaired anticipations (cf. Nooteboom 2005).

For the purpose of this paper the relevance of the above reasoning is that it makes little sense to keep anticipations and exchanges separate as they have been in the corpus of speech errors. It would make sense to keep separate the anticipations and exchanges as they are made in internal speech, because the dependent measure in the further analysis, *fraction repaired*, apparently is not the same for these two classes of errors. Unfortunately there is no way to tell which repaired anticipations stem from misclassified exchanges and which do not. For this reason anticipations and exchanges were collapsed into a single category, *anticipations+*, to be kept separate from the category of perseverations. This leads to the breakdown of the data presented in Figure 3.

The data in Figure 3 were analyzed with a logistic regression using effect coding, with as dependent binomial variable *fraction repaired* and as

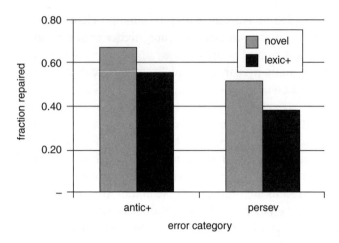

Figure 3. *Fractions repaired of speech errors made in anticipations plus exchanges (antic+; N = 333) and perseverations (persev; N = 134), separately for novel and lexicalized (lexic+) expressions. Both main effects are significant.*

Table 1. *Estimated parameters for the best fitting binomial logistic regression model of fraction repaired using effect coding. The grand mean was used as 'intercept'. For fixed effects, regression coefficients are given, with standard errors, t values and p values. Due to the structure of the data set with no repetitions for speakers or for word sequences, there are no random effects.*

effects	coef.	s.e.	t	p
intercept = grand mean	0.594	0.024	24.01	<0.001
novel/lexic+:	+/−0.129	0.055	−2.33	<0.020
antic+/persev:	+/−0.151	0.049	−3.05	<0.003
interaction:	0.020	0.110	0.18	<0.860

fixed factors *novel versus lexicalized+* and *anticipation+ versus perseveration*. The grand mean was used as intercept. The best fitting model showed no interaction between the two fixed factors, and showed a significant effect of both '*anticip+* versus *persev*' ($p < 0.003$) and '*novel* versus *lexic+*' ($p < 0.02$). Table 1 gives the relevant analysis results. For a discussion of this type of logistic regression see Johnson 2008.

That the *fraction repaired* is considerably and significantly higher for anticipations plus exchanges than for perseverations can be explained by the many errors in this category that are half-way repaired exchanges for which the fraction repaired is expected to be much higher than for perseverations. That the fraction repaired is significantly higher for novel phrases than for PLIs confirms the main hypothesis tested in this paper.

3. Discussion

The basic assumption underlying the current study is that the preparation and production of PLIs such as proverbs, sayings, idiomatic expressions, collocations and clichés is more automatic than the preparation and production of novel phrases. This assumption is captured in the superlemma theory of Levelt & Meyer (2000). As it is known that automatic processes in the human mind are more efficient and less error prone than novel processes, one would expect that fewer speech errors are made in PLIs than in novel phrases. Whether this is indeed the case is yet to be investigated. But it is also known that more automatic processes are less guided by monitoring than novel processes (Wheatley and Wegner 2001). One therefore expects that, if speech errors are made in PLIs, they will be less often detected and repaired by self-monitoring than speech errors in novel phrases. The current study of repaired and unrepaired phonological speech errors in spontaneous Dutch shows that this is indeed the case.

In a first attempt to demonstrate the hypothesized lower fraction repaired for PLIs than for novel phrases, the effect was found for phonological anticipations and perseverations but not for exchanges. This potentially weakened the conclusion. Therefore the deviant pattern in exchanges was in need of explanation. It was observed that speech errors classified as repaired exchanges were less frequent, and speech errors classified as repaired anticipations were more frequent than one would expect. This can be explained by assuming that impending exchanges in internal speech that are repaired after the first and before the second part of the speech error is spoken, are classified as repaired anticipations from which they cannot be distinguished. If one corrects for this misclassification, on the basis of the distribution of repaired and unrepaired perseverations, it turns out that all three classes of speech errors, anticipations, perseverations and exchanges, have a more similar distribution (cf. Nooteboom 2005). This implies that in internal speech there are more exchanges than one would derive from the classification of overt errors in corpora. Following further data analysis, sets of repaired anticipations and repaired exchanges had to be collapsed because one has no way of knowing whether specific repaired anticipations in the corpus in fact were or were not half-way repaired exchanges in inner speech. However, the hypothesized lower fraction repaired for PLIs than for novel phrases clearly stands out in the final analysis, thus confirming the main hypothesis of the current study.

The fact that common phonological (and lexical) speech errors are made in PLIs such as proverbs, sayings, idiomatic expressions, collocations and clichés supports those theories of phrasal lexical expressions that assume that each such expression not only has its own lexical entry, called *superlemma* by Levelt & Meyer (2000), but also that each superlemma activates the lemmas for the words that are constituents of the expression. The finding that such speech errors are significantly less often repaired in lexicalized than in novel expressions can be explained by assuming that these errors are less often detected either in inner speech (cf. Nooteboom & Quené 2008) or in overt speech (for the difference between self-monitoring inner and overt speech, see Nooteboom 2010). This suggests that, as one might expect, the preparation and production of PLIs is more automatic and less closely monitored than the preparation and production of novel phrases, supporting the main assumption underlying this investigation.

Utrecht University, The Netherlands

Acknowledgement

The author is grateful to Hugo Quené for his assistance in running the logistic regression analysis, and for his helpful comments on the investigation and on an earlier version of this ms.

Access to list of word sequences:

http://www.let.uu.nl/~Sieb.Nooteboom/personal/
PLIs&NovelPhrasesWordSequences.xls
 [Data in sheet 1, explanation of column headers in sheet2]

Note

Correspondence address: S.G.Nooteboom@let.uu.nl

References

Bolinger, Dwight. 1975. *Aspects of language*. New York: Harcourt, Brace, Jovanovich.
Cacciari, Cristina. & Patrizia Tabossi. 1988. The comprehension of idioms. *Journal of Memory and Language* 27. 668–683.
Cutler, Anne. 1982. The reliability of speech error data. *Linguistics* 19. 561–582.
Cutting, J. Cooper & J. Kathryn Bock. 1997. That's the way the cookie bounces: Syntactic and semantic components of experimentally controlled idiom blends. *Memory and Cognition* 25(1). 57–71.
Fraser, Bruce. 1970. Idioms within a transformational grammar. *Foundations of Language* 6. 22–42.
Fromkin, Victoria A. 1973. Appendix. In Victoria A. Fromkin (ed.) *Speech errors as linguistic evidence*, 243–269. The Hague: Mouton.
Jackendoff, Ray S. 1995. The boundaries of the lexicon. In Martin Everaert, Evert-Jan Van der Linden, André Schenk & Rob Schreuder (eds.), *Idioms: Structural and psychological perspectives*, 133–169. Hillsdale, NJ: Lawrence Erlbaum Associates.
Janetzko, Dietmar. 2008. Objectivity, reliability, and validity of search engine count estimates. *International Journal of Internet Science* 3(1), 7–33. http://www.ijis.net/ijis3_1/ijis3_1_janetzko.pdf. (Accessed 19 October 2010).
Johnson, Keith. 2008. *Quantitative methods in linguistics*. Malden, MA: Blackwell.
Ketko, Hazel. 2000. Importance of 'MultiWord Chunks' in facilitating communicative competence and its pedagogic implications. In *The Language Teacher online, December 2000*. http://www.jalt-publications.org/tlt/articles/2000/12/ketko. (Accessed 22 February 2010).
Kuiper, Koenraad. 2009. *Formulaic genres*. Basingstoke: Palgrave Macmillan.
Kuiper, Koenraad, Marie-Elaine Van Egmond, Gerard Kempen & Simone A. Sprenger. 2007. Slipping on superlemmas: Multiword lexical items in speech production. *The Mental Lexicon* 2(3). 313–357.
Levelt, Willem J.M. & Antje Meyer. 2000. Word for word: Multiple lexical access in speech production. *European Journal of Cognitive Psychology* 12(4). 433–452.
Nooteboom, Sieb G. 2005. Listening to one-self: Monitoring speech production. In Robert J. Hartsuiker, Roelien Bastiaanse, Albert Postma & Frank Wijnen (eds.) *Phonological encoding and monitoring in normal and pathological speech*, 167–186. Hove and New York: Psychology Press, Taylor & Francis Group.
Nooteboom, Sieb G. 2010. Monitoring for speech errors has different functions in inner and overt speech. In Martin Everaert, Tom Lentz, Hannah de Mulder, Oystein Nilsen & Arjen Zondervan (eds.) *The linguistic enterprise: From knowledge of language to knowledge in linguistics*, 213–233. Amsterdam and Philadelphia: John Benjamins Publishing Company.
Nooteboom, Sieb & Hugo Quené. 2008. Self-monitoring and feedback: A new attempt to find the main cause of lexical bias in phonological speech errors. *Journal of Memory and Language* 58. 837–861.

Nunberg, Geoffrey, Ivan Sag & Thomas Wasow. 1994. Idioms. *Language* 70. 491–537.
Oostdijk, Nelleke & Daan Broeder. 2004. The spoken Dutch corpus and its exploitation environment. In *Proceedings of the 4th International Workshop on Linguistically Interpreted Corpora (LINC-03)*. 14 April, 2003. Budapest, Hungary: EACL-03.
Pawley, Andrew K. & Frances H. Syder, 1983. Two puzzles for linguistic theory: Nativelike selection and nativelike fluency. In Jack C. Richards & Richard Schmidt (eds.) *Language and communication*, 191–225. London: Longman.
Rossi, Mario & Évelyne Peter-Defare. 1998. *Les lapsus ou comment notre fourche a langué* [Speech errors or how our slip has tongued]. Paris: Presses Universitaires de France.
Schelvis, Marianne. 1985. *The collection, categorisation, storage and retrieval of spontaneous speech error material at the Institute of Phonetics*, Utrecht: PRIPU 10. 3–14.
Sprenger, Simone A., Willem J.M. Levelt & Gerard Kempen. 2006. Lexical access during the production of idiomatic phrases. *Journal of Memory and Language* 54. 161–184.
Swinney, David A. & Anne Cutler. 1979. The access and processing of idiomatic expressions. *Journal of Verbal Learning and Verbal Behavior* 18. 523–534.
Van Lancker-Sidtis, Diana. 2004. When novel sentences spoken or heard for the first time in the history of the universe are not enough: Toward a dual-process model of language. *International Journal of Language and Communication Disorders* 39(1). 1–44.
Wheatley, Thalia & Daniel M. Wegner. 2001. Automaticity of action, Psychology of. *International Encyclopedia of the Social and Behavioral Sciences,* 991–993. Amsterdam: Elsevier.

The paradoxical success of *can (-ed) not help but V*: When the extragrammatical meets the non-compositional

MATHILDE PINSON

Abstract

This paper is a study of the expression can help, *meaning 'can refrain/ avoid'. It focuses on the polarity and the fixedness of this expression and on its complex complementation. A diachronic corpus study shows that this item is no longer best described as a negative polarity item and that it has undergone a process of lexicalization. The second half of this article deals with the complex complementation of* can (-ed) not help *and, more specifically, with the* can (-ed) not help but V-*structure. This structure is extragrammatical because there exists no similar construction in contemporary English. However, as will be shown, its use has recently increased at the expense of* can (-ed) not help + gerund. *This paper will demonstrate that a combination of sociolinguistic, semantic and pragmatic factors, coupled with criteria related to processing ease, may have played a decisive part in this somewhat paradoxical success.*

Keywords: idiom; lexicalization; negative polarity item; complementation; extragrammaticality.

1. Introduction

Multi-word expressions are pervasive in natural speech and writing and more than half of word choices are in fact predetermined by the word's appearance in a prefabricated expression (Erman & Warren 2000). In this paper I provide a case study of a particular instance of a multi-word expression, in the hope that a detailed analysis of this rather peculiar but frequently used sequence may shed some light on the processes of phrasal lexicalization.

The following sentence:

(1) *I couldn't help but cry.*

is semantically unambiguous and is used quite freely by most English speakers. Yet, straightforward as it may seem to most native speakers, it exhibits several particularities which are of interest to phraseologists. Firstly, it is noticeable that the verb *help* is not used in its core meaning here (this particular meaning of *help* will be referred to as *help$_2$*, as opposed to the core meaning of *help*, hereafter called *help$_1$*). Secondly, the presence of *can* + a negation seems to be a pre-requisite for this particular meaning to occur. However, it is obviously possible to use *can* + a negation with the meaning of *help$_1$* (e.g. *Sorry, I can't help you with this.*), which shows that the type of complement clause used after *help* is also essential to bring about this particular meaning.

These basic facts give rise to a number of questions:

– How can the meaning of *help$_2$* be accounted for?
– How fixed is this verb phrase?
– Why is *but* used here to introduce a complement clause?
– How does this type of complement differ from the gerund?

A corpus study based on a variety of sources, both diachronic (*Lexicons of Early Modern English, Old Bailey Proceedings, Corpus of Historical American English*) and synchronic (*British National Corpus, Corpus of Contemporary American English*), seems to be the most suitable way to probe these issues. I will address the first two questions in the first half of this paper, which is devoted to the string *can (-ed) not help$_2$* itself, and in particular to the question of the +/– compositionality (Section 2) and the gradual lexicalization (Section 3) of this multi-word expression. The second half of this paper will broach the complex complementation of *can (-ed) not help$_2$* and will focus more specifically on the extragrammaticality of *can (-ed) not help but V* as well as the sociolinguistic distinction between *can (-ed) not help but V* and *can (-ed) not help V-ing* (Section 4). The final section (Section 5) covers the semantic and pragmatic distinctions between the two variants.

2. *Can (-ed) not help$_2$*: status and +/– compositionality

Can (-ed) not help$_2$ is a verbal word combination that exhibits some degree of semantic opacity. It is an idiom in Huddleston and Pullum (2002)'s sense and is often included in dictionaries of idioms (e.g. Ammer 1997; Makkai 1987; Cowie, Mackin & McCaig 1983; Henderson 1954).

Compositionality is a semantic measure which refers to the degree of predictability of the meaning of a whole from the meaning of its component parts (Langacker 1987). The meaning of the string *can (-ed) not help$_2$* is not fully predictable, as it describes the subject's inability to refrain from performing the process encoded in the complement clause. It does not correspond to the association of the meaning of *can* with that of *not* and that of *help$_1$*, namely the 'inability to assist or succour'. Indeed, the replacement of *help* with one of its synonyms in example (1) does not produce the intended meaning and is even impossible to decode, as is shown in example (2).

(2)   *I couldn't assist/aid but cry.*

This string is, however, more compositional than the classic idiom *kick the bucket*, which is entirely unpredictable. Contrary to this idiom – or to less non-compositional, metaphorical idioms, such as *spill the beans* or *pull strings* – it is quite clear that the lack of predictability of *can (-ed) not help$_2$* is attributable to one item alone, the verb *help* itself. One may therefore hypothesize that the non-compositionality of *can (-ed) not help$_2$* is in fact due to a semantic shift which has affected the verb *help*. A close examination of an Early Modern English corpus, such as the *Lexicons of Early Modern English* (LEME), helps us to understand how the meaning of *help$_2$* ('avoid/refrain') arose. This corpus is a collection of multilingual dictionaries, technical lexicons and, more importantly for our purposes, medical treatises, which proved essential in understanding this semantic shift.

Originally, the verb *help* was prototypically followed by an animate recipient in the dative, to which was optionally added an adverbial clause denoting purpose. Then, it became a ditransitive verb, as the possible *wh*-extraction of (a part of) the object suggests (cf. Chomsky 1980):[1]

(3)   *He helped [you] [to build a house].*
(4)   *What did he help you to build?*
(5)   *You need his help [(in order) to build a house].*
(6)   **What do you need his help (in order) to build?*

In Early Modern English, a monotransitive use started to appear. From the original meaning of *help* derived the sense 'to facilitate', present in (7), and 'to alleviate/cure', present in (8):

(7) *Myrtles are [...] verye profitable to helpe the restoring of broken bones,* (Lanfranco of Milan, *Chirurgia,* 1565)
(8) *If it be strened, it helpeth and swageth the sores in a mannes mouthe* (Anonymous, *Banckes's Herbal,* 1525)

The latter meaning is particularly transparent in the following sentence, where *help* is used as a ditransitive verb:

(9) *[This herb] shall helpe hym of the yelowe euyll.* (Anonymous, *Banckes's Herbal,* 1525)

In (9), the use of an indirect object introduced by *of* (*of the yelowe euyll*) indicates that the sentence can be paraphrased as:

(10) *[This herb] shall cure hym of the yelowe euyll.*

From this meaning derived the passive form *It can't be helped,* meaning *It can't be remedied.*

The numerous medical treatises included in LEME offer various indications as to how the sense 'to cure' could lead to a notion of protection or prevention, as the following sentence suggests:

(11) *The floures of Lavander [...] mixed with Cinnamon, Nutmegs, and Cloves, made into pouder, and given to drinke in the distilled water thereof, doth helpe the panting and passion of the heart.* (Thomas Johnson, *The Herbal or General History of Plants,* 1633)

It is possible to imagine that such a remedy, used primarily to treat tachycardia and shortness of breath, was thereafter used to prevent such symptoms from occurring. Indeed, nothing in the syntactic structure of the sentence explicitly specifies if the beverage is used to cure such conditions or if it is supposed to stave off their occurrence. Similarly, in the following sentence, with a prepositional object, it is not made explicit whether the medicine is used for its curative or for its preventive properties.

(12) *It helpeth against the bitings of any venomous beast, either taken in drinke, or outwardly applied.* (Thomas Johnson, *The Herbal or General History of Plants,* 1633)

Although it would seem more logical to use this drug after an insect bite, it is not specifically encoded in the sentence. Furthermore, the use of the preposition *against* resembles the syntax of the verb *protect* and this suggests some ambiguity regarding the precise moment when the medicine should be used.

One can therefore hypothesize that the lack of semantic explicitness of such structures, coupled with the frequent use of therapeutic drugs for prophylactic purposes, led to the advent of $help_2$.

The semantic ambiguity between $help_1$ and $help_2$ is also conspicuous in other types of discourse, as can be seen in the following excerpt from a multilingual dictionary dating back to 1574,

(13) *To decaie: to go to naught [e.g.] To helpe the common weale falling in decay.* (John Baret, *An Alveary or Triple Dictionary, in English, Latin, and French*, 1574)

The original in Latin reads as follows:

(14) F   re   præsidium   labenti   Reipublicae.
Bring-IMP thing-ABL protection-ACC stumbling-DAT republic-DAT
Bring true protection to the stumbling republic.

Literally, *praesidio* means 'to sit in front of something' and, by extension, 'to watch over, to protect', so there seems to be a certain ambiguity between the two meanings of *help* here. The republic is said to be "stumbling", so it has already experienced difficulties, but if it needs protection, it means that further difficulties are still expected and may still be avoided.

The course of action intended to improve a situation can be taken either subsequently or prior to the unfortunate event(s). The common semantic feature between $help_1$ and $help_2$ lies in the euphoric denotations associated with this verb and could be conceived as a kind of *problem-solving* concept. Whether a problem was solved after it occurred or solved by avoiding its occurrence was considered irrelevant and was conceptually backgrounded at the time when the semantic shift took place.

Finally, the secondary meaning of *help* became clearly distinct from its core meaning, as can be seen in the following sentence (from the *Old Bailey*), which unambiguously corresponds to the meaning 'avoid/prevent':

(15) *I do not believe the prisoner could help the accident.* (*Old Bailey*, 1834)

3. Gradual fixation

Today, *help₂* prototypically occurs in the string *can (-ed) not help*, but it is important to ascertain to what extent this item is actually fixed and to understand the processes of fixation resulting in this sequence. One of the most complex issues related to this expression is the question of polarity.

3.1. *Polarity*

As Bybee (2010) explains,

> [i]n general, we expect affirmative uses to be more common than negative ones, based on the cross-linguistic finding that all languages 'mark' negative with an overt marker, but no languages mark affirmative and leave the negative unmarked. As markedness relations correlate very highly with relative frequency (Greenberg 1963), we expect to find more affirmatives than negatives in any batch of data examined.
> (Bybee 2010: 152)

However, in the case of *can help₂*, the proportion of negative cases is much higher than that of positive cases.

3.1.1. *Free combination and lack of polarity sensitiveness.* As can be noticed, examples (11) and (12), which were identified as potential sources of this particular lexical shift, did not involve negative polarity. This is also the case in example (16):

(16) One thing there is [...] which I fear will touch me; but I shall help it, I hope. (Pepys, *Diary*, 1668).

This type of sentence is nevertheless very rare and only a few cases of free combinations can be observed in corpora, becoming extremely infrequent in the 19th century.[2]

3.1.2. *Licensing contexts.* Rather early on, *can (-ed) not help₂* became a collocation and may even be considered a colligation, since it displays a high degree of compatibility not only between individual graphic units but also between lexical and syntactic items.[3] Indeed, the collocation *can help* colligates with a negation and can even be deemed a Negative Polarity

Item (NPI). NPIs are items which never occur in positive assertions using the simple past (Giannakidou 1998). Conversely, such items occur when they are in the syntactic scope of a) a negative particle (including cases of non-clausemate negation), b) a restrictive particle, c) a subject containing a negative quantifier, d) a subject containing a restrictive quantifier. They are also licensed by e) a negation with inverse scope, i.e. when the item is "within the semantic scope of an expression which does not c-command it at S-structure" (de Swart 1998: 179), f) *wh-* and *yes/no* questions, g) *if*-clauses, h) *than-*clauses and i) *before*-clauses. All these licensing contexts can be found in the case of *can (-ed) not help$_2$*, as can be seen in the following examples, which illustrate each type of licensing context:

(17) a. *He couldn't help crying.*
    a'. *I don't think that she can help doing what she does.* (Linebarger 1980: 24) (negative raising)
    b. *He could hardly help knowing it.* (COCA 2008, FIC)
    c. *No one can help but be shocked.* (COCA 1996, SPOK)
    d. *Few who followed the unraveling details could help but wonder...* (COCA 1992, NEWS)
    e. *She can help doing none of those things.* (de Swart 1998: 179)
    f. *How can you help but hate such people?* (COCA 1990, FIC)
    g. *Never climb shale or slate if you can help it.* (COCA 2009, FIC)
    h. *They could not help it any more than his skin could help what was happening to it.* (COHA 1955, FIC)
    i. *The curtain whooshed back. Caitlin tensed before she could help herself.* (COHA 2009, FIC)

Yet, this list of licensing contexts does not accurately reflect acceptability judgements.

3.1.3. *Acceptability judgements.* In order to analyse native speakers' reactions towards these licensing contexts, I conducted a pilot study on twenty Anglophones, asking them to evaluate the acceptability of these sentences from 1 ("perfectly normal") to 5 ("wrong") and I calculated the average grade obtained for each of these sentences. Three different groups of sentences emerge from this study. Sentences (17a), (17a') and (17g) have a low score (1.1 to 1.4) and are therefore considered very acceptable; sentence (17e) has the highest score (3.5 "very strange"); the remaining sentences have an intermediate score, ranging from 2.5 to 2.7 ("a bit strange"). As a result, it appears that *can help₂* is only totally acceptable when it is in the scope of a negative particle – with or without negative raising – or when it occurs in an *if*-clause.[4]

It also appears that the sentence made up by de Swart, with inverse scope, is problematic. It was labelled "wrong" by nearly one quarter of the informants.

These results confirm that a distinction needs to be made between grammaticality and acceptability. Most of these sentences are grammatical but they are very rarely employed. As Bybee (2010) explains,

> in usage-based theory, [...] acceptability judgements within a language are postulated to be based on familiarity, where familiarity rests on two factors: the frequency of a word, construction or specific phrase, and similarity to existing words, constructions or phrases. Items will be judged as acceptable to the extent that they are frequent in the subject's experience or similar to frequent items.
>
> (Bybee 2010: 214)

This is precisely why a corpus study is essential at this stage. An analysis based on COCA shows that all of the above contexts are in fact statistically marginal (around 2%), with the exception of prototypical cases of negative particles (cf. De Beaugrande [2008], who only finds *can help₂* in negative contexts in his corpus).[5] One may therefore question to what extent it is appropriate to label this item an NPI. Indeed, several elements indicate that it would be more adequate to consider it a lexicalized verb phrase.

3.2. Lexicalization

"Lexicalization is the change whereby in certain linguistic contexts speakers use a syntactic construction or word formation as a new contentful form with formal and semantic properties that are not completely derivable or predictable from the constituents of the construction or the word formation pattern. Over time there may be further loss of internal constituency [...]" (Brinton and Traugott 2005: 96). The first element that suggests that this item is undergoing lexicalization is the fact that in earlier periods the expression of inability exhibited some variation which no longer appears today.

(18) *This was a heavy piece of news to my nephew, but <u>there was no way</u> to help it but to comply.* (William Defoe, *Robinson Crusoe*, 1719)

(19) *The Prisoner deny'd the Fact, as to the Murther of the Child, and said, that she knew not that she was so near her Time and that it dropp'd from her at the Vault, when <u>uncapable</u> to help it. Upon a full Hearing of the Matter, the Jury acquitted her.* (Old Bailey, 1729)

(20) *[T]o say all in a word, he doats upon you; and I begin to see <u>it is not in his power</u> to help it.* (Samuel Richardson, *Pamela*, 1740)

(21) *It is <u>impossible</u> to help lamenting the unhappiness of Sir Edward.* (Charlotte Smith, *Ethelinde*, 1789)

This suggests that non-prototypical expressions of inability have decreased over time and that the use of *can (-ed) not* has become obligatory. For an expression to become obligatory is, indeed, one of the characteristics of its being lexicalized (see, for instance, Heine and Narrog 2009: 404).

Furthermore, it can be noticed that the incidence of the negative adverb *never* with *can help* is significantly lower than that of *not*. The use of *never* is not ungrammatical, but its compatibility with *can help$_2$* is in no way comparable to its incidence with a typical NPI such as *anything*. The figures found in COCA demonstrate that *anything* is as compatible with *never* as it is with *not* ($N_{not\ x\ anything}$ = 3842; $N_{never\ x\ anything}$ = 4038). By way of contrast, in the same corpus, *can (-ed) not help$_2$* appears 1288 times, while only 3 instances of *can (-ed) never help$_2$* can be found.[6] The fact that *never* is so rare with *can help$_2$* raises serious doubt as to the legitimacy of labelling *can help$_2$* a prototypical NPI.

These two elements – earlier variation in the expression of inability and the extremely low frequency of *never* – demonstrate that the item under scrutiny is fairly frozen and that it exhibited more variability in the past. One may therefore wonder whether the proportion of the non-prototypical licensing contexts mentioned above has also decreased over time.

I have conducted a diachronic study on COHA, to see whether the proportion of non-prototypical licensing contexts is stable. If the item in question is an NPI, there is no reason why it should have evolved over time. Conversely, if cases which differ from the prototypical *can (-ed) not help$_2$* are declining in number, it would suggest that this item is no longer a true NPI but that it is lexicalizing into a fixed phrase. This study is based on instances of "help [vvg]", i.e. uninflected forms of *help* followed by a *V-ing* form.[7] The sentences are coded as prototypical if they contain the exact string *can (-ed) not help$_2$* (and contracted forms) and as non-prototypical if they correspond to licensing contexts (17a') to (17i) or to any other alternative forms, such as other negative constructions (e.g. *Nor/neither could he help laughing*), affirmative forms (e.g. *I can help crying*) or alternative expressions of inability (e.g. *It was impossible to help thinking*). Strings which are interrupted by a constituent (e.g. *I could not, despite my fears, help laughing*) were also coded as non-prototypical because the adjacency of verbal components is another characteristic of lexicalization. The non-prototypical cases were subsumed under a) interrogatives, b) non-prototypical negatives and c) other non-lexicalized cases. Figure 1 shows the diachronic tendency which can be observed in COHA.

As can be seen, in the 1830s–1840s, non-prototypical cases accounted for 16% of all occurrences of *help$_2$ V-ing*. Since then, the proportion of non-prototypical cases has steadily decreased and only amounts to around 2% today.

In the early 19th century, *can help$_2$ V-ing* exhibited a relatively high degree of syntactic flexibility and, like prototypical negative polarity items such as *anything* or *ever*, was found in a variety of NPI licensing contexts. Today it is practically never used in licensing contexts other than the prototypical clause-mate negation with *not*. Likewise, alternative expressions of inability and strings that are interrupted by a constituent have become extremely rare in recent years. Put together, these two types of non-lexicalized forms only represent 0.5% of all occurrences of *help$_2$ V-ing*.

The lexicalization of this string is probably linked to a general tendency towards improved processing. For instance, it has been demonstrated (Drenhaus, Błaszczak and Schütte 2007: 190) that interrogative sentences

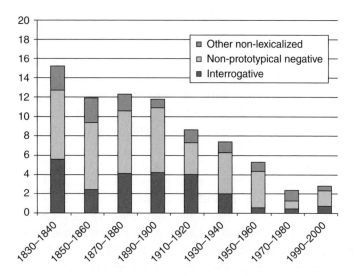

Figure 1. *Percentage of non-prototypical forms of* help$_2$ + V-ing *(COHA)*

containing an NPI are harder to process than negative sentences containing an NPI. This probably explains why interrogative contexts are, on the whole, less frequent and are disappearing more rapidly than non-prototypical negative contexts, as can be seen in Figure 1.

Moreover, questions of proximity (cf. Hawkins 2004, Rohdenburg 1996) are also paramount in accounting for the ease and speed of processing. It seems fairly logical that sentences like the following ones should be avoided.

(22) *He could **no** more help going on to further heights of success than his "gilt-edged" securities, stored in thick parcels in his safe-deposit boxes, **could help bearing** interest.* (COHA 1899, FIC)
(23) ***No** man, outside of a deaf and dumb asylum, who is awakened at midnight on the 3d of July with – a hideous din that he knows will grow worse and worse for the next twenty-four hours, **can help feeling** that the Declaration of Independence was a terrible mistake, and that slavery and quiet are infinitely preferable to freedom and fire-crackers.* (COHA 1876, NEWS)

Although these two sentences are interpretable, as the reader can reread them if necessary, the amount of effort required in order to process them is exceptionally high.

Today non-prototypical licensing contexts are so infrequently encountered that speakers have become unfamiliar with them. Some people are in fact so uncomfortable with these structures that they want to add an extra negation or even fail to interpret them correctly, as the following comments by native speakers show:

(17) c. *No one can help but be shocked.* "OK if the point is to say that no one was shocked."
 d. *Few who followed the unraveling details could help but wonder...* "Don't you need a negation *couldn't?*"

Indeed, two out of the four interrogative sentences containing *help$_2$ but V* found in COCA 2005–2010 contain an extraneous negation:

(24) *Tyler's face and the smiles and, I mean, how can you **not** help but fall in love with this family?* (COCA 2010, SPOK)
(24') *He wanted to be me. And I? How could I **not** help but be drawn to him, his wife, his daughters?* (COCA 2010, FIC)

These developments strongly suggest that this multi-word expression is no longer an NPI but that it is on the verge of becoming a fully lexicalized verb phrase. As such, it is now "stored and retrieved whole from memory at time of use, rather than being subject to generation or analysis by the language grammar" (Wray 2002: 9). In view of this, it is clear that it has become easier to process than its NPI ancestor. As an NPI, it had to be parsed as *can* + negation + *help*, whereas it is now processed as an unanalyzable chunk, the use of which improves fluency and provides time for discourse planning (cf. Bolinger 1975, Kuiper 1996).

Another development which has contributed to the fixedness of the structure concerns the type of objects compatible with *can (-ed) not help$_2$*.

3.3. Evolution of objects: the gradual disappearance of non-pronominal NPs

A further change in the syntax of *can (-ed) not help$_2$* is the type of complement that is compatible with this verbal sequence. Quite early on, gerunds started to be used as an alternative to NPs, as can be seen in the following sentence:

(25) *We cannot help acknowledging the Great and Good Creator and Governour of the Universe.* (John Rotheram The Force of the Argument for the Truth of Christianity 1653)

Many instances of *can (-ed) not help$_2$* were still followed by full NPs in the 18th and 19th centuries, whereas today these NPs would undoubtedly be replaced by phrasal complements, as the following examples show:

(26) *This is because they call me a Molly, and say I am more like a Woman than a Man, and how can I help <u>my face</u>?* (Old Bailey, 1738)
(27) *I cannot help <u>the thought which tells me thou hast not yet learned truly to decipher its language.</u>* (COHA 1839, FIC)
(28) *But Ottila cannot help <u>her beauty.</u>* (COHA 1864, FIC)

These sentences would be respectively replaced by:

(26') *This is because they call me a Molly, and say I am more like a Woman than a Man, and how can I help <u>looking the way I do</u>?*
(27') *I cannot help <u>thinking that thou hast not yet learned truly to decipher its language.</u>*
(28') *But Ottila cannot help <u>being beautiful.</u>*

Table 1, based on the *Old Bailey Corpus*, documents the gradual disappearance of full NPs in this construction.

This phenomenon is partly due to the general development of gerunds, but it also appears to be related to a gradual decline in nouniness on the part of the object of *can (-ed) not help$_2$*. This process can be observed in the following manipulation, based on a sentence adapted from COHA (1859):

(29) *I won't stay here and be quiet Mrs. Ralph Huntington, No. 2 [...]. I tell you I feel within me that my destiny is elsewhere. I cannot help my fate.*

If one replaces the NP *my fate* with the anaphora *it*, it should theoretically be possible to interpret this proform as being co-referential with *my destiny*, which is the closest preceding salient NP. However, the use of an anaphora actually produces a different result:

(29') *I won't stay here and be quiet Mrs. Ralph Huntington, No. 2 [...]. I tell you I feel within me that my destiny is elsewhere. I cannot help it.*

In this sentence, a modern reader is more likely to consider that *it* refers to the VP *feel within me that my destiny is elsewhere* than to interpret it as co-referential with *my destiny*. This suggests that the object of *can (-ed) not help$_2$* is no longer perceived as an entity, but that it is now prototypically a process, which explains why its compatibility with full NPs has gradually diminished.

Today, the proportion of full NPs as objects of *can (-ed) not help$_2$* is extremely low and only accounts for 1.2% (N = 10) of all cases *of can (-ed) not help$_2$* in COHA for the period 2000–2010. The vast majority of objects are phrasal complements (*but* V and gerunds), which represent 71.3% of cases (N = 598). *It* is used 15.7% of the time (N = 132) and reflexive pronouns occur in 10.37% of cases (N = 87). The remaining objects are

Table 1. *Proportion of* can (-ed) not help$_2$ + *full NP and* can (-ed) not help$_2$ + V-ing *in the 18th and 19th centuries (Source Old Bailey)*

	Can (-ed) not help + NP (except it)	Can (-ed) not help V-ing
1700–1750	41% (12/29)	59% (17/29)
1800–1840	14,3% (8/56)	85,7% (48/56)

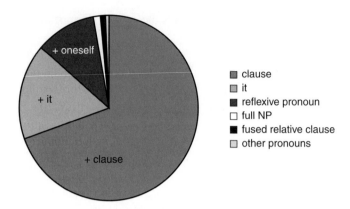

Figure 2. *Types of objects of* can (-ed) not help$_2$ *(COHA 2000s)*

pronouns other than *it* (0.6%; N = 5) and fused relative clauses (0.8%; N = 7). Figure 2 illustrates this distribution.

Let us now turn more specifically to the two types of phrasal complements that are compatible with *can (-ed) not help$_2$*, and in particular to the construction involving *but* plus a bare infinitive.

4. The use of *can (-ed) not help but V*

4.1. The extragrammaticality of can (-ed) not help but V

Figure 3 illustrates the success of *can (-ed) not help but V* in British and American corpora, using data from The Times and Time Magazine. As Jespersen (1917) and Thomas (1948) noticed, the *but*-version was primarily used in American English, but its proportion has increased dramatically in the two varieties over the 19th and 20th centuries.

The statistical success of the *but*-version seems somewhat astonishing given the fact that it is extragrammatical (or asyntactic [Cruse 1986]). According to Fillmore et al. (1988), an idiom is said to be extragrammatical when it does not obey the syntactic rules of contemporary English. This is, for example, the case for multi-word expressions such as *let alone* or *by and large*.

It is also the case for *can (-ed) not help but V*, since this construction is the only structure in which the morpheme *but* acts as a complementizer in unmarked contemporary English. Indeed, it is a syntactic fossil. Studies devoted to the use of *but* as a complementizer either deal with Middle and

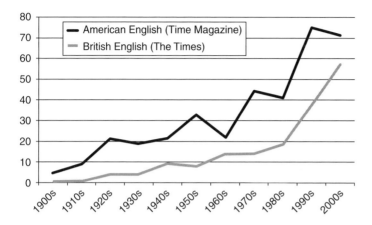

Figure 3. *Evolution of the percentage of* but V *after* can (-ed) not help, *as opposed to* V-ing, *in American English (Time Magazine) and in British English (The Times)*

Early Modern English (Lopez-Couso & Mendez-Naya 1998) or underline its markedness in contemporary English (Cotte 2004).

It is therefore rather surprising that this structure, which is unique in contemporary English, should be experiencing such a vigorous revival, particularly as there already exists a well-established alternative, the gerund form, which appears in many other verbal constructions.

4.2. But *as a complementizer*

Throughout its history, *but* has been a preposition, an adverb, a coordinating conjunction, an adverbial subordinator, a (negative) complementizer and a negative relative pronoun. Semantically speaking, *but* was (or still is) abessive, exceptive, restrictive and contrastive and was also used to express negative condition. The common feature between these different meanings clearly lies in their closeness to a negative meaning. All these different meanings are appropriately subsumed by Joly (1980) under the notion of "reversal".

As a complementizer, the use of *but* illustrates what Croft (2000) calls cryptanalysis. *But* was traditionally compatible only with inherently negative verbs such as verbs of abstention, doubt and denial. In cryptanalysis, a grammatical morpheme is employed to reinforce a particular meaning which is already encoded by the lexicon. To improve expressivity or facilitate processing, the negative meaning of these verbs is reinforced by a (semi-) negative grammatical morpheme, like *but*. The use of *but* as a complementizer after abstention verbs resembles the Latin morpheme *quin*, and this structure may have derived from it, as Warner (1982) suggests (although see Lopez-Couso and Mendez-Naya 1998 for discussion).

The use of *but* as a complementizer is very complex insofar as it may or may not be negative:

(30) *My master knows not but I am gone hence.* (= *that I am not gone*) (Shakespeare, *Romeo and Juliet*, V, iii, 1597)
(31) *I doubt not but you can put me into the best way to obtain that favour.* (not negative) (John Hawles, *Englishman's Right*, 1680)

The extreme complexity of this complementizer partly explains why it has died out. What is more, its more or less negative meaning also explains why *can (-ed) not help but V* was for a long time rejected by American purists, who considered it a case of double negation (e.g. Genung 1893: 317).

Let us now study in more detail the sociolinguistic dimension of these two variants.

4.3. Sociolinguistic distinction between can (-ed) not help but V and can (-ed) not help V-ing

The average proportion of *can (-ed) not help but V* observed in *The Times* during the 1990s is higher (37%) than that of the British National Corpus (22.7%). Seeing that the BNC includes a variety of genres (spoken, fiction, etc.), it is clearly a less formal corpus than *The Times*. This therefore suggests that the *but*-construction is rather formal in British English.

Furthermore, the comparison between contracted and non-contracted forms of *can (-ed) not* in the BNC confirms this trend, as can be seen in Table 2.

The proportion of *but* is higher (30.6) when *can (-ed) not* is not contracted than when it is (18.6).

Table 2. *Percentage of* V-ing *and* but V *after contracted and non-contracted forms of* can (-ed) not help *in the BNC*

	V-ing	But + V
Contracted forms	81.4% (477/586)	18.6% (109/586)
Non-contracted forms	69.4% (215/310)	30.6% (95/310)

The relative formality of *can (-ed) not help but V* is also suggested by a remark from Lawler (1996), who considers it "a little precious" and labels it a "parvenu construction".

In American English the sociolinguistic pattern is rather different. In 1948, Thomas said that the *but*-construction was fairly well implanted in American English, both in informal and formal dialects. He nevertheless stated that, "the one which appears most frequently in standard written English is *cannot help* plus gerund". In COCA the highest proportion of *cannot/could not help but V* can be found in the spoken sub-corpus, where it accounts for 90% of occurrences.[8] It is therefore evident that *can (-ed) not help but V* is not a formal construction in American English.

Nevertheless, the stylistic pattern of use observed in American English is more complex than one might expect and, under close analysis, provides us with a better understanding of the semantic particularities of *can (-ed) not help but V*.

5. Semantic and pragmatic distinctions

5.1. *Semantic distinctions*

In view of the high proportion of *cannot/could not help but V* found in the spoken sub-section of COCA, one may expect the proportion of *cannot/could not help but V* to be ranked, in decreasing order, as follows: spoken > fiction > academic. And yet, this is clearly not the case in practice, as can be seen in Table 3. The order observed actually follows this pattern: spoken (90%) > academic (68.4%) > fiction (55.2%).

These somewhat unexpected results can be partially explained when compared with the proportion of [- human] subjects used with *cannot/could not help$_2$* in each of these sub-corpora, the figures of which are shown in Table 4.

Table 3. *Percentage of* but + V *after* cannot/could not help$_2$ *in three sub-sections of COCA*

	% cannot/could not help$_2$ but V *(as opposed to* cannot/could not help$_2$ V-ing*)*
Spoken	90% (47/52)
Academic	68.4% (193/282)
Fiction	55.2% (221/400)

Table 4. *Percentage of [- human] subject with* cannot/could not help$_2$ + *phrasal complement in three sub-sections of COCA*

	% *[- human] subject with* cannot/could not help$_2$ + *phrasal complement*
Spoken	7.6% (4/52)
Academic	18% (51/282)
Fiction	1.7% (7/400)

As can be seen, the proportion of [- human] subjects with *cannot/could not help$_2$* is much higher in the academic sub-corpus. This observation therefore suggests a high compatibility between the use of *but* and [- human] subjects, which, in turn, provides us with some insight into the meaning of *can (-ed) not help but V*.

According to Thomas (1948), *can (-ed) not help V-ing* and *can (-ed) not help but V* are totally interchangeable. Yet, the prevalence of *but* with a [- human] subject, together with the high proportion of *V-ing* in fiction, clearly suggest that there exists some sort of semantic nuance between the two constructions.

For instance, with a [- human] subject, the use of a gerund seems problematic:

(32) *The result is friction and ill feeling which cannot help but have unfortunate effects.* (COHA 1923, MAG)
(33) ?* *The result is friction and ill feeling which cannot help having unfortunate effects.*

With *but*, there seems to be a notion of inevitable logical consequence, whereas the high proportion of gerunds in fiction suggests that *V-ing* conveys a rather subjective inability to act otherwise. One might even suggest that there exists a fundamental binary opposition between the two constructions. The use of the gerund is oriented towards the expression of subjectivity and feelings, and is more suitable for narrations, whereas the *but*-form is more objective. It is directed towards the intellect and seems particularly appropriate in argumentation. Although argumentative discourse may also rely heavily on subjectivity, speakers/writers of argumentative discourse generally seek to emphasize the objectivity of their position. The use of the *but*-form thus constitutes a powerful strategy to inconspicuously impose one's viewpoint by presenting it as objective.

This semantic distinction can be related to the fact that the bare infinitive, which accompanies *but* in this structure, prototypically refers to a concept or a notion (cf. Chuquet 1986), while the *V-ing* form is often said to convey the inner point of view of the speaker (cf. Adamczewski 1982).

This binary opposition remains, however, a little simplistic and it would thus be fruitful to compare these two structures with a third one, *can (-ed) not but V*, in order to gain a better understanding of the meaning of these forms. For instance, it can be noticed that sentence (32) strongly resembles the following one:

(34) *That officers of the Government [...] should refuse to be governed themselves by the laws, [...] cannot but have an injurious effect upon a people too prone to avoid or refuse obedience to authority.* (COHA 1860, NEWS)

Other such pairs of sentences abound in COHA, as these examples illustrate.

(35) a. *If so, the success of the experiment **cannot but encourage** her to go forward.* (COHA 1852, MAG)
b. *Confronting indifference on a cosmic scale **cannot help but encourage** feelings of diminishment, abandonment, implacable solitude.* (COHA 1995, MAG)
(36) a. *We have described the Serpent Mound, and although we are ignorant of its object, it **cannot but recall** the important place which the symbol of the serpent held in the ancient Mexican superstition.* (COHA1849, MAG)
b. *Indeed, the panels of the inner room, which represent the arts and sciences, are entirely peopled by babies: plump, coy infant poets; chubby infant astronomers and musicians – figures which **cannot help but recall** Wendy's obsession with the possible genius of her unborn child.* (COHA 1974, FIC)

The similarity between these pairs of sentences results from the presence of a [- human] subject and from the notion of inevitable logical consequence. One may therefore suggest that *can (-ed) not help but V* and *can (-ed) not but V* are synonymous. In fact, it appears that *can (-ed) not help but V* constitutes a syncretism of the meanings of *can (-ed) not help V* and *can (-ed) not but V*, as can be seen in Figure 4.

The three constructions presented in Figure 4 span between two distinct semantic poles: involuntary physical reaction and inevitable logical consequence. The three predicates chosen (*cry*, *wonder* and *have an effect*) are illustrative of each of the three categories identified: [+ involuntary physical

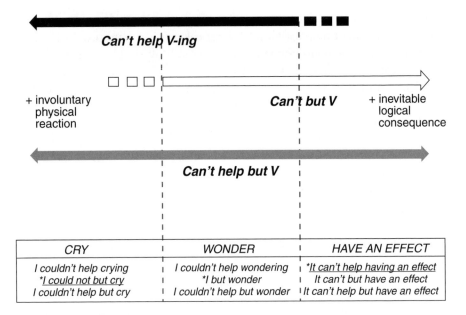

Figure 4. *A semantic representation of* can (-ed) not help but V

reaction] is exemplified by the predicate *cry*, [+ inevitable logical consequence] is illustrated by the predicate *have an effect*, while *wonder* [+P] is fairly neutral, as it can correspond to both an irrepressible subjective reaction and an inevitable objective consequence. These examples show that *can (-ed) not help but V* constitutes a syncretism of the other two structures.

To get a full picture of the competition between these variants, I have conducted a study on COHA, based on the proportion of these three structures, with 5 frequent verbs (*wonder, notice, feel, be* and *think*).

Data on *can (-ed) but* was also included in Figure 5, but given its very low frequency, it will not be addressed here. The overall tendency revealed by the graph reflects the total disappearance of *can (-ed) not but V* and the steady increase in the use of *can (-ed) help but V*. The first stage (1820–1900) illustrates the gradual replacement of *can (-ed) not but V* with *can (-ed) not help V-ing* (in neutral contexts). The success of the gerund form probably corresponds to the gradual loss of the object's nouniness (cf. Section 3.3), since the prior structure *can (-ed) not help* + NP was less likely to replace a structure containing a verb. Since the beginning of the 20th century, the *can (-ed) not help but V*-structure has increased and has also contributed to replacing *can (-ed) not but V*. From the 1950s onwards, the success of the *can (-ed) not help but V*-structure has notably participated in

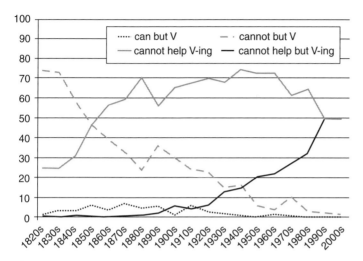

Figure 5. *Distribution of 4 alternative constructions in COHA (5 verbs)*

reducing the proportion of *can (-ed) not help V-ing* in American English.

The slight semantic distinction between the two forms is associated with different pragmatic values which directly derive from the dichotomy between objectivity and subjectivity mentioned above.

5.2. *Pragmatic distinctions*

Those speakers whose repertoire includes both complement types often exploit the slight semantic difference between the two forms for pragmatic purposes. For instance, as far as politeness is concerned, one can notice a slight nuance between the two following sentences:

(37) *I couldn't help noticing that you haven't paid for your drinks.*
(37') *I couldn't help but notice that you haven't paid for your drinks.*

Given that the *but*-version is more objective, it highlights the conspicuousness of the action described in the sentence. Being more direct and therefore potentially less polite than the first, the second sentence infers that the speaker's observation is inevitable. It may even be interpreted as an insinuation that the person who forgot to pay did it on purpose.

Furthermore, the objectivity encoded by the *but*-version gives it stronger argumentative force. When *but* is used, the object of the multi-word verb is presented as an inevitable consequence, which is therefore much harder to challenge than a mere subjective statement. The use of the *but*-form enables the speaker/writer to enforce her point of view on the hearer/reader by presenting it as an objective fact.

Similarly, when the subject of *can (-ed) not help* refers to the speaker, the notion of objectivity added by the *but*-structure also constitutes an effective strategy which enables the speaker to reinforce her lack of responsibility. In

(38) *I couldn't help doing it.*

The speaker insists on her non-responsibility, but by using

(38') *I couldn't help but do it.*

the speaker further strengthens her position of non-responsibility by suggesting that the event encoded in the object-clause was objectively unavoidable. This pragmatic effect partly explains why this form has increased dramatically in recent years.

6. Conclusion

In this paper, the multi-word expression *can (-ed) not help$_2$* has been studied from different angles. First, it has been shown that the non-compositionality of this idiomatic expression is due to a semantic shift undergone by the verb *help*. It has subsequently been demonstrated that this string has almost ceased to constitute an NPI in its own right, since it has lost virtually all of its erstwhile syntactic flexibility and is practically never used in licensing contexts other than the prototypical clausemate negation with *not*. This string has now become lexicalized; it has gradually lost its variability and the adjacency of its components has now become the rule.

The second half of this paper has been devoted to the factors which have contributed to the success of the *but*-form. As shown in this study, *can (-ed) not help but V* possesses a broader semantic content and is therefore more economical from the point of view of production than the gerund form. In addition, compared to the *V-ing* structure, the use of the *but*-form provides the speaker with a more efficient means of strategically signalling her non-responsibility.

Moreover, the *but*-structure is more likely to obey the principle of rhythmic alternation than the gerund. This principle, which was identified by

Schlüter (2003), predicts that, all things being equal, the preferred variant is the one which displays an alternation of stressed and unstressed syllables. Schlüter demonstrates this principle in her study of the alternation between the past participles *lighted* and *lit* and the structure "determiner + *not* + adjective" *(*a 'not 'happy 'person* vs. *a 'not-ex'cessive 'price)*. Interestingly, this principle can also be observed in the alternation between *can (-ed) not help V-ing* and *can (-ed) not help but V*. For instance,

(39) *I couldn't help but feel...*

is more satisfying rhythmically and is easier to process than

(40) *I couldn't help feeling...*

which exhibits a stress-clash between *help* and *feel*. Given that English includes a great number of monosyllabic verbs, together with many verbs stressed on the first syllable, this factor may have played a significant role in the decrease in gerunds after *help*. This principle may also explain why the *can (-ed) not but V*-structure, which entails a stress on *but*, has disappeared,

(41) *I couldn't but feel...*

The principle of rhythmic alternation therefore proves to be a very useful tool in analysing the evolution of a variety of morphosyntactic variables. This principle is founded on neurological experiments which show that the activation of neurons is followed by a refractory phase, during which they are harder to reactivate. According to Schlüter (2003), this would explain why the immediate co-occurrence of two similar elements (here two stressed syllables) tends to be rare.

To summarize, the success of the *can (-ed) not help but V*-structure appears to be multi-causal. Indeed, it has been demonstrated that a combination of semantic and extra-semantic factors have brought about the unlikely yet vigorous revival of this syntactic fossil.

University Paris 3-Sorbonne Nouvelle, France

Notes

Correspondence address: mathilde_pinson@hotmail.com

1. Obviously the verb *help* can still be followed by a purposive clause today, see Mair (1990) and Quirk et al. (1985) for discussion.
2. In my study of *help$_2$* + gerund in COHA (cf. Section 3.2.), affirmative cases represent only 0.35% of occurrences in the 19th century.
3. The term colligation refers to the frequent co-occurrence of a particular lexical item with a specific grammatical category (Legallois 2008).
4. The latter context can only be found when *it* is used as the object of *can help$_2$*. The proportion of *if*-clauses with the string *help$_2$ it* in COCA for the period 2005–2010 is quite high: 17% (N = 61). Interestingly, most of these sentences (59/61) contain an additional licensor, such as *never* in sentence (17g). Consequently, one may conclude that *if* is not a sufficient licensor for this item. This explains why sentence (17g) was readily accepted by the informants, whereas conditionals are known to be weaker licensors than negations and interrogations. We observe a similar pattern with *than*-clauses, which are only compatible with *can help* when they appear in conjunction with a negation.
5. *If*-clauses are also fairly frequent in the case of *can help it* (cf. note 4).
6. The incompatibility between *never* and *can help* does not seem to be due to problems related to meaning, since the rare occurrences that do include *never* do not appear to exhibit any semantic incompatibility:
   (i) *I can never help marveling at people like that, who hold their own, remain themselves, no matter what.* (COHA 1969, FIC)
   (ii) *When she stopped in on her tenants to make her hated monthly call, she could never help being bemused by the fact that Isaac may have been at a particular apartment the night before.* (COHA 1993, FIC)
   (iii) *She could never help smiling when complimented.* (COHA 1970, FIC).
7. The V-*ing* form has been chosen for this study because its use has been more stable over the past two centuries than the *but*-form, as is shown in Section 4.1.
8. Most of the spoken section of COCA is composed of unscripted interactions. However, the fact that it is entirely based on TV and radio programs entails that it is far from being fully representative of spoken American English in general.

Corpora

The British National Corpus, version 3 (BNC XML Edition). 2007. Distributed by Oxford University Computing Services on behalf of the BNC Consortium. URL: http://www.natcorp.ox.ac.uk/ (accessed 15/02/2009).

Davies, Mark. 2007-. TIME Magazine Corpus (100 million words, 1920s-2000s). Available online at http://corpus.byu.edu/time (accessed 20/07/2010).

Davies, Mark. 2008-. *The Corpus of Contemporary American English (COCA)*: 410 + million words, 1990-present. Available online at http://www.americancorpus.org (accessed 14/09/2010).

Davies, Mark. 2010-. *The Corpus of Historical American English (COHA)*: 400+ million words, 1810–2009. Available online at http://corpus.byu.edu/coha (accessed 10/10/2010).
Lancashire, Ian. 1999. *Lexicons of Early Modern English*. Universtity of Toronto Press. http://leme.library.utoronto.ca/ (accessed 1/07/2009).
Old Bailey Proceedings Online. 1674–1913. www.oldbaileyonline.org (accessed 20/08/2010).
The Times Digital Archive 1785–1985. Gale. http://www.galeuk.com/times/remote.htm (accessed 5/03/2009).
Web concordancer. http://vlc.polyu.edu.hk/concordance/wwwconcappe.htm (accessed 7/03/2009).

References

Adamczewski, Henri. 1982. *Grammaire linguistique de l'anglais*. Paris: Armand Colin.
Ammer, Christine. 1997. *American heritage dictionary of idioms*. Boston: Houghton Mifflin Company.
de Beaugrande, Robert. 2008. A lexicogrammar of processes in clauses. In *A friendly grammar of English*. www.beaugrande.com/ (accessed 2/07/2009).
Bolinger, Dwight. 1975. *Aspects of language*. New York: Harcourt, Brace, Jovanovich.
Brinton, Laurel J. & Elizabeth Closs Traugott. 2005. *Lexicalization and language change*. Cambridge: Cambridge University Press.
Bybee, Joan. 2010. *Language usage and cognition*. Cambridge: Cambridge University Press.
Chomsky, Noam. 1980. *Rules and representations*. New York: Columbia University Press.
Chuquet, Jean. 1986. *To et l'infinitif anglais*. Gap & Paris: Ophrys.
Cotte, Pierre. 2004. Les subordonnées en but : La genèse et le linéaire. In Jean-Marie Merle & Lucie Gournay. *Contrastes: Mélanges offerts à Jacqueline Guillemin-Flescher*, 213–220. Gap & Paris: Ophrys.
Cowie, Anthony Paul, Ronald Mackin & Isabel R McCaig. 1983. *Oxford dictionary of current idiomatic English, 2: English idioms*. Oxford: Oxford University Press.
Croft, William. 2000. *Explaining language change: An evolutionary approach*. Harlow: Longman Linguistic Library.
Cruse, D. Alan. 1986. *Lexical semantics*. Cambridge: Cambridge University Press.
Drenhaus, Heiner, Joanna Bła & Julianne Schütte. 2007. Some psychological comments on NPI licensing. In Estella Puig-Waldmüller (ed.), *Proceedings of sinn und bedeutung 11*, 180–193. Barcelona: Universitat Pompeu Fabra.
Erman, Britt & Beatrice Warren. 2000. The idiom principle and the open choice principle. *Text* 20. 29–62.

Fillmore, Charles J., Paul Kay & Mary Catherine O'Connor. 1988. Regularity and idiomaticity in grammatical constructions: The case of *let alone*. *Language* 64(3). 501–538.
Genung, John Franklin. 1893. *Outlines of rhetoric*. Boston: Ginn and Company.
Giannakidou, Anastasia. 1998. *Polarity sensitivity as (non)veridical dependency*. Amsterdam & Philadelphia: John Benjamins.
Greenberg, Joseph H. 1963. Some universals of grammar with particular reference to the order of meaningful elements. In Joseph H. Greenberg (ed.). *Universals of language*, 73–113. Cambridge, MA: MIT Press.
Hawkins, John A. 2004. *Efficiency and complexity in grammars*. Oxford: Oxford University Press.
Heine, Bernd & Heiko Narrog. 2009. *The Oxford handbook of linguistic analysis*. Oxford: Oxford University Press.
Henderson, Bernard Lionel Kinghorn. 1954. *A dictionary of English idioms. part 1: Verbal idioms*. London: James Blackwood & Co Ltd.
Huddleston, Rodney & Geoffrey K. Pullum. 2002. *The Cambridge grammar of the English language*. London: Cambridge University Press.
Jespersen, Otto. 1917. *Negation in English and other languages*. Copenhagen: Host.
Joly, André. 1980. *But:* morphème de la subordination de l'anglais. *Travaux de linguistique et de littérature XVIII.1*. 269–285.
Kuiper, Koenraad. 1996. *Smooth talkers: The linguistic performance of auctioneers and sportscasters*. Mahwah, NJ: Erlbaum.
Langacker, Ronald. 1987. *Foundations of cognitive grammar: Theoretical prerequisites, vol. 1*. Stanford, CA: Stanford University Press.
Lawler, John. 1996. www-personal.umich.edu/~jlawler/aue/canthelp.html (accessed 18/08/2009).
Legallois, Dominique. 2008. Peut-on mesurer la naturalité des énoncés?. *Mémoire de la Société de Linguistique de Paris* 16.
Linebarger, Maria C. 1980. *The grammar of negative polarity*, Cambridge, MA: MIT PhD thesis.
López-Couso, Maria José & Belén Méndez-Naya. 1998. On minor declarative complementizers in the history of English: The case of *but*. In Jacek Fisiak & Marcin Krygier. *Advances in English historical linguistics*, 161–171. Berlin & New York: Mouton de Gruyter.
Mair, Christian. 1990. *Infinitival complement clauses in English: A study of syntax in discourse*. Cambridge: Cambridge University Press.
Makkai, Adam. 1987. *A dictionary of American idioms*. New York, London, Toronto & Sydney: Barron's.
Quirk, Randolph, Sydney Greenbaum, Geoffrey Leech & Jan Svartvik. 1985. *A comprehensive grammar of the English language*. London: Longman.
Rohdenburg, Günter. 1996. Cognitive complexity and grammatical explicitness in English. *Cognitive Linguistics* 7. 149–182.
Schlüter, Julia. 2003. Phonological determinants of grammatical variation in English: Chomsky's worst possible case. In Günter Rohdenburg & Britta

Mondorf (eds.), *Determinants of grammatical variation in English*, 69–118. Berlin & New York: Mouton de Gruyter.

de Swart, Henriëtte. 1998. Licensing of negative polarity items under inverse scope. *Lingua* 105(3–4). 175–200.

Thomas, Russel. 1948. Cannot help but. *College English* 10(1). 38–39.

Warner, Anthony R. 1982. *Complementation in Middle English and the methodology of historical syntax*. London: Croom Helm.

Wray, Alison. 2002. *Formulaic language and the lexicon*. New York: Cambridge University Press.

Changes in the phrasal lexicon of Māori: *mauri* and *moe*

JEANETTE KING and CAROLINE SYDDALL

Abstract

Māori, the indigenous language of New Zealand, has been in considerable contact with English for over one hundred years. Over that time there have been documented changes in the pronunciation, grammar and lexicon of Māori. As a result we would also expect evidence of changes to the phrasal lexicon. A study of the words mauri *and* moe *in the Māori language over the last 150 years shows that older formulae are becoming more restricted in their use and that formulae calqued from English have also appeared.*

Keywords: Māori; phrasal lexicon; formulae; language change; formulaic genre.

1. Introduction

Māori is an indigenous language which has been in considerable contact with English for over 150 years. As a consequence of this language contact, Māori has become an endangered language (Harlow 2007). However, unlike many other endangered languages Māori has been well documented throughout the time it has been in contact with English, with good dictionaries and grammars and increasing access to a wealth of archival material, with much of this written by Māori themselves (Orbell 1995: 19).

However, despite the good level of documentation there has been not been much investigation on the extent and features of the phrasal lexicon of Māori. Nevertheless, with the scale of documented material available in Māori it is possible not just to document features of the historical phrasal lexicon but to compare this with usage today, in other words to investigate changes in the phrasal lexicon over time.

1.1. The Māori language

Māori is a member of the Austronesian family of languages and is spoken by the indigenous inhabitants of New Zealand, a group of islands in the South Pacific. An expansion of Polynesian settlement across the Pacific lead to the discovery and settlement of New Zealand by Polynesian voyagers about 800 years ago (Sutton 1994). Since the arrival of European missionaries and whalers and sealers from the beginning of the 19th century, and large scale European settlement from the 1840s onwards, the Māori people and their language have been in increasing contact with English language and culture.

Massive urbanisation by Māori in the middle of the 20th century lead to English becoming the language in which Māori children were raised (Benton 1991). This shift lead to a break in the intergenerational transmission of Māori which has been somewhat staunched by a range of successful language revitalisation initiatives introduced from the late 1970s (Reedy 2000). The most well-known of these are the Māori medium education initiatives kōhanga reo (pre-school language nests) and kura kaupapa Māori (primary schools) (King 2001; King 1999). In summary, we can say that most Māori were monolingual speakers of Māori in the 19th century, increasingly bilingual in the first part of the 20th century, and increasingly monolingual in English until the 1980s.

However, despite revitalisation initiatives, the numbers of competent speakers of Māori is low. Although 24% of the Māori population of 565,000 can speak some Māori (Statistics New Zealand 2007), it is estimated that only 14% speak the language well or very well (Te Puni Kōkiri 2008: 22) and that these levels are not high enough to retain the vitality of the language (Bauer 2008). There are only a few communities where Māori is still the language of communication among older adults.

Many of those involved in revitalisation efforts, particularly in urban areas, are second language speakers of Māori. Even present day elders who were raised in Māori environments until the end of their teenage years, have not generally had a continuous or full access to community socialisation in Māori during their adult lives. For younger speakers today the domains where Māori can be used, and are being used, are quite restricted. As in other similar revitalisation situations, the language of peer socialisation for young people is largely English (Lewis & Smallwood 2010).

As a result of the close relationship with English, it is not surprising that there have been a number of documented changes to the Māori language over the last 150 years. The pronunciation of Māori has changed considerably over this time period with many of the changes attributable to the effect of New Zealand English (Harlow & Keegan et al. 2009). Grammatical changes have also been noted (Kāretu 1995), as well as changes in vocabulary as new words were required with the advent of Māori medium schooling in the 1980s (Harlow 2007: 212–16). There is also awareness that the close association of the Māori language with English has implications for Māori syntax and forms of expression (Kāretu 1995: 7).

1.2. *Terminology*

Terminology used in this paper follows definitions by Kuiper (2009). This study focuses on phrasal lexical items (PLIs), and in particular, formulae. A PLI is a structurally complex lexical item with syntactic structure. In other words, it is a grouping of two or more words which has 'syntactic categories which determine where they may be used in sentences' (Kuiper 2009: 5). The phrasal lexicon of a language comprises the PLIs of that language. A formula is a type of PLI which has non-linguistic conditions of use, that is, cultural knowledge which determines when and how it can appropriately be used. It is worth noting that not all PLIs are formulae. A formulaic genre is a variety of a language in which a significant amount of the discourse consists of formulae. Formulaic genre may be written or spoken, and include formats such as newspaper death notices and rugby commentaries.

1.3. *The phrasal lexicon of Māori*

The phrasal inventory of native speakers of any language is huge. Various estimates for English, for example, range between 'the same order of magnitude as the single words of the vocabulary' (Jackendoff 1995: 137) to the phrasal vocabulary being 'more numerous than words by a ratio of at least 10:1' (Mel'cuk 1995: 169). While we have no estimates about the extent of the phrasal lexicon of the Māori language we would expect that, before colonisation, it was considerable, especially in a number of formulaic genre, some of which are still practised today. What is also to be expected is that as a result of the contact between Māori and English that there will have been appreciable changes in the content and extent of the phrasal lexicon.

The Māori Language Commission has produced a book of idiomatic and formulaic phrases which notes the important role of formulae in the character of the Māori language.

Ko ngā kīwaha nei te aka o te reo Māori, te kāwai e tuituia ai, e kawea ai ngā whakaaro o te tangata ki te taiao, ki te ao mārama
(Te Taura Whiri i te reo Māori 1999: 6).

'These formulaic expressions are the vine of the Māori language, the tendril that holds together and conveys a person's thoughts to the wider world.'

This book was intended to increase the phrasal lexicon of proficient second language speakers and its existence indicates awareness that the phrasal lexicon of younger speakers is restricted.

Taking into account the situation of the Māori language as outlined above, we can put forward three hypotheses of how the phrasal lexicon of Māori may have been altered through the increasing contact with English and the more restricted use of Māori over the last 150 years:

1. That many Māori PLIs will not be used as frequently as formerly;
2. That new PLIs will have been calqued from English;
3. That overall the numbers of PLIs in Māori will have decreased.

The first two hypotheses are the subject of this paper. The third hypothesis is, of course, impossible to test conclusively. However, its accuracy can be deduced from the fact that a number of activities which are likely to have had associated formulaic genres, such as traditional bird-snaring (Best 1942), Māori birth rituals (Best 1904), certain types of weaving (Wallace 2009), are no longer practised. Considering that some of these activities were attended by ritual it is highly likely that they were characterised by a range of formulae. Although new genres have appeared in the Māori language it seems unlikely that the teaching of mathematics, for example, would be associated with much formulaic language. Furthermore, while some new genre such as broadcast rugby commentaries in Māori contain formulae, it is not clear that these are much more than calquing from English.

2. Corpora

The ability to study changes in the phrasal lexicon over time is facilitated by access to an increasing number of searchable corpora (many of which are available online). The analysis presented here includes material from two quite different corpora of the Māori language: the Māori newspaper corpus and the Māori Broadcast Corpus.

The Māori newspaper corpus (Niupepa Māori) is a written corpus comprising issues of 34 Māori newspapers printed between 1842 and 1932. The corpus contains approximately 10 million written words, about 85% of which is in Māori (Curnow 2002). The corpus comprises newspapers from three main sources: the government, Māori themselves, and religious organisations. Although there are overlaps, the newspapers from these three sources largely fall into three time bands: government 1842–1877, Māori 1862–1913 and religious 1898–1932. Results from the analysis presented here are shown in three time bands which closely align with these dates. The corpus is available online (Keegan et al. 2001) at www.nzdl.org/niupepa.

The Māori Broadcast Corpus (MBC) contains 1 million words transcribed from oral broadcast speech recorded in 1995 (Boyce 2006). Although a proportion of this corpus will be scripted or semi-scripted material the majority is unscripted spoken language. Both corpora are searchable: the newspaper corpus is searchable online and the broadcast corpus, available on CD, is searchable using proprietary concordance software.

3. Loss of PLIs – the case of *mauri*

We will examine the loss of PLIs in Māori through an analysis of the changing uses and meanings of the word *mauri* in 19th and 20th century sources.

3.1. *Definition of* mauri

In order to discuss changes in the use of *mauri* it is necessary to begin with defining *mauri* in English. However, definitions, especially for this particular word are problematic. For our purposes at this point we will accept modern definitions of the word, the main ones being 'life principle' (H. Williams 1971), 'life force' (Hikuroa et al. 2010) and 'life essence' (Barlow 1991). The nature of these definitions of *mauri* will be discussed in Section 3.4.

Both humans and natural resources have *mauri*. In the case of fishing spots, forests and other natural resources the *mauri* resides in a physical object such as a special stone (Best 1922). With humans, the *mauri* resides inside the person, thus lending itself to metaphysical translations, as above.

Contrary to much modern use of the term, the most important aspect of a *mauri* in 19th century was not that a *mauri* existed, but what state the *mauri* was in:

> Anything that supported human existence had a *mauri* (life force) whose condition was an index of success. A *mauri* for a fishing ground,

for example, represented the life in fish. *Mauri* are now often conflated with *wairua*, which describes an immortal soul, but formerly the difference between them was absolute: *mauri* were mortal.

(Head 2006: 138)

If the condition of *mauri* was important, we can assume that there would be PLIs to describe the condition of the *mauri*, and, furthermore, that there would be positive and negative descriptors.

3.2. Mauri *in the 19th century*

The two main 19th century sources which we will use to study the word *mauri* are the Māori newspaper corpus and dictionary entries for the word *mauri* in successive editions of the Williams' dictionary of Māori.

An online search of the newspaper corpus revealed 573 tokens of *mauri* but a large proportion of these were rejected. This is because the newspapers have been digitized using Optical Character Recognition (OCR) and are estimated to be 75–96% correct depending on the varying quality of the original image (Keegan et al. 2001). Because the online resource also has facsimile copies of each page of the newspaper it was possible to check the word in context. This check revealed that many of the tokens identified by the online search software were mistakes made by the OCR software, most commonly mistaking the words *Māori* or *mauria* for *mauri*. A number of tokens (175) were also eliminated due to the repeated use of one of the formulae in a newspaper banner (*Te Wānanga*). Examples of names (17 examples) or references to a time in the month (11) were also omitted from the analysis. There were only two examples of the word *mauri* referring to a physical object.

In total, 245 examples of *mauri* in the newspaper collection were analysed for this study. As expected, the majority of these tokens (225) were PLIs and only 20 were mono-morphemic. Despite the low numbers of single word uses of *mauri* it is interesting to note that these have increased over time, especially in the last time period (70% of mono-morphemic tokens occurred in the final time period).

Mauri was used in PLIs and formulae with three collocates: *oho* (to startle, surprise), *tau* (to become calm) and *ora* (to be healthy, alive). This accords with expectations, as these words describe a *mauri* in various states of ease or unease.

Of the three collocates *oho* was the most frequent, occurring 122 times (54%), then *ora* occurring 53 times (24%) and *tau* occurring 50 times (22%). The reason for *oho* being the most frequent collocate is perhaps because a startled or surprised *mauri* is more worthy of comment than one which is calmed down or healthy.

The frequency of the three main collocates over the three time periods is shown in Figure 1. These three time periods roughly equate to the main periods of publication of the three types of Māori newspaper: those published by the government or allied sources, those published by Māori themselves and those published by religious groups and individuals.

Oho is the most frequent collocate with *mauri* in all three time bands. However, within each time period, the proportion of tokens of *oho* has reduced from 81% to 56% to 44% over the three time bands. In contrast, the proportion of tokens with *ora* has increased over time. The next three sections will examine how these three collocates are used with *mauri*.

3.2.1. *Use of* mauri *with* oho. The use of *oho* with *mauri* refers to a *mauri* that has been awoken or startled, and is the most frequent collocate of *mauri* in the newspaper database. The first occurrence of *oho* with *mauri* occurs in the Māori newspapers in 1843. In the first edition of Williams Dictionary published by William Williams in 1844 the entry for *mauri* gives two examples with translations, repeated as examples (1) and (2) below, both of which are PLIs using the word *oho* (1844: 139).

(1) *Ka oho   taku mauri   i te pū-hanga   o te pū.*
    TAM startle my *mauri*   cause the shoot-NOM of the gun
    'I got a fright when the gun discharged.'

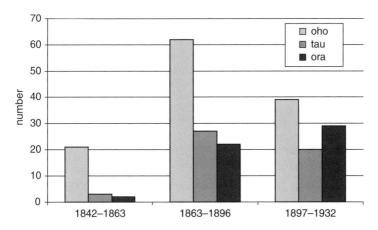

Figure 1. *Frequency of collocates of* mauri *in the Māori newspapers by time period*

(2) Kei oho mauri   ngā tāngata   o te kāinga.
    TAM startle *mauri*   the(PL) people   of the village
    'In case the people of that village get a fright.'

These sentences are representative of those found in the newspaper corpus, the typical form of which is shown in example (3). Optional elements are indicted in round brackets, alternative elements are indicated by a forward slash.

(3) (TAM) *oho* (*rere*) (TAM) DET/POSSPRONOUN *mauri* (*o* NP) (*i* NP).

This formula generates a wide range of possible expressions with some typical example phrases shown in examples (4) to (6).

(4) Ka oho   taku mauri.
    TAM startle   my *mauri*
    'I got a fright.'
(5) Oho ana   taku mauri   i te tae-nga   o te rongo.
    startle TAM my *mauri*   at the arrive-NOM of the news
    'I was startled when I heard the news.'
(6) Oho-rere ana   te mauri   o ngā mokopuna.
    startle-suddenly TAM   the *mauri*   of the(PL) grandchildren
    'The grandchildren got a big fright.'

Twenty-three percent of all the tokens of *oho* occurring with *mauri* included a result phrase introduced by '*i*' indicating what caused the *mauri* to be startled. An example of this sort of sentence is shown as example (7).

(7) Oho ana   taku mauri   i te wehi.
    startle TAM my *mauri*   cause the fear
    'I was startled with fear.'

Forty-six percent of the tokens were the compound, *ohomauri*, which first appears in the newspapers in 1857. This word is used both as a noun and verb as shown in examples (8) and (9) respectively.

(8) Oho-mauri ana   rātou.
    startle-*mauri* TAM   they
    'They were startled.'

(9) Kei te pōrangi   ia i te kaha rawa   o tōna oho-mauri.
    TAM beside oneself she cause the strong INTENS of her startle-*mauri*
    'The woman was beside herself because she was so startled.'

3.2.2. *Use of* mauri *with* tau. With 50 occurrences, the word *tau* (or variations thereof) was the least common collocate of *mauri* in PLIs in the newspaper database. The word *tau* indicates that the *mauri* has been calmed or settled down. The first occurrence of *tau* with *mauri* was in 1862, over twenty years after the first example with *oho*. Considering that the meaning of *tau* is to calm or settle down, it is perhaps not surprising that it is the least frequent collocate as the fact of a *mauri* being awoken or startled (*oho*) is far more noteworthy than the reverse state. Like *oho*, *tau* occurred in very productive constructions, the basic form shown in example (10) with sample examples (11) and (12).

(10) (TAM) *tau* DET/POSSPRONOUN *mauri* (*o* NP) (*ki reira/raro*).
(11) Kua tau   te mauri   o te tangata.
     TAM settle the *mauri* of the man.
     'The man calmed down.'
(12) Ka tau   taku mauri ki raro.
     TAM settle my *mauri* to below
     'I calmed down.'

Example (12) shows an interesting calque from the English phrasal verb 'to calm down' with 'down' being rendered by the phrase *ki raro* which traditionally would refer only to a physical location. A phrase with *ki* indicating the location of the action occurs in nine of the 50 examples. In fifteen of the 50 examples the variant *tatū* was used instead of *tau*.

3.2.3. *Use of* mauri *with* ora. The word *ora* (to be healthy or alive) was the second most frequent collocate of *mauri* in the newspaper corpus with 53 occurrences. Unlike *oho* and *tau* which occurred in PLIs which could be varied in an infinite number of ways by the writer, *ora* was found in the compound *mauri ora*. Furthermore, this compound was used in two formulae: the phrase *tihe mauri ora*, and in a proverb.

Tihe mauri ora was the most frequent formula with 35 occurrences, excluding the 175 tokens from the banner heading to the Māori newspaper *Te Wānanga* (1874–1878), shown in Figure 2. The phrase *Tihe mauri ora* (sneeze of life) is one of a number of *tauparapara* (incantations to begin a

TE WANANGA.

HE PANUITANGA TENA KIA KITE KOUTOU.

"TIHE MAURI-ORA."

NAMA, 1.	PAKOWHAI, WENEREI, AKUHATA, 5, 1874.	PUKAPUKA, 1.

He Perehi tenei mo te Motū katoa, mo nga tangata maori, kua huaina tona ingoa ko te Wananga o nga iwi katoa inaianei, kahore akau e karakia ana ki nga atua maori, hei ritenga ia mo te Perehi e | mai te mana o te tangata i te iwi, me te Rangatiratanga, me te whai taonga me te karanga ki te manuhiri. Waihoki me tenei taonga, ma koutou e kai ...

Figure 2. *Masthead of the Māori newspaper* Te Wānanga

speech) used in the formulaic genre of *whaikōrero* (oratory). The purpose of the *tauparapara* is to claim the right to speak. The first written occurrence of this formula was in 1859.

There were 12 tokens of the proverbial use of *mauri ora*, the first occurring in 1875. The proverb takes the form shown in example (13), where the word *noho* can be in variation with the word *māngere* (laziness) and *mate* with the word *matekai* (hunger).

(13) *Mauri mahi, mauri ora; mauri noho, mauri mate.*
 mauri work mauri healthy mauri sit   mauri die
 'Hard work leads to good health, idleness to affliction.'

Sometimes the proverb appears in a shortened form as *mauri mahi, mauri ora*. Considering the relative lateness of its first occurrence, the sentiments expressed in the proverb and that the proverbial use of *mauri ora* was high in religious newspapers it seems likely that the proverb was coined after colonisation.

This proverb is not in common use today. However, another version of it, shown as example (14), where *tama* replaces the word *mauri*, was the rallying idea behind Ngā Tamatoa, the Māori activist group of the 1970s.

(14) *Tama tū, tama ora, tama noho, tama mate.*
 'To stand up is to live, to sit down is to die.'

3.3. *Mauri in the 20th century*

We will now move to the use of *mauri* in the Māori Broadcast Corpus (MBC) (Boyce 2006). In contrast to the 19th century written newspaper material this corpus consists of transcripts of broadcast speech recorded in 1995. This corpus contains 157 tokens of the word *mauri*, 32% of which are PLIs. This is in direct contrast to the 19th century material where 92% of the tokens were PLIs. Figure 3 shows the different types of occurrences of *mauri* in both corpora.

We might have expected more examples of PLIs in the oral rather than the written corpus, and in fact the reverse is the case, suggesting that the change over time is even more pronounced than shown here.

A further difference is the relative proportions of the three collocates *oho, ora* and *tau*. In the 19th century material *oho* was the most frequent collocate (54%), followed by *ora* (24%, 66% of these being accounted for by the formula *tihe mauri ora*), with *tau* being the most infrequent collocate of the three, accounting for 22% of the occurrences of *mauri* as a PLI.

In contrast, the most frequent collocate of *mauri* in the MBC is *ora* (86%, all of which are examples of the formula *tihe mauri ora*). There are only 2 examples of PLIs using *oho* and 5 examples using *tau*.

Tau, which was the least frequent of the 3 collocates in the newspaper corpus has now become more common than *oho*. Furthermore it now appears in compounds, all but one of which is the form *mauri tau* which is defined as 'absence of panic' (Moorfield 2005: 85).

(15) *Ko tērā te wā   i kite   i te mauri tau.*
EQ that the time TAM see DO the absence of panic
'That was when we saw the absence of panic.'

Thus the overwhelming use of *mauri* in PLIs in modern speech appears to be accounted for by the formula *tihe mauri ora* and the compound *mauri tau*.

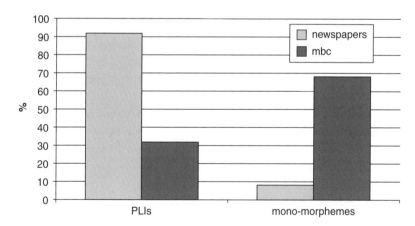

Figure 3. *Percentage use of* mauri *in PLIs and as a mono-morpheme in the Māori newspaper corpus and the Māori Broadcast Corpus*

A search of recordings in the MAONZE (Māori and New Zealand English) corpus (King et al. 2011) confirmed this finding. This corpus contains recordings of the Māori and English speech of three groups of male and female Māori born from the 1870s through to the 1980s and recorded at various times from 1938 to 2009. Amongst the speech of the 69 speakers in this corpus there were nineteen examples of *mauri*, and while 11 of these were PLIs, 6 were the compound *mauri tau*. There is only one example of the formula *tihe mauri ora* in the MAONZE corpus but this is not surprising since it contains very little oratorical material.

3.4. *Defining* mauri

So how did the change in the use of *mauri* come about? When we look back to the first four editions of the Williams' dictionary of the Māori language the entries for the word *mauri* are short with the only change over time being the addition of other obscure referents (such as 'poles', 'moon on the 29th day', etc.). The examples given in the dictionary to illustrate usage were PLIs using *oho* (see examples (1) and (2)).

However, there was a big change between the 4th and 5th editions of the Williams' dictionary (W. Williams & W. Williams 1892 and W. Williams & H. Williams 1917) when the entry for *mauri* increased from 10 lines to a whole column. In the preface to the 5th edition Herbert Williams explains Eldson Best's important role in this huge expansion.

> The most important contribution, in volume and in character is that made by Mr. Elsdon Best ... He not only supplied a very large number of words, new meanings and examples ... but has also .... rendered valuable assistance ... [with] his esoteric knowledge of the Māori being of the greatest weight.
> (W. Williams & H. Williams 1917: viii)

As was common at the time, dictionary definitions focussed on the monomorphemic use of a word, rather than the use of a word in PLIs. This practice helps to obscure the importance of the phrasal nature of many words and ignores the fact that we often parse PLIs only as far as we need to extract meaning (Wray 2002).

The original definition of *mauri* in the Williams dictionary published in 1844 (W. Williams 1844) was 'heart' and this meaning had survived up to, and including the 4th edition of the dictionary in 1892. This definition had been derived from the meanings of the two examples given in the dictionary (examples (1) and (2)). For if a gun was discharged (example (1)) was it not the heart that became startled enough to beat faster? However, under Best's interrogation, *mauri* became more metaphysical, and defined as 'life principle' reflecting Best's interest in defining and differentiating metaphysical words like *hau, manawa* and *mauri* (Best 1922).

Nowadays the word *mauri* is defined as 'life essence' or 'life principle' (Moorfield 2005: 85). Best's definition has remained the accepted meaning of *mauri* and has influenced several generations of Māori and non-Māori commentators (Holman 2010: 272–8).

Also included in the expanded dictionary entry of 1917 were three compound word forms of *mauri* of the form *mauri* + adjective: *mauri tau* ('absence of panic'), *mauri rere* ('panic stricken') and *mauri ora* (also defined as 'life principle'). These forms continue to be cited in modern dictionaries like *He Pātaka Kupu* (Te Taura Whiri i te reo Māori 2008) and *Te Aka* (Moorfield 2005).

Nevertheless, there is some indication that the concept of *mauri* still retains some sense of the early use in a range of PLIs which comment on the state of a *mauri*. For example Te Kipa Kepa Morgan (Morgan 2006) has developed a 'Mauri Model' to assess the state of natural resources within ecosystems. This model is based on the concept that the *mauri* of natural resources can fluctuate both positively and negatively and that this can be assessed.

3.5. *Summary*

Over the last 150 years the use of the word *mauri* has changed greatly. Examples from the 19th century reveal that *mauri* most commonly occurred in PLIs with three collocates. The PLIs associated with two of these collocates, *oho* and *tau,* were capable of great variation as circumstances required. At the end of the 20th century the word *mauri* is less frequently used in PLIs, apart from the formula *tihe mauri ora* which has been retained because of its use in the formulaic genre of oratory. This is one formulaic genre which is still strong in Māori culture and in which the formulae are still being learned intergenerationally. Other modern uses of *mauri* tend to be of the compound form *mauri* + adjective, in particular, *mauri tau* ('absence of panic'). The most frequent collocate from the 19th century, *oho*, occurs infrequently today with *mauri*.

Accordingly, changes in the use of *mauri* over time provide evidence to support the first hypothesis stated in Section 1.1:

1. That many Māori PLIs will not be used as frequently as formerly.

The fact that the most common modern use of *mauri* is in a PLI associated with a formulaic genre suggests that formulaic genre have an important role in the maintenance of a language's phrasal lexicon.

We also predict that other Māori words which have had productive collocates might now be more likely to have formed compound words with these collocates. With the shift to English, words in Māori have a tendency to be learnt separately as individual lexical items, and this has no doubt influenced these changes. In addition, due to the circumstances surrounding the language today, younger speakers have restricted access to a full phrasal lexicon which is expressed through a multiplicity of genres, styles, and a wide range of social contexts.

4. New formulae: the case of *moe*

The second hypothesis concerning the likely changes to the phrasal lexicon of Māori over time was that new PLIs would enter Māori via calquing from English. We will examine this by examining formulae associated with death, an aspect of Māori culture attended by many rituals (Oppenheim 1973). In particular, we will examine Māori eulogies which historically contain a good deal of formulaic language, much of which is also expressed in song (Orbell 1995: 36).

As shown in the previous section, the most unchanging use of *mauri* over time was with the formula *tihe mauri ora* from the formulaic genre of *whaikōrero*. Eulogies to the dead are another such genre so we would similarly expect this genre to be reasonably resistant to change and resilient in its phrasal repertoire.

4.1. *Māori eulogies*

Eulogies in Māori (*poroporoaki*) address the dead person directly, unlike the convention in English which is to talk about the deceased rather than to talk directly to them. In Māori culture, following death the spirit of the dead person travels north to the top of the North Island (Te Reinga), from there travelling to Hawaiki, the homeland of the Māori (Orbell 1995). The role of the speaker in addressing the dead person is to encourage the deceased's spirit to depart on this journey. As a consequence there are many formulae used in *poroporoaki* which focus on saying farewell and encouraging the spirit to depart (Oppenheim 1973:16; Salmond 1975: 183–4). The verb *haere* 'to go' is the most frequent word used in this context. Best (1905: 171–172) cites a number of examples as typical forms. Some of these are given in example (16).

(16) *Haere rā e Pa!   Haere ki ōu tīpuna.   Haere ki Hawaiki.*
go distant VOC sir go to your ancestors go to Hawaiki
'Farewell, O father! Go to your ancestors. Depart to Hawaiki.'

These PLIs, and many like them, are still used today, indicating that the formulae involved in this genre have been handed down through the generations.

4.2. *Speaking about death in English*

In English, death is often spoken of euphemistically. Nowadays people don't die, they 'pass' or 'pass away' or 'pass over'. Historically, one of the main metaphors for death in English is DEATH IS REST. It is common to see on older headstones in cemeteries the abbreviation R.I.P. (Latin: 'requiescat in pace'), commonly expressed in English as 'rest in peace'. This formula is also not uncommon in modern day death notices in newspapers.

A similar metaphor used in English is DEATH IS SLEEP. This metaphor has a long lineage, occurring in pre-Christian Greek and Latin literature. Ogle (1933) notes that,

> in Hebrew literature, as represented in the Old Testament, as early at least as the sixth century B.C., the dead are often ... denoted as "those asleep", and death as "a sleep" ... Passages from the Old Testament play an important part in the establishing of a tradition which appears in the New Testament, in the Greek and Latin Fathers, and in the liturgy of the Greek and Latin Church.
>
> (Ogle 1933: 89–90)

Accordingly, there are many examples of the DEATH IS SLEEP metaphor throughout the Bible, particularly in the Psalms.

The euphemistic use of 'sleep' for 'death' is not limited to the Bible. The English language contains a very wide range of euphemisms for death, including a range of metaphors of sleep, some religious and some not. Well over 200 euphemisms for death, including almost twenty involving sleep or rest, have been identified as being used in English in the 19th and early 20th century (Pound 1936: 197).

If the idea that DEATH IS REST and DEATH IS SLEEP have been calqued into Māori we would expect to see words like *moe* (to sleep), *takoto* (to lie down) and *okioki* (to rest) to be used in eulogistic forms. Due to the difficulty in examining all three of these words the analysis will, for the most part, restrict itself to *moe*.

4.3. *The meaning of* moe

The Māori word for 'sleep' is *moe*. Like English, it also has the meaning 'to sleep with'. However, it appears that historically this word wasn't associated with death. The form *moe* is common amongst related Polynesian languages and there is little suggestion that *moe* referred to death in any of these languages (Tregear 1891: 246; Greenhill et al. 2010).

In the Williams' dictionaries, the entry for *moe* does not include the meaning 'to die' until the 5th edition in 1917 (W. Williams & H. Williams 1917). In the first two editions (W. Williams 1844, 1852) the only translations of *moe* are 'sleep' and 'dream', and in the third edition (W. Williams & W. Williams 1871) 'marry' enters. This late entry of the meaning 'die' for *moe* in dictionary sources suggests that this meaning has been calqued from English. In an early collection of written texts in Māori first published in 1854 (Grey 1971) the word *moe* appears 103 times (Harlow 1990) but in only one of these instances does it mean 'to die.'

4.4. Moe *in the 19th century*

Although traditionally the word *moe* does not seem to have referred to death, there are relatively early examples of this word's use in death notices and obituaries in Māori newspapers. The first use of *moe* to mean 'died' or 'dead' was in 1855 in an obituary written by a non-Māori.

(17) *Ka mutu ēnei kupu āna ka moe ia.*
 TAM end these words his TAM die he
 'When these words of his were ended he died.'

There are many examples such as this where *moe* was used synonymously with, and often alongside, conventional words for death such as *mate*. The majority of examples of *moe* being used for 'died' or 'dead' were made in a religious context such as in example (18) from 1858 where *moe* is overtly linked to Christian faith.

(18) *kia moe i runga i te whakapono*
 TAM die at on DO the faith
 'to die in faith.'

Formulaic uses of *moe* began to appear at about the same time, particularly in phrases used to address the deceased. The formula *moe mai* first appeared in 1855. *Mai* is a directional particle, untranslatable in these examples, which indicates a metaphorical orientation towards the speaker.

(19) *Moe mai   e Pā!*
     sleep hither VOC sir
     'Sleep, o sir!'

Over the whole newspaper corpus there were 32 examples of *moe mai*. The formula was used both in vocative and declamatory statements, in both reports about death and *waiata tangi* (laments). The postposed deictic particles *nā* (NEARII) or *rā* (DIST) were frequently included in the phrase.

(20) *moe mai rā   i roto   i te puku   o tō maunga*
     sleep hither DIST at inside at the belly of your mountain
     'sleeping there in the belly of your mountain'

In 1876 the first printed example of the formula *moe ... i te moenga roa* ('sleep ... the long sleep') appeared in the Māori newspapers. In all there were 105 occurrences, with most appearing after the beginning of the 20th century. The structure of the formula is shown in example (20).

(21)   TAM *moe* (SUBJ) *i te moenga roa* (*o te* NP*)*

In eleven of these occurrences, the word *takoto* (to lie down) was substituted for *moe*. This formula is a close match with one of the euphemisms for death identified by Pound: sleeps the long sleep / is sleeping the final sleep (1936: 197). In Māori the formula is usually expressed in a very simple form but variation and extension facilitates a wide variety of expression. In nearly all instances this formula followed English convention in being used to talk about the dead person rather than addressing them directly. Thus the Māori version calques both the sentiment and its cultural context.

Māori calques of other well known English euphemisms cited by Pound also appear occasionally in the newspaper collection. 'Sleeps the sleep that knows no waking' is calqued into Māori as *moe i te moenga roa kāore nei he korikoringa*. The formula 'asleep in Jesus' is rendered *moe ana i runga i a te Karaiti*.

4.5. Māori literacy and print culture

At this point it is necessary to outline some of the features of Māori introduction to literacy and the effect of the development of a print culture in the Māori language. Literacy in Māori was introduced with the missionaries who by 1830 had substantially developed the phonemic orthography we know today (Parkinson 2003: 38). Māori literacy rates were high and knowledge of the Bible and associated writings spread very quickly. By 1845, when the missions reached their greatest geographical expansion, there must have been, on a numerical basis, a copy of either a Bible or a Prayer Book for every adult member of the population, believed to total about 100,000 (Barrington and Beaglehole 1974: 28). The importance of Christianity in shaping Māori thought in the second half of the 19th century is reflected in the fact that 'there was no post-1840 Māori leader with aspirations beyond the tribe who was not both literate and Christian' (Head 2005: 60).

The advent of Māori newspapers in 1842 which encouraged subscribers to submit letters and other material saw the extension of Māori literacy into the beginnings of a rich print culture in Māori. A characteristic of such contributions was the direct translation of formal oratorical conventions to the written page (Kāretu 2002). Where material was written by Europeans, there would often have been a literal translation of English concepts into Māori (Paterson 2006: 49). Applying this to the death notices, many of these writings are likely to be English ideas, structures and formulae, translated into Māori by writers whose first language was English.

Even when the author of an obituary or letter was Māori there was potential for influence from both by the style and vocabulary of other writing in the paper and expectations of what was acceptable for publication. When the writer was a member of a faith, it was likely that their use of language would also be affected by the language used in that faith.

4.6. Moe *in the 20th century*

The MBC includes some *poroporoaki*, in particular from the introductions to the documentary television programme *Waka Huia*. In these situations traditional exhortations involving the verb *haere* are used alongside expressions using *moe*. The formula *moe mai (rā)* occurred 26 times in addressing people who had died. It was not uncommon for the formula to be repeated as in example (22) as repetition plays an important role in Māori oratory (Salmond 1975: 164).

(22) *moe mai,   moe mai,   moe mai rā*
    sleep hither sleep hither sleep hither DIST
    'Sleep, sleep, sleep there'

The formula could also be used in a variety of ways to introduce supporting statements. An illustration of this is shown in example (22).

(23) *te hunga   kua mate kua moe mai   ki te pō roa*
    the people TAM die   TAM sleep hither to the night long
    'the people who have died, who have passed away to the long night.'

The compound *moenga roa* occurred 19 times in the MBC corpus, but unlike the examples from the Māori newspapers, *takoto* ('to lie down') and *okioki* ('to rest') were more frequent collocates than *moe*.

(24) *kua okioki   rātou i te moenga roa*
    TAM rest   they at the sleep long
    'They are resting in eternal sleep'
(25) *takoto mai   i tō moenga roa*
    TAM lie down at your sleep long
    'Rest in your eternal sleep'

Although example (25) illustrates a vocative use of this formula the majority of occurrences in this corpus are declamatory. However, vocative examples of all these formulae occur in collections of *poroporoaki* recorded from 1950–1970 (Rewi 2010; Brooke-White 1981) indicating that these calqued forms have entered into the formulaic genre of *poroporoaki* and been passed down through several generations to the present day to be included in the range of formulae on hand for an orator to use when required.

4.7. *Summary*

The development of newspapers printed in Māori led to a print culture in Māori and extended the formulaic genre of *poroporoaki* to the similarly formulaic English genre of the death notice and obituary. Accordingly, when reporting about deaths in the newspapers Māori correspondents combined features of both Māori and European tradition. There was often a direct addressing of the deceased in accordance with Māori convention. But conventions of the written death notices in English such as details of when and where the person died and any relevant circumstances of their death were also adopted.

Early records suggest that the meaning of *moe* was originally limited to the meanings of 'sleep' and 'to sleep with'. The Māori newspaper corpus demonstrates an increase over time in the frequency of the use of *moe* to refer to death. The formula *moe mai (rā)* was adopted into the vocative formulae of *poroporoaki*. Another formula, *moe ... i te moenga roa*, reflecting Christian thought and calqued from an English formula, is used in a more English manner in reporting about a death. These are calques from English where the metaphors DEATH IS SLEEP and DEATH IS REST are well known and associated with biblical literature. The introduction of *moe* into the group of formulae available in the formulaic genre of *poroporoaki* is an example of calquing from English, of not only the form but also the cultural context. In that this calque is strongly associated with Christianity provides further evidence of the important role that Christianity has played in Māori culture (Head 2005), particularly through Christian metaphor (King 2007).

Thus the extension of *moe* into the formulaic genre of *poroporoaki* confirms the second hypothesis with regard to changes in the phrasal lexicon of Māori over time: that the phrasal lexicon will have incorporated calques from English, in this case formulae and the non-linguistic cultural elements surrounding their use.

5. Discussion

There has been much change in the Māori language over the time that it has been in close contact with English. With regard to changes in the phrasal lexicon of Māori through an examination of the use of the word *mauri* we have found evidence of loss of PLIs and a preference in modern Māori for compound words. The PLIs which are most likely to be resistant to change are those associated with formulaic genre, like oratory and eulogy which are still practised today. These verbal rituals continue to be passed down intergenerationally, and formats and formulae associated with them remain substantially similar to that contained in early records.

However, formulaic genre such as these can still admit new forms. A strong influence in this regard has been biblical metaphors, as the Bible was the first and most dominant source of written Māori in the 19th century. Biblically based metaphors such as DEATH IS SLEEP have been calqued into Māori resulting in the verb *moe* ('to sleep') taking on the meaning 'to die'. Formulae which parallel English phrases have also become part of the formulaic genre of eulogy. Furthermore, both form and functions of this metaphor in English have been adopted into Māori.

All languages change over time, and this dynamism is a feature of both vocabulary and the phrasal lexicon. Language contact provides a context where a minority language can be greatly affected by a language of wider communication. Documentary sources of Māori which are now readily available and searchable allow us to chart aspects of change in the phrasal lexicon of Māori as it has been in increasing contact with English. We suggest that the lexicographical impulse to define words with little regard for their phrasal contexts has assisted in the loss of PLIs which could be infinitely adapted for each situation. Those PLIs which tend to be retained are compounds along with formulae associated with formulaic genre. Conversely, the important role of Christianity in Māori culture and society is underscored by the adoption of biblical formulae into Māori. Undoubtedly similar processes have affected the phrasal lexicons of other indigenous languages during colonisation. These processes of change confirm the notion that 'culture was' and is 'transmitted by formula' (Moon 1997*)*.

University of Canterbury, New Zealand

Acknowledgement

We would like to acknowledge the work of Jeffrey Holman (Holman 2010) whose examination of the pioneer ethnographer Elsdon Best and his work on defining the concept of *mauri* was the inspiration for this paper.

Note

Correspondence address: j.king@canterbury.ac.nz

References

Barrington, J. M. & Timothy H. Beaglehole. 1974. *Maori schools in a changing society: An historical review.* Wellington: New Zealand Council for Educational Research.

Barlow, Cleve. 1991. *Tikanga whakaaro: Key concepts in Māori Culture.* Oxford: Oxford University Press.

Bauer, Winifred. 2008. Is the health of te reo Māori improving? *Te Reo* 51. 33–73

Benton, Richard. A. 1991. *The Maori language: Dying or reviving?* Honolulu: East West Center. (Reprinted by New Zealand Council for Educational Research in 1997).
Best, Elsdon. 1904. *Notes on the art of war: as conducted by the Māori of New Zealand, with accounts of various customs, rites, superstitions, &c., pertaining to war, as practised and believed in by the ancient Māori.* Auckland: Reed, in association with the Polynesian Society.
Best, Elsdon. 1905. Māori eschatology: The whare pōtae and its lore. *Transactions and Proceedings of the New Zealand Institute* 38. 148–239.
Best, Elsdon. 1922. *Spiritual and mental concepts of the Māori.* Wellington: Dominion Museum.
Best, Elsdon. 1942. *Forest lore of the Maori with methods of snaring, trapping, and preserving birds and rats, uses of berries, roots, fern-root, and forest products, with mythological notes on origins, karakia used etc.* Wellington: The Polynesian Society, in collaboration with the Dominion Museum.
Boyce, Mary T. 2006. *A corpus of modern spoken Māori.* Wellington, NZ: Victoria University of Wellington PhD thesis.
Brooke-White, Val. 1981. *Whaikoorero: Ceremonial farewells to the dead.* Wellington: Continuing Education Unit Radio New Zealand.
Grey, George. 1971. *Ngā mahi a ngā tūpuna* (4th ed.). Wellington: A.H. & A.W. Reed.
Greenhill, Simon J., Ross Clark & Bruce Biggs. 2010. *Polynesian Lexicon Project Online [Pollex].* Available at: http://pollex.org.nz/.
Harlow, Ray. 1990. *A name and word index to Ngā mahi a ngā tūpuna.* Dunedin: University of Otago Press.
Harlow, Ray. 2007. *Māori: A linguistic introduction.* Cambridge: Cambridge University Press.
Harlow, Ray, Peter Keegan, Jeanette King, Margaret Maclagan & Catherine Watson. 2009. The changing sound of the Māori language. In James N. Stanford & Dennis R. Preston (eds.), *Variation in indigenous minority languages,* 129–152. Amsterdam: John Benjamins.
Head, Lyndsay. 2005. Wiremu Tamihana and the *mana* of Christianity. In John Stenhouse (ed.), *Christianity, modernity and culture: New perspectives on New Zealand history,* 58–86. Adelaide: ATF Press.
Head, Lyndsay. 2006. *Land, authority and the forgetting of being in early colonial Māori history.* Christchurch, N.Z: University of Canterbury PhD thesis.
Hikuroa, Dan, Te Kipa Kepa Morgan, Darren Gravley & Manuka Henare. 2010. Integrating indigenous values in geothermal development. In Joseph S. Te & Susan M. Healy (eds.) *Proceedings of the 4th International Traditional Knowledge Conference,* 149–152. Auckland: Ngā Pae o te Māramatanga.
Holman, Jeffrey Paparoa. 2010. *Best of both worlds: The story of Elsdon Best and Tutakangahau.* North Shore: Penguin.
Jackendoff, Ray S. 1995. The boundaries of the lexicon. In Martin Everaert, Erik-Jan van der Linden, André Schenk & Rob Schreuder (eds.), *Idioms: Structural*

and psychological perspectives, 133–166. Hillsdale, NJ: Lawrence Erlbaum Associates.

Kāretu, Tīmoti. 1995. Ākene he kōrero takurua. *He Muka* 8(2). 5–7.

Kāretu, Tīmoti. 2002. Māori print culture: The newspapers. In Jennifer Curnow, Ngapare K. Hopa & Jane McRae (eds.), *Rere atu, taku manu! Discovering history, language & politics in the Māori-language newspapers,* 1–16. Auckland: Auckland University Press.

Keegan, Te Taka, Mark Apperley, Sally Jo Cunningham & Ian Witten. 2001. The Niupepa Collection: Opening the blinds on a window to the past. In David Bearman & Franca Garzotto (eds.), *Proceedings of the International Cultural Heritage Informatics Meeting Conference ICHIM01*, Volume 1, 347–356. Available at: http://www.cs.waikato.ac.nz/~tetaka/tuhituhi.html

King, Jeanette. 1999. Lessons from Māori schooling experience – 13 years of immersion schools. In Nicholas Ostler (ed.) *Proceedings of the Third Conference of the Foundation for Endangered Languages*, 117–124. Bath: Foundation for Endangered Languages.

King, Jeanette. 2001. Te Kōhanga Reo: Māori language revitalization. In Leanne Hinton & Ken Hale (eds.), *The green book of language revitalization in practice*, 118–128. San Diego: Academic Press.

King, Jeanette. 2007. *Eke ki runga i te waka: The use of dominant metaphors by newly-fluent Māori speakers in historical perspective.* Christchurch, NZ: University of Canterbury PhD thesis.

King, Jeanette, Margaret Maclagan, Ray Harlow, Peter Keegan & Catherine Watson. 2011. The MAONZE project: Changing uses of an indigenous language database. *Corpus Linguistics and Linguistic Theory* 7(1). 37–57.

Kuiper, Koenraad. 2009. *Formulaic genres.* Basingstoke: Palgrave Macmillan.

Lewis, Gari & Jeni Smallwood. 2010. Pobl Ifanc: Ymbweru er mwyn Gweithredu Young people: Empowering for action. In Hywel Glyn & Nicholas Ostler (eds.), *Proceedings of the fourteenth conference of the Foundation for Endangered Languages*, 141–147. Reading, England: The Foundation for Endangered Languages.

Mel'čuk, Igor. 1995. Phrasemes in language and phraseology in linguistics. In Martin Everaert, Erik-Jan van der Linden, André Schenk & Rob Schreuder (eds.), *Idioms: Structural and psychological perspectives,* 167–232. Hillsdale, NJ: Lawrence Erlbaum Associates.

Moon, Paul. 1997. Traditional Māori proverbs: Some general themes. *Deep South* 3(1). Available at: http://www.otago.ac.nz/DeepSouth/vol3no1/moon2.html

Moorfield, John C. 2005. *Te Aka Māori-English, English-Māori dictionary and index.* Auckland: Pearson Education New Zealand.

Morgan, Te Kepa Brian. 2006. Decision-support tools and the indigenous paradigm. *Engineering Sustainability* 159. 169–177.

Ogle, Marbury B. 1933. The sleep of death. *Memoirs of the American Academy in Rome* 11. 81–117.

Oppenheim, Roger S. 1973. *Māori death customs.* Wellington: A.H. & A.W. Reed Ltd.
Orbell, Margaret. 1995. *The illustrated encyclopedia of Māori myth and legend.* Christchurch: Canterbury University Press.
Parkinson, Phil. 2003. The Māori grammars and vocabularies of Thomas Kendall and John Gare Butler. Part 3: Kendall's revised grammar, 1827–32. *Rongorongo Studies* 13(2). 37–55.
Paterson, Lachy. 2006. *Colonial discourses: Niupepa Māori 1855–1863.* Dunedin: Otago University Press.
Pound, Louise. 1936. American euphemisms for dying, death, and burial. *American Speech* 11(3). 195–202. Retrieved from: http://www.jstor.org/pss/452239
Reedy, Tamati. 2000. Te Reo Maori: The past 20 years and looking forward. *Oceanic Linguistics* 39(1). 157–169.
Rewi, Poia. 2010. *Whaikōrero: The word of Māori oratory.* Auckland: Auckland University Press.
Salmond, Anne. 1975. *Hui: A study of Māori ceremonial gatherings.* Wellington: A.H. & A.W. Reed Ltd.
Statistics New Zealand. 2007. *QuickStats about Māori.* Wellington: Author.
Sutton, Doug. G. 1994. *The origin of the first New Zealanders.* Auckland: Auckland University Press.
Te Puni Kōkiri. 2008. *The health of the Māori language in 2006.* Wellington: Author.
Te Taura Whiri i te Reo Māori. 1999. *He kohinga kīwaha.* Auckland: Reed.
Te Taura Whiri i te Reo Māori. 2008. *He pātaka kupu: Te kai a te rangatira.* North Shore: Reed.
Tregear, Edward. 1891. *The Māori-Polynesian comparative dictionary.* Wellington: Lyon and Blair.
Wallace, Patricia T. 2009. Changing usage of kiekie (Freycinetia banksii) and challenges to sustainability. In C. A. Wilson & R. M. Laing, *Natural fibres in Australasia: Proceedings of the combined (NZ and AUS) conference of The Textile Institute,* 127–131. Dunedin: The Textile Institute (NZ).
Williams, Herbert W. 1971. *Dictionary of the Māori language* (7th ed.). Wellington: Government Printer.
Williams, William. 1844. *A dictionary of the New-Zealand language, and a concise grammar: to which is added a selection of colloquial sentences.* Paihia, N.Z.: Printed at the Press of the Church Missionary Society.
Williams, William. 1852. *A dictionary of the New Zealand language and a concise grammar: to which is added a selection of colloquial sentences* (2nd ed.). London: Williams and Norgate.
Williams, William & Herbert W. Williams. 1917. *A dictionary of the Māori language* (5th ed.). Wellington: Govt. Printer.
Williams, William & William L. Williams. 1871. *A dictionary of the New Zealand language: to which is added a selection of colloquial sentences* (3rd ed.). London: Williams and Norgate.

Williams, William & William L. Williams. 1892. *A dictionary of the New Zealand language* (4th ed.). Wellington: Whitcombe & Tombs.

Wray, Alison. 2002. *Formulaic language and the lexicon*. Cambridge: Cambridge University Press.

Helvetismen: Nationale und areale Varianten? Kodifizierung und sprachliche Realität.[1]

BRITTA JUSKA-BACHER

Abstract

The concept of pluricentricity – introduced by Michael Clyne in its modern form – is widely accepted for the German language area. It states that German is an official language in three nations – Germany, Switzerland and Austria – where it has evolved into discrete standard varieties. This is also reflected in lexicography, e.g. in the Variantenwörterbuch des Deutschen, *which lists national lexical variants from the three countries.*

Despite agreement on pluricentricity, there is controversy among linguists about what determines geographical boundaries between language varieties, in particular about the relative importance of national or dialect areas such as Bavarian and Alemannic, either of which transcend the borders between two and three countries (Austria/South-East Germany, and Switzerland/Eastern Austria/South-West Germany). Among the linguists who have tried to resolve the controversy, Ingo Reiffenstein emphasises the overlap of national and areal variation.

This article addresses the co-existence of national and dialect-area influences. It investigates the spatial distribution of familiarity with a set of phrasemes which relevant contemporary dictionaries have defined as Helvetisms.

A survey of 1,000 individuals from Switzerland, Germany and Austria examined their familiarity with 18 alleged phraseological Helvetisms; participants were also asked to guess at the phrasemes' spatial distribution. On the basis of this empirical data, we sought to confirm whether the phrasemes are in fact restricted to Switzerland, or whether they occur in (parts of) the other standard variety areas, paying particular attention to areas adjacent to Switzerland, i.e. Austria and Baden-Württemberg in Germany.

The definition of a (phraseological) Helvetism implies two main assumptions: firstly, the phraseme needs to be part of this standard variety of German, expressed by its codification in dictionaries, with Koller also requiring that speakers be aware of the phraseme being a Swiss variant. Secondly, the phraseme needs to be widely used in German-speaking Switzerland, and only here.

Three criteria – e.g. existing dictionaries, expert opinion, and empirical data (corpus linguistics or survey data) – indicate codification of phrasemes in dictionaries. While the lexicographers of three dictionaries relevant for national phraseme variants, i.e. Duden Redewendungen (Dudenredaktion 2008), Schweizer Wörterbuch (Meyer 2006), and Variantenwörterbuch (Ammon et al. 2004), refer to all three of these criteria, including empirical data collected from corpora, none have ascertained whether informants from the relevant regions are familiar with the phrasemes. Hence, the three dictionaries can establish only an approximate relation between relevant phrasemes and national language areas; none of them contain reliable data on the spatial distribution of phraseological units, particularly in crossborder dialect areas. Another problem in dealing with phraseological Helvetisms is that of terminological imprecision due to insufficient knowledge of spatial distribution; phrasemes known to be in use across the entire Alemannic area (German and Austrian border areas with Switzerland) are nevertheless defined as Helvetisms in contemporary dictionaries. A third problem is our limited knowledge of speaker awareness. Several studies have found evidence for low awareness by Swiss speakers of their national variety and its variants, which was one reason for Koller to entirely negate the existence of a Swiss national variety.

The survey

We conducted a survey on the knowledge of a group of 18 phrasemes codified as Helvetisms in the above-mentioned dictionaries. Almost 1,000 informants from Austria, Germany and Switzerland (the largest cohort) answered multiple-choice questions regarding their familiarity with the phrasemes, and the form or meaning of phrasemes; participants were also asked to guess at the spatial distribution of the phrasemes in German-speaking countries, and to supply personal information on age, gender, education and place of residence. We used the data to create maps showing the spatial distribution of these supposed Helvetisms.

Results

1. The data collected from Swiss, German and Austrian speakers regarding their familiarity with so-called phraseological Helvetisms show both national and areal influences, and therefore confirm the co-existence of national and areal concepts. Three groups of phrasemes were distinguished according to their spatial distribution, with the first group restricted to but widespread within the Swiss language area (e.g. dastehen wie der Esel am Berg *– literally: 'to stand like a donkey at the foot of the mountain', English equivalent: 'to look like a [dying] duck in a thunderstorm'), and therefore Helvetisms sensu stricto. A second group of phrasemes (e.g.* durchs Band weg *– literally: 'off through the band', meaning 'every single one') was known outside Switzerland to relevant degrees (i.e. > 40% of participants), which means that, taking their actual spatial distribution into account, they can be named more appropriately, e.g. Austro-Helvetism (known in Switzerland and Austria), Alemannism (well-known throughout the Allemannic dialect region), etc. The third group of phrasemes was re-stricted to some regions of Switzerland but unknown in the other German speaking areas (e.g.* das Feuer im Elsass sehen *– literally: 'to see the fire in Alsace', meaning 'to be in great pain'), and may therefore be considered regional Helvetisms or Swiss regionalisms to indicate their restricted distribution in Switzerland.*

2. The empirical data give an impression of Swiss speakers' awareness of their national variants. Average awareness of a phraseme's status as a Helvetism was 50%, which means one in two Swiss informants correctly identified a Helvetism – a comparatively low value that confirms outcomes of other studies. However, these awareness values should be interpreted with caution since classification as a Helvetism may be influenced by several factors, e.g. correct classification was highly correlated with familiarity of the phrasemes; well-known phrasemes were more often correctly classified as Helvetisms.

Moreover, our findings suggest that even relatively low awareness need not be a criterion for the general denial of a standard variety, as Koller does for Switzerland.

Linguists can and should support speakers' awareness of the national variety, and reinforce their linguistic self-confidence in the non-dominant language community. To use a Swiss example, the codification of national variants can demonstrate that common French loan words for Bürgersteig, Hähnchen, Fahrrad *– i.e.* Trottoir, Poulet, Velo *(pavement, chicken, bicycle) – are fully equivalent to their German counterparts.*

1. Plurizentrik der deutschen Sprache: Plurinationalität oder Pluriarealität?

Grundlage der heutigen Plurizentrikdiskussion[2] stellen die Ausführungen von Clyne dar (1984, siehe auch 1992), in denen das Deutsche als plurizentrische, im Sinne einer plurinationalen Sprache mit den drei Vollzentren Deutschland, Österreich und der Schweiz beschrieben wird.[3] In diesen Ländern haben sich aufgrund der unterschiedlichen nationalen Entwicklung je eigene standardsprachliche Varietäten herausgebildet. Dies Konzept der nationalen Varietäten ist prinzipiell akzeptiert und belegt, wovon u.a. verschiedene Wörterbücher zeugen, die sich die Erfassung der Lexik dieser Varietäten zum Ziel gesetzt haben: Das *Variantenwörterbuch des Deutschen* von Ammon et al. (2004), *Wie sagt man in Österreich?* von Ebner (2009) und das *Schweizer Wörterbuch* von Meyer (2006), Neuauflage von *Wie sagt man in der Schweiz?*, Meyer (1989).

Die zentrale Gewichtung des nationalen Einflusses ist allerdings verschiedentlich auch auf Kritik gestoßen. So wurde argumentiert, dass die räumliche Komponente einerseits nur eine von zahlreichen sozialen Dimensionen darstelle (siehe beispielsweise Koller 1999: 156) und dass andererseits bei der räumlichen Gliederung des deutschen Sprachraums die areale Komponente (sprich der Einfluss der Dialekträume auf die Standardsprache dieser Gebiete) schwerer gewichte als die nationale (Scharloth 2005: 237).[4] Es wurde vorgeschlagen, die Begriffe „Plurizentrik" und „Plurinationalität" durch „Pluriarealität" zu ersetzen beziehungsweise zu konkretisieren (Ammon 1995: 49; Scheuringer 1997: 339ff). Diesem Gedanken widerspricht wiederum von Polenz (1999: 126), der auf den Abbau älterer Dialekt- und Regionalkontinua, die Scheuringer (1990) für das bairische Dialektkontinuum (Deutschland und Österreich) sowie Schifferle (1995) und Seidelmann (1983) für das alemannischen Dialektkontinuum (Deutschland und die Schweiz) aufgezeigt haben, und auf die zunehmende soziolinguistische Bedeutung der heutigen Staatsgrenzen hinweist. Eine Synthese der Positionen in der Plurinationalitäts- vs. Pluriarealität-Diskussion versucht Reiffenstein (2001: 88; siehe auch Hofer 2003: 479), indem er das Nebeneinander beider Konzepte herausstellt, dahingehend dass nationale Varietät und regionale Variation sich überlappen.

In Abbildung 1 wird diese Situation vereinfacht grafisch dargestellt. Dabei symbolisieren die durchgezogenen Linien die nationalen Grenzen und die von ihnen eingeschlossenen Flächen die nationalen Varietäten, d.h. das deutsche, Deutschschweizer und österreichische Vollzentrum. Die gestrichelten Linien umgeben den alemannischen Dialektraum (die areale alemannische Varietät), die gepunkteten Linien den bairischen Dialektraum (die areale bairische Varietät). Der Terminus *areale* Verbreitung bezeichnet im Folgenden eine Verbreitung innerhalb des alemannischen beziehungsweise barischen Dialektraums (zur räumlichen Erstreckung dieser Areale siehe Kapitel 2).

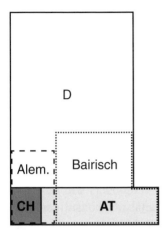

Abbildung 1. *Das Deutsche als plurinationale und pluriareale Sprache*
Innerhalb der durchgezogenen Linien in verschiedenen Graustufen: die nationalen Varietäten (D = Deutschland, CH = Deutschschweiz, AT = Österreich). Die gestrichelten Linien markieren den alemannischen, die gepunkteten Linien den bairischen Dialektraum.

Im vorliegenden Artikel wird exemplarisch anhand einiger Phraseme, die in aktuellen Wörterbüchern der Schweizer nationalen Varietät zugeschrieben sind, überprüft, ob diese Zuschreibung korrekt ist, d.h. sie sich wirklich auf den Schweizer Raum beschränken oder aber in (bestimmten Regionen von) Österreich und Deutschland ebenfalls bekannt sind. Dabei werden grenzüberschreitend besonders der alemannische und der bairische Raum berücksichtigt, um zu untersuchen, wie groß jeweils arealer und nationaler Einfluss sind.

2. Helvetismus und phraseologischer Helvetismus

Nach der Betrachtung der Aufteilung der deutschen Sprache in verschiedene räumliche Varietäten soll der Blick auf die Bezeichnung der sprachlichen Einheiten oder Merkmale[5], die diesen Regionen zuzuordnen sind, d.h. die nationalen Varianten, gewendet werden. Auf nationaler Ebene bezeichnen Helvetismen sprachliche Varianten, die für die Standardsprache der Deutschschweiz charakteristisch sind, Austriazismen stehen für österreichische und Teutonismen für bundesdeutsche Besonderheiten. Sprachliche Einheiten, die nicht auf eine oder zwei nationale Varietäten begrenzt sind, werden in diesem Artikel als gemeindeutsch bezeichnet.[6] Was aber heißt

„für die Standardvarietät der Deutschschweiz charakteristisch"? Darin stecken zwei Komponenten:

1. Die Zugehörigkeit zur Standardsprache. Nach Burger (1995: 13) sind (phraseologische) Helvetismen „standardsprachlich akzeptierte lexikalische und phraseologische Besonderheiten der Schweiz". Ammon (1986: 17–39) diskutiert im Hinblick auf den standardsprachlichen Aspekt eine Reihe potentieller Definitionsmerkmale, nämlich Überregionalität, Verwendung durch die Oberschicht, Invarianz, Ausbau, Schriftlichkeit, und hebt als zentrales Merkmal die Kodifizierung der sprachlichen Einheiten hervor. Neben dieser betont Koller (1999: 156) besonders das Bewusstsein der Sprechenden um ihre nationale Varietät als konstituierendes Kriterium für diese Varietät.[7] Diese beiden Merkmale werden in den Kapiteln 3 und 5.2 beziehungsweise 4 und 5.3 in diesem Artikel ausführlich behandelt.
2. Die geografische Verbreitung der sprachlichen Einheiten oder Merkmale. Diese wird sowohl durch eine maximale als auch eine minimale Erstreckung definiert. Haas (1982: 114) zielt auf die maximale Erstreckung, wenn er lexikalische Helvetismen als „jene Wörter, die ausschließlich in der Schweiz vorkommen" charakterisiert, Ammon (1986: 17–22) spricht eine Mindestgrenze an, indem er innerhalb der Schweiz eine überregionale geografische Verbreitung verlangt (zur geografischen Verbreitung exemplarischer Phraseme siehe Kapitel 2).

Auf der arealen Ebene sind für diese Arbeit die Begriffe Alemannismus (zum alemannischen Dialektraum gehören: die Deutschschweiz, Liechtenstein, das österreichische Bundesland Vorarlberg, die südlichen zwei Drittel Baden-Württembergs und das südwestliche Bayern, besonders Schwaben, siehe Ammon 1995) und Bavarismus (aus Österreich, ohne Vorarlberg, sowie Bayern, besonders Ober- und Niederbayern, Oberpfalz, Oberfranken, siehe Ammon 1995) von Bedeutung.

Bei einem phraseologischen Helvetismus handelt es sich um ein standardsprachliches Phrasem der deutschen Schweiz.[8] Phraseme und ihr Vorkommen in nationalsprachlichen Varietäten wurden empirisch bisher sehr zurückhaltend untersucht (und noch weniger in arealen Varietäten). Zu phraseologischen Helvetismen siehe Arbeiten von Burger (1995, 1996, 1998) und Häcki Buhofer (1998), zu Austriazismen von Földes (1992, 1996), zu Teutonismen von Schmidlin (2004, 2007).

Bei der Arbeit mit phraseologischen Helvetismen ergeben sich zwei zentrale Probleme, die bereits Burger (2007: 209f) anspricht: Einerseits gibt es in der

Schweiz wie in Österreich Phraseme, die als nationale Varianten klassifiziert werden, sich aber über die Nationengrenzen hinaus (besonders den alemannischen und bairischen Dialektraum) erstrecken (siehe auch Meyer 2006: 20; Földes 1992: 11).[9] Diese terminologischen Ungenauigkeiten hinsichtlich der Verbreitung der Phraseme sind auf bisher fehlende gesicherte empirische Daten zurückzuführen. Andererseits bereitet die Abgrenzung standardsprachlicher von aus der Mundart übersetzten Phrasemen Schwierigkeiten (Burger 1998: 50, 2007: 218), weil die Informanten in der Abgrenzung häufig unsicher sind und die Wörterbücher in Folge ebenfalls Schwierigkeiten bei der Zuordnung haben. Dieses Abgrenzungsproblem konnte bisher nicht gelöst werden[10] und wurde auch in der im Folgenden beschriebenen empirischen Untersuchung, in der ausschließlich mit Material gearbeitet wurde, das in Wörterbüchern als standardsprachlich klassifiziert war, wiederholt thematisiert.[11]

3. Die Kodifizierung nationaler Varianten

Als zentrale Bedingung für die Zugehörigkeit einer sprachlichen Einheit oder eines Merkmals zur Standardsprache und damit als Voraussetzung für eine Klassifizierung als nationale Variante wurde in Kapitel 2 die Kodifizierung angesprochen. Ammon diskutiert bereits 1986 (37–50) ausführlich Bedeutung und Relevanz einer Kodifizierung der standardsprachlichen Einheiten. Kodifizierung definiert er (1986: 43) als „die Darstellung der Sprachnormen [...] in Regeln", die präskriptiven Charakter haben. Im Jahr 1995 (250–253) nennt derselbe Autor explizit, aber nicht abschließend, diejenigen Wörterbücher, in die ein Helvetismus aufgenommen und in denen er als solcher klassifiziert sein muss, um als kodifiziert zu gelten. Dazu gehören in erster Linie eine Reihe von Duden-Bänden (Dudenredaktion 1990, 1991; *Schweizer Schülerduden 1978, 1980*), aber auch verschiedene andere Nachschlagewerke (z.B. Siebs 1969). Für Phraseme werden speziell Dudenredaktion (1992) und Meyer (1989, ebenfalls Duden-Reihe) angeführt. Ist eine Einheit in diesen Wörterbüchern nicht verzeichnet, so kann sie ebenfalls als Helvetismus gelten, wenn sie „aufgrund einer anderen Quelle [...] als Helvetismus identifizierbar" ist (Ammon 1995: 253). Ammon (ebd.) geht davon aus, dass „Helvetismen [...] außerhalb ihres eigenen nationalen Zentrums wenig bekannt [sind], abgesehen von einzelnen Ausnahmen". Wenn diese Annahme stimmt, dann sollte eine Befragung nach der Bekanntheit von Phrasemen für tatsächliche Helvetismen außerhalb der Schweiz sehr geringe Werte liefern, die mit einer ebenfalls sehr geringen Verwendungshäufigkeit korrelieren sollten.

Das Wörterbuch, das diese Kodifizierungen beinhaltet, bezeichnet Ammon (1986: 49) als „linguistisches Regelwerk [...] für mindestens einen grammatischen Rang" (d.h. Schreibung, Aussprache, Grammatik oder Lexik, siehe Fußnote 5). Die Regeln haben offizielle Gültigkeit und werden beispielsweise in der Schule vermittelt. Auf der einen Seite hat die Kodifizierung also präskriptive Verbindlichkeit, auf der anderen Seite sollte sich das Regelwerk möglichst weitgehend an der Sprachwirklichkeit orientieren.[12] Dieses Ziel spricht Drosdowski im Vorwort des Herausgebers zur Duden-Grammatik (Dudenredaktion 1984: o. S.) für ein linguistisches Regelwerk explizit an: „[Die Grammatik] beschreibt primär, sie führt die Breite des Üblichen vor, verschweigt nicht konkurrierende Wortformen und Verwendungsweisen, sondern erläutert sie, und sie achtet darauf, daß Sprachgebrauch und kodifizierte Norm nicht auseinanderklaffen."

Es ist also von einer gegenseitigen Einflussnahme von Kodifizierenden und Sprachgemeinschaft auszugehen. Wie dicht Wörterbuch und Sprachgebrauch aber tatsächlich beieinander liegen, hängt wesentlich von den Zielen und Methoden der Lexikografen sowie vom Alter des Wörterbuchs ab.

In diesem Artikel sollen Wörterbuch und sprachliche Wirklichkeit in der lexikografischen Praxis am Beispiel phraseologischer Einheiten untersucht werden. Für die lexikografische Seite stehen diejenigen aktuellen (phraseologischen) Nachschlagewerke, die in Ammons Sinn gegenwärtig die relevanten Wörterbücher für eine Kodifizierung von Helvetismen sind und die als Grundlage für die hier vorgestellte Arbeit dienten: die Neuauflage des Dudenbandes 11 (Dudenredaktion 2008), die Neuauflage von Meyer (2006) sowie das *Variantenwörterbuch* (Ammon et al. 2004, das erst rund 10 Jahre nach dem oben zitierten Beitrag von Ammon erschien). Es handelt sich bei allen drei Werken um relativ neue Ausgaben oder Überarbeitungen, die unterschiedlich differenziert ihr methodisches Vorgehen referieren. Die sprachliche Wirklichkeit wird anhand von Befragungsdaten in Kapitel 5 vorgestellt.

Prinzipiell gibt es drei Möglichkeiten, wie Phraseme Eingang in Wörterbücher finden können:

1. Sie können aus anderen Wörterbüchern und älteren Auflagen übernommen werden,
2. sie können aufgrund von Expertenwissen (u.a. der Phraseografen) aufgenommen oder
3. aufgrund empirischer Daten, d.h. anhand von Korpusanalysen oder Informantenbefragungen, Eingang ins Wörterbuch finden.

Ziel aller drei hier genannten Wörterbücher war die Abbildung des aktuellen Sprachgebrauchs (Dudenredaktion 2008: 15; Meyer 2006: 19; implizit Ammon et al. 2004: VII). Methodisch haben die Bearbeiter des Dudenbandes sowohl auf die bereits vorhandenen lexiko- wie phraseografischen Werke, d.h. die vorangehende Auflage des Bandes sowie auf andere Duden-Wörterbücher, und einschlägige Fachliteratur zurückgegriffen als auch wurden empirische Daten, auf der Grundlage korpuslinguistischer Analysen im Duden-Korpus, herangezogen (ebd.). Meyer (2006: 20f) gibt als Quellen einerseits das eigene Expertenwissen sowie eine umfassende Belegsammlung (aus Zeitungen, Zeitschriften, Sachbüchern und (Fach-) Literatur, aus der sich keine Gebrauchshäufigkeiten ablesen ließen) an. Ammon et al. (2004: VIIf) schließlich rekurrieren ebenfalls auf Expertenwissen (nämlich sowohl der 14 Autor(inn)en als auch einer Reihe weiterer Mitarbeitender aus unterschiedlichen Teilen des deutschsprachigen Raums) sowie auf Internetrecherchen. Weitere Publikationen der einzelnen Autoren und Autorinnen liefern spezifischere Informationen zum Vorgehen: Das Expertenwissen wurde genutzt, indem umfangreiches schriftsprachliches nicht-digitales Quellenmaterial von den einzelnen Bearbeitern aus der Fremdperspektive exzerpiert wurde. D.h. beurteilt wurde je eine fremde Varietät (Bickel 2006; Schmidlin 2004a). Außerdem wurden die Zuweisungen der Wörter und Phrasen zu den jeweiligen Varietäten anhand der Vorkommensfrequenzen der Varianten im Internet in den jeweiligen Domänen in AltaVista und Google rücküberprüft (Bickel 2006; Hofer 2003).

Umfassende Informantenbefragungen, die etwas über die kleinräumigere geografische Verbreitung oder das Bewusstsein der Sprechenden um die nationale Varietät aussagen könnten, wurden, soweit ersichtlich, in keinem der Wörterbuchprojekte durchgeführt. Die beste Chance auf eine in groben Zügen zuverlässige räumliche Zuordnung hat das *Variantenwörterbuch*, das mit einer räumlich gut gestreuten und relativ großen Zahl von Experten arbeitet. Die Analyse der Vorkommenshäufigkeit der Varianten, die mit Hilfe der Suchmaschinen ermittelt wurden, erlaubt ebenfalls nur eine grobe Zuordnung auf der Ebene der nationalen Varietäten, aber keine Differenzierung innerhalb dieser. So kann beispielsweise die Bekanntheit eines Phrasems im grenznahen Raum (z.B. im alemannischen Teil Deutschlands) nicht zufriedenstellend berücksichtigt werden, da die Frequenzangabe sich auf den gesamten bundesdeutschen Raum bezieht und die Konzentration in einem Teilgebiet nicht sichtbar macht. Zum Bewusstsein der Sprechenden hinsichtlich ihrer Varietät beziehungsweise der gängigen Varianten kann mit den verwendeten Verfahren ebenfalls keine Aussage gemacht werden.

Die erste Frage, die in Kapitel 5 anhand von Daten aus einer Informantenbefragung exemplarisch beantwortet werden soll, bezieht sich auf die räumliche Verbreitung einer Reihe phraseologischer Helvetismen innerhalb wie außerhalb der Schweiz und damit darauf, wie genau die o.g. Wörterbücher die sprachliche Wirklichkeit wiedergeben. Wir wollen uns also nicht wie Ammon damit zufrieden geben, dass die Phraseme in Wörterbüchern kodifiziert sind, sondern möchten die sprachliche Wirklichkeit direkt und eben nicht über den Umweg der Wörterbücher untersuchen, um herauszufinden, ob die als Helvetismus kodifizierten Varianten tatsächlich nationale oder aber eventuell auch grenzüberschreitende areale Einheiten sind.

4. Das Bewusstsein der Sprechenden

In Kapitel 2 wurde neben der Kodifizierung mit dem Bewusstsein der Sprechenden um ihre nationale Varietät bereits ein weiteres Kriterium für die Zugehörigkeit einer sprachlichen Variante zur Standardsprache und damit als Bedingung für die Klassifizierung als Helvetismus genannt (siehe Koller 1999: 156). In diesem Bereich lassen sich zwei Ebenen unterscheiden: einerseits ein prinzipielles Bewusstsein auf der Ebene der nationalen Varietät, wie es Koller anspricht, und andererseits ein konkretes Bewusstsein auf der Ebene der sprachlichen Einheiten, in unserem Falle der phraseologischer Helvetismen.

Auf der Ebene des Varietätenbewusstseins spricht Koller (1999: 156) dem Schweizer Standarddeutschen den Status einer nationalen Varietät ab, da sie den Deutschschweizern nicht hinreichend bewusst sei. Zudem finde keinerlei Identifikation der Sprechenden mit der Schweizer Schriftsprache, sondern vielmehr mit den Dialekten (1999: 139), d.h. mit regionalen Räumen anstatt mit einem nationalen (Teil-)Raum statt. Das Plurizentrizitätsbewusstsein der Deutschschweizer in einer empirischen Studie erfragt und getestet (Lesen und Beurteilen von Testsätzen mit Helvetismen auf ihre Korrektheit) hat Scharloth (2004, 2005). Während in einer Befragung 99,7% seiner Informanten angaben, dass sich Schweizer und Deutsche beim Sprechen der Standardsprache unterscheiden, kam Scharloth auf der Grundlage von Sprachbewusstseinstests zu dem Ergebnis, dass Schweizer Helvetismen systematisch (in gut 70% der Fälle) als schlechtere oder nicht korrekte Standardsprache und eben nicht als gleichberechtigte Schweizer Varianten einstufen (2004: o. S.). Scharloth schließt aus diesen Ergebnissen, dass von einem Plurizentrizitäts- oder

Varietätenbewusstsein der Deutschschweizer nicht gesprochen werden kann (2004: o. S., 2005: 263).

Auf der Ebene des Helvetismenbewusstseins geht wiederum Koller (1999: 159) davon aus, dass die Schweizer Varianten den Sprechenden sehr unterschiedlich bewusst sind. Zum Teil seien sie es gar nicht bewusst, zum Teil würden sie in der Schule wie Vokabeln erlernt und zum Teil würden sie auch als dialektal statt als standardsprachlich eingestuft. Im Bereich der Phraseologie geht Burger (1998: 52) davon aus, dass phraseologische (standardsprachliche) Helvetismen (im Gegensatz zu den aus dem Dialekt in die Standardsprache übersetzten Phrasemen) den Sprechenden in der Regel nicht bewusst sind. Eine Befragung von 79 Schweizer Germanistikstudierenden, die 15 gemeindeutsche und 15 Schweizerische Phraseme mit hohem Bekanntheitsgrad hinsichtlich ihrer nationalen Verbreitung zuordnen sollten, ergab, dass es sich bei den am schlechtesten zugeordneten fünf Phrasemen um Helvetismen handelte (23 bis 57% richtige Zuordnung), d.h. dieses Drittel der allgemein bekannten Schweizer Phraseme lag sehr deutlich unter oder nur gering über der zufälligen Trefferwahrscheinlichkeit von 50%. Der Mittelwert der korrekten Einstufung der 15 phraseologischen Helvetismen lag bei 76%. Hinsichtlich einer Verallgemeinerbarkeit dieses Ergebnisses von Philologiestudierenden geht Burger von einem allgemein eher bescheidenen Bewusstsein für Helvetismen in der gesamten Sprachgemeinschaft aus (1998: 72–74).

Was das Verhältnis dieser beiden Bewusstseinsebenen zueinander angeht, sollte man davon ausgehen können, dass sie prinzipiell korrelieren. Je größer das Bewusstsein auf der Variantenebene (d.h. je mehr Varianten der Sprechende als nationale Besonderheit auf der Ebene der Standardsprache einstuft), desto größer sollte auch das Varietätenbewusstsein sein (d.h. desto größer die Wahrscheinlichkeit, dass er/sie ein plurizentrisches Bewusstsein entwickelt hat). Und auf der anderen Seite sollte ein Informant mit ausgeprägtem Varietätenbewusstsein eher dazu neigen, Varianten als national einzustufen.

Da in der im Folgenden beschriebenen empirischen Untersuchung nur das Helvetismenbewusstsein, nicht aber das Varietätenbewusstsein erfragt wurde, ist letzteres nur tendenziell im Rückschluss von der Varianten- auf die Varietätenebene möglich. Die zweite Frage an die empirischen Daten bezieht sich also auf das Sprachbewusstsein auf Phrasemebene, d.h. wie bewusst ist es den Schweizer Sprechenden, dass es sich bei den abgefragten Phrasemen um Helvetismen handelt? Dieser Frage wird in Abschnitt 5.3 nachgegangen.

5. Empirische Daten zur räumlichen Verbreitung phraseologischer Helvetismen und zum Bewusstsein der Sprechenden

5.1. Material und Methoden

Da in dieser Studie eine möglichst genaue räumliche Zuordnung der Informanten (zu Kantonen oder Bundesländern) und damit ihrer Angaben vorgenommen werden sollte, wurde mit einer Informantenbefragung gearbeitet. Die Daten wurden in einer Online-Befragung[13] zur Bekanntheit[14] einer Auswahl von phraseologischen Helvetismen im Frühling 2009 gemeinsam mit Germanistikstudierenden der Universität Basel erhoben.[15] Die vorgestellten Phraseme wurden mit den Studierenden als typische phraseologische Helvetismen ausgewählt (Expertenwissen) und sind in mindestens einem der in Kapitel 3 genannten Wörterbücher (Ammon et al. 2004; Dudenredaktion 2008; Meyer 2006) als Schweizer Varianten kodifiziert. Mit dem Fragebogen wurde im Multiple-choice-Verfahren die Form (in Ergänzungstests)[16] beziehungsweise die Bedeutung[17] von 18 helvetischen Phrasemen erhoben (Auflistung siehe Anhang 1). Außerdem wurden die Informanten zu einem Teil der Phraseme gefragt, ob es sich ihrer Meinung nach um Helvetismen handle,[18] und sie wurden gebeten, eine Reihe von soziodemografischen Angaben zu machen (für eine areale Zuordnung: Sozialisierung mit/ohne Dialekt und Ort, an dem der größte Teil des Lebens verbracht wurde, sowie Alter, Geschlecht, Ausbildung). Zur Teilnahme an der Befragung wurde in einer kostenlosen Online-Zeitung aufgerufen und die Fragebögen wurden im Schneeballprinzip als E-Mails an Bekannte verschickt.

Im folgenden Kapitel werden exemplarisch die Ergebnisse zur räumlichen Verbreitung von sechs der abgefragten Helvetismen vorgestellt (Auflistung der Phraseme siehe Tabelle 1), die teilweise Varianten zu bundesdeutschen Phrasemen und teilweise eigenständige Schweizer Phraseme ohne strukturell ähnliches Äquivalent im Bundesdeutschen darstellen (zu diesen Kategorien siehe Burger 1995: 17). Diese sechs Phraseme wurden wegen ihrer unterschiedlichen räumlichen Verbreitung ausgewählt.

An der Befragung haben sich rund 1000 Personen beteiligt, von denen 981 bei der Auswertung berücksichtigt werden konnten.[19] 863 von ihnen stammten aus der Schweiz (bis auf Obwalden wurden alle Deutschschweizer Kantone abgedeckt), 118 aus Deutschland, Österreich und Liechtenstein (zur Verteilung der Informanten auf die einzelnen Kantone und Bundesländer siehe Anhang 2). Wegen der geringen Teilnehmerzahlen aus Österreich in dieser Untersuchung (5) ist eine gewisse Vorsicht bei der Interpretation der österreichischen Daten geboten.

Helvetismen: Nationale und areale Varianten? 83

Tabelle 1. *Auswahl der in Kapitel 5.2 behandelten Phraseme inkl. Bedeutungsangabe, ggf. gemein-/bundesdeutschem Äquivalent und Klassifizierung in Wörterbüchern*

abgefragtes Phrasem	Bedeutung	gemein-/bundesdeutsches Äquivalent	als Helvetismus klassifiziert von
1. dastehen wie der Esel am Berg	„von einer neuen Situation überfordert, ratlos sein"	dastehen wie der Ochs am/vorm Berg	Ammon et al. (2004) Dudenredaktion (2008) Meyer (2006)
2. durchs Band weg	„ausnahmslos"	durch die Bank weg	Ammon et al. (2004) Dudenredaktion (2008) Meyer (2006)
3. Jetzt jagt es den Zapfen ab!	„Jetzt ist genug!"	–	Ammon et al. (2004) Meyer (2006: *Der Zapfen ist ab.*)
4. kein Büro aufmachen	„keine Umstände machen"	–	Ammon et al. (2004)
5. Jmd. kann mir in die Schuhe blasen.	„Jmd. soll mich in Ruhe lassen."	–	Ammon et al. (2004) Dudenredaktion (2008: *Er/sie [...] kann mir den Schuh/die Schuhe aufblasen.*) Meyer (2006)
6. das Feuer im Elsass sehen	„starke Schmerzen haben"	–	Ammon et al. (2004)

5.2. Die räumliche Verbreitung der phraseologischen Helvetismen

Ein erster Blick auf den Bekanntheitsgrad der sechs exemplarischen Phraseme innerhalb und außerhalb der Schweiz (siehe Abbildung 2) zeigt, dass alle Phraseme in der Schweiz deutlich mehr Informanten bekannt waren als in Österreich und Deutschland. Dieser Unterschied lässt sich mit Hilfe eines t-Tests auch statistisch nachweisen (p = 0.007). Diese Verteilung spricht prinzipiell für eine Kategorisierung der Phraseme als Helvetismen. Der Bekanntheitsgrad der einzelnen Phraseme außerhalb der Schweiz fällt allerdings sehr unterschiedlich aus. Was besonders bei den Phrasemen 4 und 5 einen ersten Hinweis darauf gibt, dass die Bezeichnung „Helvetismus" unter Umständen zu eng gefasst sein könnte.

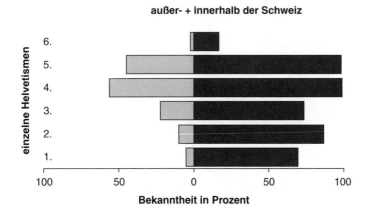

Abbildung 2. *Bekanntheit der sechs exemplarischen Phraseme außerhalb (graue Balken links, durchschnittlicher Bekanntheitsgrad 23%) und innerhalb (schwarze Balken rechts, durchschnittlicher Bekanntheitsgrad 74%) der Schweiz (die Nummerierung entspricht derjenigen in Tabelle 1 und der folgenden Beispiele).*

Zu den folgenden Karten[20] (Abbildungen 3–8)
Da in dieser Untersuchung zwei Ebenen der räumlichen Verbreitung untersucht werden sollten, nämlich sowohl die Verteilung innerhalb der Nationen, insbesondere in der Schweiz, als auch in den Arealen des Alemannischen und des Bairischen, müssen aus den kartografischen Darstellungen beide Bereiche ersichtlich sein. Es werden daher in den Abbildungen 3–8 die Schweizer Informanten nach Kantonen gezeigt, die deutschen Informanten

den drei Bereichen Baden-Württemberg[21], Bayern[22] oder Rest-Deutschland zugeordnet. Da aus Österreich und Liechtenstein mit fünf und sieben nur sehr wenige Informanten teilgenommen haben, werden diese nach Ländern zusammengefasst.[23]

Beispiel 1: dastehen wie der Esel am Berg[24]
Dieses Verbalphrasem mit der Bedeutung „von einer neuen Situation überfordert, ratlos sein", das eine Variante zu *dastehen wie der Ochs am/vorm Berg* darstellt, wird sowohl von Ammon (2004) als auch von der Dudenredaktion (2008) und Meyer (2006) als Helvetismus klassifiziert (siehe Tabelle 1). Die empirischen Daten (kartografisch dargestellt in Abbildung 3) zeigen in der Deutschschweiz einen Bekanntheitsgrad zwischen 20 und 100%, wobei abgesehen von den Kantonen Bern, Freiburg und im Wallis im Westen und im Thurgau und in Graubünden im Osten, wo die Bekanntheit zwischen 20 und 60% liegt, ein Bekanntheitsgrad zwischen 60 und 100% erreicht wird. In den Gebieten außerhalb der Schweiz, d.h. sowohl in Österreich (und Liechtenstein) als auch im gesamten Raum der Bundesrepublik Deutschland, also auch im Alemannischen und Bairischen, ist dieses Phrasem nicht bekannt (Bekanntheit < 20%).[25]

Auf der Grundlage dieser überregionalen Verbreitung in der Schweiz und der (tendenziellen) Unbekanntheit außerhalb der Schweiz ist *dastehen wie der Esel am Berg*, wie in den Wörterbüchern geschehen, eindeutig als (absoluter)[26] Helvetismus einzustufen.

Beispiel 2: *durchs Band weg*
Dieses Phrasem in der Bedeutung „ausnahmslos" wird im bundesdeutschen Raum in der Variante *durch die Bank weg* verwendet. *Durchs Band weg* wird von allen drei konsultierten Wörterbüchern als Helvetismus eingestuft. Aus den Informantendaten (siehe Abbildung 4.) ergibt sich für die Schweiz ein sehr einheitliches Bild: In der überwiegenden Zahl der Kantone hat das Phrasem einen Bekanntheitsgrad von 81–100%, nur im Wallis und in Nidwalden (auch in Liechtenstein) ist es nur 61–80% der Befragten bekannt. Jenseits der Schweizer Landesgrenzen ist es in Österreich der Hälfte der Informanten bekannt (41–60%), im bundesdeutschen Raum hingegen herrscht eindeutig die Variante *durch die Bank weg* vor (das Schweizer Phrasem wird von nur 0–20% angegeben).

Da das Phrasem neben der flächendeckenden Verbreitung in der Schweiz auch in Österreich etwa der Hälfte der Informanten bekannt ist, während es in Deutschland nicht vorzukommen scheint, scheint es – unter

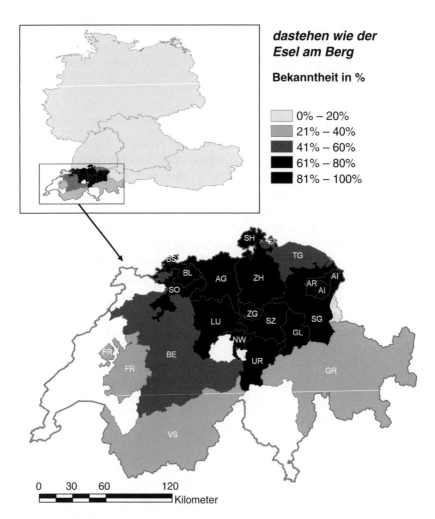

Abbildung 3. *Bekanntheit von* dastehen wie der Esel am Berg *innerhalb und außerhalb der Schweiz*

Annahme der Verallgemeinerbarkeit der Angaben der wenigen Informanten auf die Sprachgemeinschaft – korrekter, es statt als Helvetismus als Austro-Helvetismus zu kategorisieren.

Beispiel 3: *Jetzt jagt es den Zapfen ab.*
Dieses satzwertige Phrasem mit der Bedeutung „Jetzt reicht es!", ohne strukturell ähnliche gemeindeutsche Variante, wird von Ammon et al.

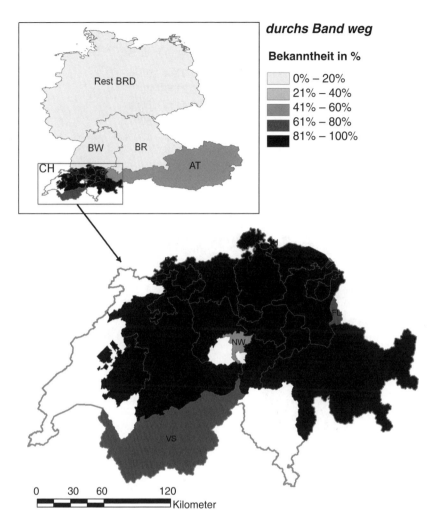

Abbildung 4. *Bekanntheit von* durchs Band weg *innerhalb und außerhalb der Schweiz*

(2004) und Meyer (2006, in der Variante: *Der Zapfen ist ab.*) als Helvetismus klassifiziert, in Dudenredaktion (2008) ist es nicht verzeichnet. Die Visualisierung der Befragungsdaten in Abbildung 5 zeigt für die Schweiz ein uneinheitlicheres Bild als für die vorangehenden Phraseme. In den (auch) deutschsprachigen Westschweizer Kantonen Fribourg, Bern, Solothurn und Wallis sowie in Schwyz und Appenzell Ausserrhoden (wie auch in Liechtenstein) ist es zwischen 81 und 100% der Befragten bekannt, in den

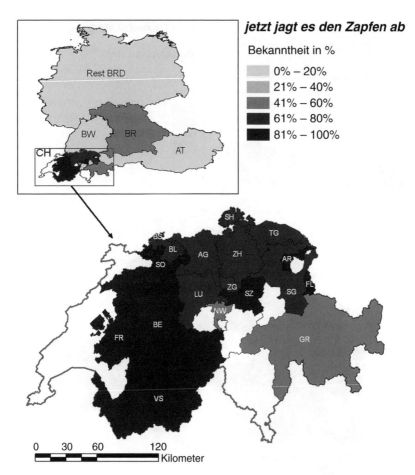

Abbildung 5. *Bekanntheit von* Jetzt jagt es den Zapfen ab. *innerhalb und außerhalb der Schweiz*

nördlichen Kantonen (Baselland, Baselstadt, Aargau, Luzern, Schaffhausen, Zürich, Zug, Thurgau, St. Gallen) zwischen 61 und 80%, in Graubünden zwischen 41 und 60% und in den übrigen Kantonen 40% und weniger. Außerhalb der Schweiz kannten nur 41–60% der bairischen Informanten dieses Phrasem, in den übrigen Regionen war es (nahezu) unbekannt (0–20%).

Aufgrund der überregionalen Verbreitung in der Schweiz und einem Bekanntheitsgrad von 50% in Bayern neben der Unbekanntheit im übrigen deutschsprachigen Raum, wird – in Abweichung von den Wörterbüchern – vorgeschlagen, dieses Phrasem als Bavaro-Helvetismus zu klassifizieren.

Helvetismen: Nationale und areale Varianten? 89

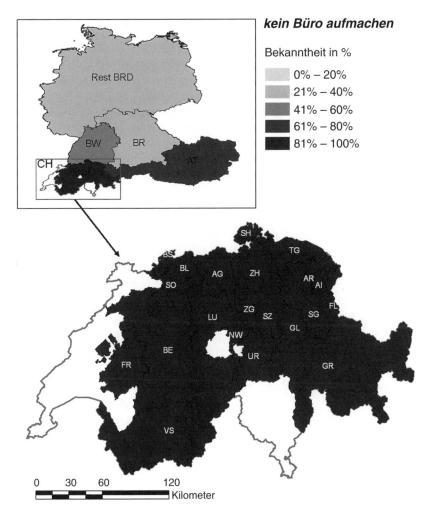

Abbildung 6. *Bekanntheit von* kein Büro aufmachen *innerhalb und außerhalb der Schweiz*

Beispiel 4: *kein Büro aufmachen*
Das Verbalphrasem *kein Büro aufmachen* mit der Bedeutung „keine Umstände machen", das ebenfalls keine strukturell äquivalente Variante im Gemeindeutschen hat, wird nur von Ammon et al. (2004) als Helvetismus aufgeführt, in den beiden anderen Wörterbüchern fehlt es. Den empirischen Daten zufolge (siehe Abbildung 6) ist das Phrasem in der gesamten Schweiz

und Liechtenstein allgemein bekannt (81–100%). Darüber hinaus ist es in Österreich 61–80% und in Baden-Württemberg 41–60% der Informanten bekannt. Im übrigen deutschen Raum erreichte es einen Bekanntheitsgrad von 21–40%. Wegen seiner Verbreitung in der ganzen Schweiz und des größeren Bekanntheitsgrades in Österreich und Baden-Württemberg als im übrigen bundesdeutschen Raum wird in Abweichung von Ammon et al. (2004) vorgeschlagen, dieses Phrasem als Austro-Alemannismus zu bezeichnen.

Beispiel 5: *Jmd. kann mir in die Schuhe blasen.*
Dieses satzwertige Phrasem mit der Bedeutung „Jmd. soll mich in Ruhe lassen." ist in den Wörterbüchern von Ammon et al. (2004) und Meyer (2006) als Helvetismus angegeben. In Dudenredaktion (2008) wird mit der gleichen Bedeutung die Variante *Er/sie […] kann mir den Schuh/die Schuhe aufblasen.* (ohne Angabe der räumlichen Erstreckung) genannt. Die Befragung (siehe Abbildung 7) ergab eine allgemeine Bekanntheit dieses Phrasems in der Schweiz wie in Österreich (und Liechtenstein, überall 81–100%). In Baden-Württemberg und Bayern erreichte es eine Bekanntheit von immerhin 61–80%, im restlichen bundesdeutschen Raum blieb es mit 21–40% deutlich dahinter zurück.

Aufgrund des hohen Bekanntheitsgrades nicht nur in der Schweiz, sondern in Österreich und auch den beiden südlichen Bundesländern Deutschlands wird vorgeschlagen, statt von einem Helvetismus von einem Phrasem, das im gesamten süddeutschen Raum verbreitet ist, zu sprechen.

Beispiel 6: *das Feuer im Elsass sehen*
Als letztes Beispiel sei das Verbalphrasem *das Feuer im Elsass sehen*, wiederum ohne gemeindeutsche Variante („große Schmerzen haben"), angeführt. Dieses ist nur bei Ammon et al. (2004) angeführt und als Helvetismus eingestuft. Den Informantenangaben zufolge (siehe Abbildung 8) ist dieses Phrasem nur in wenigen Regionen der Schweiz bekannt.[27] Es wurde – wegen seiner räumlichen Nähe zum Elsass nicht ganz überraschend – in den nordwestlichen Kantonen Baselland und Baselstadt, Aargau, im nördlichsten Kanton Schaffhausen sowie im Wallis von weniger als der Hälfte der Informanten (21–40%) als bekannt angeführt. In den übrigen Schweizer Kantonen sowie im restlichen deutschsprachigen Raum war es (nahezu) unbekannt (in der Schweiz: 0–20%, in Österreich, Deutschland und Liechtenstein: 0–4%).

Aufgrund der regionalen Beschränkung auf wenige Kantone und des auch hier vergleichsweise geringen Bekanntheitsgrads wird vorgeschlagen,

Helvetismen: Nationale und areale Varianten? 91

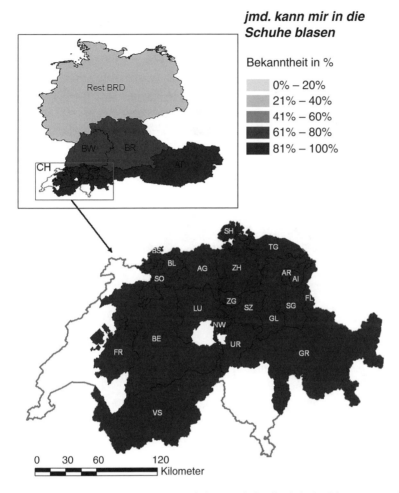

Abbildung 7. *Bekanntheit von* Jmd. kann mir in die Schuhe blasen. *innerhalb und außerhalb der Schweiz*

nicht von einem Helvetismus, sondern von einem regionalen Helvetismus oder einem Schweizer Regionalismus zu sprechen.[28]

Ammons (1995: 253) Annahme, dass Helvetismen in der Regel außerhalb der Schweiz wenig bekannt sind, kann – abgesehen von denjenigen Einheiten, die hier als grenzüberschreitend klassifiziert wurden – anhand der phraseologischen Daten bestätigt werden.

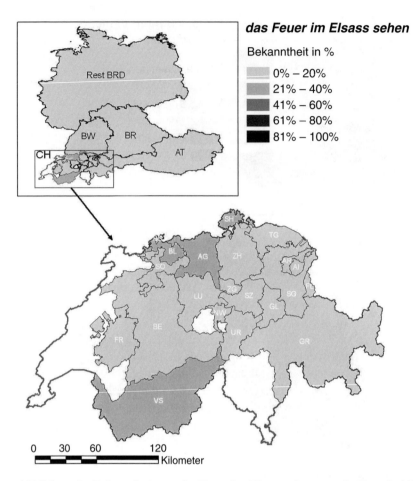

Abbildung 8. *Bekanntheit von* das Feuer im Elsass sehen *innerhalb und außerhalb der Schweiz*

5.3. *Das Helvetismenbewusstsein der Sprechenden*

In Kapitel 4 wurde die Frage nach dem Bewusstsein der Sprechenden um den Status der Phraseme als Helvetismus aufgeworfen. Den Ausgangspunkt bildet die Aussage Burgers (1998: 74), der von einem unauffälligen Bestand der Schweizer Varianten und damit einem geringen Bewusstsein für phraseologische Helvetismen ausgeht. Daran schließt sich die Frage an, ob sich Faktoren identifizieren lassen, die mit besonders hohen oder geringen Werten für die Einschätzung eines Phrasems als Helvetismus in Zusammenhang stehen.

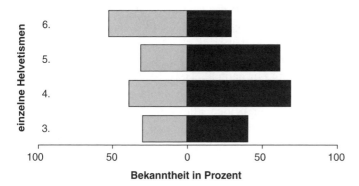

Abbildung 9. *Einschätzung von vier der sechs exemplarischen Phraseme als Helvetismus außerhalb (graue Balken links, Mittelwert 49%) und innerhalb (schwarze Balken rechts, Mittelwert 38%) der Schweiz. Nr. 3: Jetzt jagt es den Zapfen ab., Nr. 4 kein Büro aufmachen, Nr. 5 Jmd. kann mir in die Schuhe blasen., Nr. 6 Das Feuer im Elsass sehen.*

Auf der Datengrundlage von vier der sechs in Tabelle 1 angeführten Phraseme (zu den anderen zwei Phrasemen wurde der Status als Helvetismus nicht abgefragt) wird in Abbildung 9 die Zuordnung als Helvetismus vs. gemeindeutsches Phrasem durch die Informanten dargestellt. Vergleicht man zunächst einmal die varietäteninterne Einstufung der Schweizer Informanten mit der varietätenexternen Beurteilung der deutschen und österreichischen Befragten, lässt sich prinzipiell feststellen, dass diese vier Phraseme (wie auch sieben weitere, hier nicht aufgeführte, die im Fragebogen hinsichtlich der räumlichen Verbreitung einzustufen waren, siehe Fußnote 29) in der Regel in der Schweiz von einem größeren Prozentsatz der Informanten als Helvetismen eingestuft wurden. Das Bewusstsein für Helvetismen scheint also innerhalb der Varietät größer zu sein als außerhalb der Varietät (p-Wert für alle elf Phraseme[29] < 0.001).[30] Die einzige Ausnahme bildet das Phrasem *das Feuer im Elsass sehen*.

Die durchschnittliche Klassifizierung der vier Phraseme als Helvetismen beträgt knapp 50% (und entspricht etwa derjenigen aller 11 Phraseme, die als nationale Varianten zugeordnet wurden: 47%). Im Vergleich zu den von Burger befragten Studierenden (76% korrekte Einstufung als Helvetismus, siehe Kapitel 4) liegt der sich aus diesen Daten ergebende Mittelwert – wie von Burger für die durchschnittliche Bevölkerung vermutet – deutlich niedriger.

Im Vergleich dazu wurde ein gemeindeutsches, weniger bekanntes Phrasem (*Der Krug geht zum Brunnen, bis er bricht.* mit einem Bekanntheitsgrad von 26%) von nur 4% und ein Phantasiephrasem (*Der Storch fliegt vorbei.*) von 5% der Schweizer Informanten als Helvetismus eingestuft. Diese geringen Werte könnten ein Hinweis darauf sein, dass die Schweizer Informanten relativ verlässlich ein Phrasem nur dann als Helvetismus einstufen, wenn sie sich bei der Zuordnung sicher sind. Die Werte könnten aber auch mit dem geringen Bekanntheitsgrad dieser beiden Phraseme in Zusammenhang stehen, denn je mehr Informanten eine Einheit kennen, desto mehr können sie begründet als Helvetismus bewerten (ein unbekanntes Phrasem ist schwer zu klassifizieren). Um diese Hypothese zu prüfen, wurden nicht nur die entsprechenden Daten der vier oben genannten, sondern aller elf Helvetismen, die von den Informanten auf ihre räumliche Verbreitung hin beurteilt wurden, korreliert (siehe Abbildung 10). Durch die größere Zahl der Helvetismen konnte die statistische Power erhöht werden. Die Regression belegt deutlich einen statistisch signifikanten linearen Zusammenhang zwischen den Datensätzen (p = 0.008): Phraseme werden mit zunehmendem Bekanntheitsgrad häufigerer korrekt als Helvetismus eingeschätzt (siehe Verlauf der Regressionsgeraden). Das Bestimmtheitsmaß $R^2 = 0.56$ gibt an, dass immerhin 56% der Variabilität der Einschätzung als Helvetismus durch den Bekanntheitsgrad der Phraseme erklärt werden.

Diese Korrelation kann ein Grund für die deutlich höheren Bewusstseinswerte in Burgers Studie (1998, siehe Kapitel 4) sein, denn bei den von

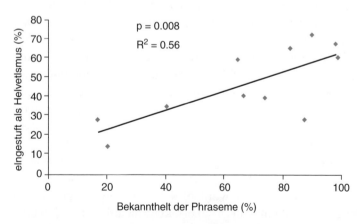

Abbildung 10. *Korrelation der Bekanntheit der Phraseme in der Schweiz (in Prozent) und der Einstufung als Helvetismus durch Schweizer Informanten (in Prozent)*

ihm vorgegebenen Phrasemen handelte es sich durchweg um Einheiten mit einem sehr hohen Bekanntheitsgrad (1998: 72).[31]

Dass *das Feuer im Elsass sehen* in der Schweiz von relativ wenigen Informanten als Helvetismus eingeschätzt wurde, scheint daher auch damit zusammenzuhängen, dass es innerhalb der Schweiz eine geringe räumliche Verbreitung und einen beschränkten Bekanntheitsgrad hat. Der relativ große Anteil Nicht-Schweizer, der dieses Phrasem als Helvetismus ansieht, könnte andererseits in diesem Fall möglicherweise auf die räumliche Nähe der im Phrasem enthaltenen Ortsangabe (Elsass) zur Schweiz zurückzuführen sein, der die Nicht-Schweizer verführt haben könnte, auf seinen Status als Helvetismus rückzuschließen. Solche landestypischen Hinweise (geografische Angaben, aber auch politische, gesellschaftliche u.a. Besonderheiten) können die nationale Zuordnung beeinflussen. Einen ähnlichen Einfluss dürfte es haben, wenn einzelne Komponenten eines Phrasems Helvetismenstatus haben. So ist es beispielsweise bei *Jetzt jagt es den Zapfen ab.* möglich, dass *Zapfen* als Flaschenverschluss die Informanten zur Klassifizierung des Phrasems als Helvetismus veranlasst hat.

Und schließlich könnte für die Einschätzung auch der Phrasemtyp relevant sein, d.h. ob es sich bei den Phrasemen um eigenständige Schweizer Einheiten (ohne Varianten in den anderen nationalen Varietäten), um Sonderphraseologie (mit Varianten) oder um falsche Freunde handelt (vgl. Fußnote 8). Hier reicht das Material dieser Untersuchung für eine statistische Auswertung nicht aus. Das Bewusstsein im Hinblick auf das einzige im Material enthaltene Phrasem, das zur Sonderphraseologie gehört (*in kurzen Hosen dastehen*) und das national zugeordnet werden sollte, liegt deutlich unterhalb der in Abbildung 10 enthaltenen Geraden (Bekanntheit 87%, Einstufung als Helvetismus 28%). Das gilt auch für den phraseologischen falschen Freund *jmdm. die Stange halten* in der Bedeutung „jmdn. unterstützen" (Bekanntheit 20%, Einstufung als Helvetismus 14%). Diese beiden Beispiele weisen im Verhältnis zur Bekanntheit die geringsten Bewusstseinswerte auf, was ein Hinweis darauf sein könnte, dass Schweizer Sonderphraseologie und falsche Freunde den Schweizer Probanden weniger häufig als Helvetismen bewusst sind als die dritte Gruppe der eigenständigen Schweizer Phraseme – was als Hypothese für umfangreichere Untersuchungen dienen kann.

Bisher wurde in diesem Abschnitt vom absoluten, d.h. tatsächlich auf die Schweiz begrenzten Helvetismus ausgegangen. Die in 4.5.2. dargestellten Ergebnisse haben aber gezeigt, dass einige Phraseme durchaus auch in angrenzenden Räumen anderer Nationen geläufig sind. Neben der räumlichen Verbreitung und Bekanntheit innerhalb der Schweiz könnte daher auch ein

Zusammenhang zwischen der Klassifizierung als Helvetismus und der Verbreitung außerhalb der Schweiz bestehen, denn wenn die Informanten mit einem Phrasem auch grenzübergreifend in Berührung kommen (unter der Annahme, dass Nichtschweizer diese Einheiten nicht nur kennen, sondern auch verwenden), werden sie ihn möglicherweise nicht mehr als Helvetismus einstufen. Hier sollte in erster Linie die eigene Spracherfahrung, nicht die Kodifizierung in Wörterbüchern ausschlaggebend sein. Diese These konnte wegen der geringen Zahl der untersuchten Phraseme ebenfalls nicht statistisch untersucht werden. Ein Blick auf die relative Lage der Punkte in Abbildung 10 zeigt aber, dass sich zwischen den Gruppen der Phraseme, die gemäß Befragungsdaten als Helvetismen beziehungsweise Austro-, Bavaro-Helvetismen oder Alemannismen charakterisiert wurden, keine systematischen Unterschiede ausmachen lassen. Zu denjenigen Phrasemen, deren Einstufung als Helvetismus weniger häufig erfolgte, als dem Modell zufolge zu erwarten gewesen wäre (d.h. die Punkte liegen unterhalb der Geraden), zählten sowohl solche, die auf die Schweiz beschränkt sind, als auch solche mit grenzüberschreitender Verbreitung.[32] Diesem kleinen Datensatz zufolge würde es für die Einstufung als Helvetismus prinzipiell keinen Unterschied machen, welche Reichweite ein Helvetismus im angrenzenden Ausland hat – was ebenfalls anhand einer größeren Datengrundlage zu überprüfen ist.

Es mag deutlich geworden sein, dass die Klassifizierung eines Phrasems als Helvetismus durch eine ganze Reihe unterschiedlicher Kriterien beeinflusst werden kann. Neben diesen Einflussfaktoren ist auch auf die methodische Schwierigkeit der Erfassung des Helvetismenbewusstseins aufmerksam zu machen. Auch wenn im Fragebogen neben den Kategorien des Vorkommens „nur innerhalb der Schweiz" und „auch außerhalb der Schweiz" auch die Antwortmöglichkeit „weiss nicht" vorgegeben war, ist nicht auszuschließen, dass diese Möglichkeit bei Unwissenheit selten angegeben und stattdessen geraten wurde. Die Kategorie „weiss nicht" wurde von den Schweizer Informanten in 28% der Fälle, von Nicht-Schweizern in 47% der Fälle angekreuzt.

Für die in dieser Studie erfragten Phraseme ergab sich innerhalb der Schweiz eine Bewusstseinsrate von rund 50% (für die hier berücksichtigten vier Phraseme: 49%, für alle elf: 46%) bei einem durchschnittlichen Bekanntheitsgrad von 74%. Mit anderen Worten: etwa jedem zweiten Sprechenden war der Helvetismenstatus eines Phrasems bewusst (im Einleitungstext zum Fragebogen wurde nur erwähnt, dass es um „Redewendungen" ging, es wurde aber kein Bezug zu nationalen Varietäten hergestellt). Im Allgemeinen kann man wohl davon ausgehen, dass ein gewisser Bekanntheitsgrad die Voraussetzung für das Bewusstsein als Helvetismus darstellt.

6. Nationale wie areale Verbreitung phraseologischer Helvetismen

6.1. *Räumliche Verbreitung und Ausdifferenzierung des Helvetismenbegriffs*

Die erste Frage an die empirischen Daten, die in Kapitel 3 gestellt wurde, bezog sich auf die räumliche Verbreitung von Phrasemen, die in den Wörterbüchern (Ammon et al. 2004; Dudenredaktion 2008; Meyer 2006) als Helvetismen kodifiziert sind. Die in Kapitel 5.2 dargestellten Ergebnisse haben gezeigt, dass diese Kodifizierungen nicht immer zuverlässig die tatsächliche Verbreitung der betreffenden Phraseme beschreibt. Exemplarisch wurde mit Hilfe empirischer Daten für sechs Phraseme gezeigt, dass die als Helvetismen klassifizierten Phraseme drei Gruppen angehören:

1. Phraseme, die nur in der Schweiz und hier überregional bekannt sind,
2. Phraseme, die in der Schweiz überregional, aber auch im angrenzenden österreichischen und/oder (einem Teil des) bundesdeutschen Raum(s) bekannt sind, und
3. Phraseme, die in der Schweiz nur regional bekannt sind.

Es konnte damit im phraseologischen Bereich gezeigt werden, dass sprachliche Einheiten und Merkmale sowohl für Nationen als auch grenzübergreifend für Areale charakteristisch sein können und damit für das Deutsche sowohl die Bezeichnungen Pluri*nationalität* als auch Pluri*arealität* ihre Berechtigung haben. Dies beeinflusst den Status der Phraseme als Helvetismus nicht prinzipiell. Es wurde aber vorgeschlagen, bisherige terminologische Ungenauigkeiten zu konkretisieren, indem auch die areale Komponente bei der Bezeichnung der Phraseme berücksichtigt wird, und die Einheiten der 2. und 3. Gruppe nicht (nur) als Helvetismen zu bezeichnen, sondern ihre Verbreitung in der Bezeichnung genauer zu berücksichtigen, z.B. durch Benennungen wie Austro-Helvetismus, Alemannismus etc. Auf der Grundlage der geringen Phrasemzahl in dieser Studie ist selbstverständlich nicht quantifizierbar, ob nationale oder areale (Alemannisch, Bairisch) Grenzen den größeren Einfluss haben.

6.2. *Bewusstsein*

Die zweite Frage, die anhand der empirischen Daten untersucht werden sollte (siehe Kapitel 4), bezog sich auf das Sprachbewusstsein der Schweizer Informanten hinsichtlich ihrer Varietät, das auf der Ebene der einzelnen

Helvetismen geprüft wurde. Es konnte gezeigt werden, dass die Einstufung durch eine Reihe verschiedener Faktoren beeinflusst werden kann. Ein zentraler Faktor, der 56% der Variabilität in der Einstufung eines Phrasems erklärt, ist seine Bekanntheit. Ob und eine wie große Rolle andere Faktoren wie der Phrasemtyp (eigenständige Schweizer Einheiten, Schweizer Sonderphraseologie oder falsche Freunde), landestypische Hinweise und der Helvetismenstatus von Komponenten spielen, bleibt anhand umfangreicherer empirischer Untersuchungen zu erforschen.

Durchschnittlich hatten die in dieser Studie berücksichtigten phraseologischen Helvetismen, die von den Informanten räumlich zugeordnet wurden, einen Bewusstseinsgrad von 50%, d.h. jedem zweiten Informanten war der Status eines Phrasems als Helvetismus bewusst. Ein Rückschluss vom Helvetismen- auf das Varietätenbewusstsein lässt sich insofern ziehen, als bei dem relativ geringen Bewusstsein auf der Phrasemebene davon auszugehen ist, dass das Bewusstsein der Schweizer Sprechenden um ihre nationalsprachliche Varietät nicht besonders stark ausgeprägt ist oder nach Scharloth (2004: o.S.) „das Plurizentrizitätskonzept [ist] noch auf dem Weg von den Köpfen der Linguisten in die Köpfe der Sprecher".[33] Demnach erwüchse im Falle der Schweiz das Varietätenbewusstsein also nicht in erster Linie aus dem Bedürfnis des Sprechenden um nationale Identität und würde in seiner Folge vom Linguisten aufgenommen, sondern ginge tendenziell von der Linguistik – beispielsweise über Kodifzierungen – in Richtung der Sprechenden. Damit wäre das Kriterium des Sprechendenbewusstseins um die eigene Schweizer Varietät, das Koller (199:156, siehe Kapitel 2 und 4) als Voraussetzung für die Existenz einer nationalen Varietät fordert, nicht erfüllt. Das bisher begrenzte Bewusstsein der Sprechenden und seine Förderung von linguistischer Seite scheint meiner Meinung nach jedoch kein Ausschlusskriterium für das Bestehen einer nationalen Varietät zu sein. Vielmehr mag der Einzug von Schweizer Varianten in die Wörterbücher dazu führen, dass diese Varianten im nicht-dominanten Zentrum Schweiz eben nicht mehr als minderwertig (Scharloth 2004, 2005), sondern zunehmend als gleichberechtigt betrachtet werden. Die Kodifizierung dieser Varianten ermöglicht eine Entwicklung dahingehend, dass die Varianten des dominanten bundesdeutschen Zentrums keinen präskriptiven Charakter mehr haben und Kinder in Deutschschweizer Schulen lernen, dass *Trottoir*, *Poulet* und *Velo* keine Fehler, sondern gleichberechtigte Schweizer Besonderheiten neben dem bundesdeutschen *Bürger-/Gehsteig*, dem *Hähnchen* und dem *Fahrrad* darstellen. Gegen dieses bewusstseinsunterstützende oder z.T. -bildende Vorgehen von Linguistenseite, das das sprachliche (Selbst-)Bewusstsein der Sprechenden stärkt, ist nichts einzuwenden.

Universität Basel, Switzerland

Anmerkungen

Kontaktadresse: Britta.Juska-Bacher@unibas.ch

1. Mein Dank geht an die zwei anonymen Referent(inn)en für ihre sorgfältige Lektüre und konstruktiven Kritikpunkte zu einer früheren Version dieses Artikels.
2. Einen Überblick über die Herausbildung und Entwicklung des Konzepts Plurizentrik gibt Ammon (1995: 42–48).
3. Zu anderen plurizentrischen Sprachen siehe Clyne (1992).
4. Ein Beleg der Vermutung, dass die Gemeinsamkeiten zwischen Regionen unterschiedlicher nationaler Varietäten (z.b. im grenzüberschreitenden alemannischen oder bairischen Dialektraum) größer sind als die Gemeinsamkeiten innerhalb einer nationalen Varietät (z.b. im Schweizerdeutschen oder im österreichischen Standarddeutsch), müsste in den verschiedenen linguistischen Dimensionen wie Lexik, Semantik, Aussprache, Orthografie, Grammatik und Pragmatik quantifiziert werden.
5. Es kann sich dabei um Besonderheiten in der Schreibung, Aussprache, Grammatik oder Lexik der jeweiligen Varietät handeln.
6. In der lexikografischen Praxis werden beispielsweise im phraseologischen Bereich Helvetismen und Austriazismen als solche markiert, Teutonismen hingegen werden tendenziell eher als gemeindeutsch eingestuft.
7. Als weitere wichtige Bedingungen fordert Koller (1999: 156) ein zahlenmäßiges Gewicht der Schweizer Varianten und ihren Bezug auf zentrale Lebensbereiche der Sprechenden. Zu diesen Kriterien kann die in Kapitel 4.5 beschriebene Studie keine Hinweise liefern, da nur mit einer exemplarischen Auswahl von Phrasemen gearbeitet wird.
8. Burger (1995: 17) unterscheidet drei Typen: erstens „Sonderphraseologie", d.h. Phraseme, die strukturelle Varianten zu bundesdeutschen und/oder österreichischen Einheiten darstellen, zweitens eigenständige Schweizer Phraseme (ohne Varianten in den anderen nationalen Varietäten) und drittens eine beschränkte Zahl von falschen Freunden.
9. In der Literatur wird daher auch zwischen sprachlichen Einheiten, die auf die Schweiz beschränkt sind, und solchen, die überwiegend, aber nicht ausschließlich in der Schweiz vorkommen, unterschieden. Haas (2000: 10) bezeichnet erstere als „absolute" Helvetismen, Ammon (1995: 65) spricht von „spezifischen" und Meyer (2001: 1191) von „arealgenauen" Helvetismen. Einheiten, die nicht auf die Schweiz beschränkt sind, nennt Haas (2000: 10) „Frequenzhelvetismen", Ammon (1995: 65) „unspezifische" und Meyer (2001: 1191) „übergreifende" Helvetismen, ohne dass dabei in der Bezeichnung die räumliche Erstreckung außerhalb der Schweiz konkretisiert würde. Die hier vorgeschlagenen Benennungen stellen eine Möglichkeit in dieser Richtung dar.
10. Meyer (1989, 2006) behilft sich daher mit der Kategorie „mundartnah".

11. Dies sowohl bei der Fragebogenerstellung (in der Diskussion mit den muttersprachlichen Studierenden) als auch von Seiten der Probanden, die gelegentlich Phraseme im Dialekt angaben: Beispielsweise wurde statt *Jetzt ist genug Heu (dr)unten.* auch *Jetz isch gnueg heu dunde/donde/dunnä.* genannt. Statt *Jmd. kann mir in die Schuhe blasen.* gaben Probanden auch an: *Blas mer doch id Schue!* und *Du kasch mir in dschueh blose.*
12. Dies verlangt indirekt auch Burger (1995: 14), wenn er für einen phraseologischen Helvetismus dessen Gebräuchlichkeit in der Sprachgemeinschaft fordert.
13. Zur Methode der Online-Befragung sowie zu ihren Vor- und Nachteilen siehe Juska-Bacher (2010). Die Probandengruppe ist nicht repräsentativ für die Grundgesamtheit der Sprechenden. Die bisher für Online-Erhebungen herausgestellten abweichenden Faktoren vom Bevölkerungsdurchschnitt hinsichtlich Alter, Geschlecht und Ausbildung (siehe Bandilla 1999: 15) wurden aber erfasst und gelten für alle hier untersuchten arealen Räume gleichermaßen, so dass eine Vergleichbarkeit wiederum gewährleistet ist. Hinsichtlich des Alters zeigte sich wie in verschiedenen anderen Erhebungen zur Bekanntheit von Phrasemen (z.B. Grzybek 1991: 247, Häcki Buhofer/Burger 1994: 15f, Juska-Bacher 2009: 171f), dass ältere Informanten von der Gesamtheit der abgefragten Phraseme durchschnittlich mehr kannten als jüngere. Bei einer Gruppierung der Informanten nach Alter in 10-Jahres-Schritten war ein Anstieg der durchschnittlichen Kenntnis von der Altersgruppe der 11- bis 20-Jährigen bis zur Gruppe der 61- bis 70-Jährigen, mit leichtem Abfall der durchschnittlichen Kenntnis der über 70-Jährigen zu erkennen. Im Hinblick auf die einzelnen Phraseme gab es aber durchaus solche, bei denen dieses Prinzip nicht galt (z.B. *Zupf/züpf ich!*) mit dem höchsten Bekanntheitsgrad in der Gruppe der 21- bis 30-Jährigen und dem geringsten in der Gruppe der über 70-jährigen Informanten und *jmdm. die Stange halten* in der Bedeutung „sich mit jmdm. messen" mit dem größten Bekanntheitsgrad in der Gruppe der 21- bis 30-Jährigen und der 11- bis 20-Jährigen und einem deutlichen Abfall des Bekanntheitsgrades bis zur Unbekanntheit dieses Phrasems ab der Gruppe der 61-Jährigen. An der Befragung haben sich 545 Frauen und 432 Männer beteiligt (von fünf Informanten fehlen entsprechende Angaben), 435 der Informanten haben keine Universität besucht, 546 hingegen haben an einer Universität studiert (von einem Informanten fehlt diese Angabe).
14. Da davon ausgegangen wird, dass das Testen der Bekanntheit (durch Ergänzungstests oder Abfrage der Bedeutung) deutlich zuverlässiger ist als eine Selbsteinschätzung der Bekanntheit, der Verwendung oder der Verwendungshäufigkeit, wurde mit dem Testen der Bekanntheit gearbeitet.
15. Ihnen allen danke ich für ihr Interesse an diesem Thema und ihren Einsatz bei der Erarbeitung, Diskussion und Verbreitung des Fragebogens. Ebenso gedankt sei den 1000 Probanden, die an der Befragung teilgenommen haben.
16. Einleitungstext zu diesem Abschnitt:
    „Bitte füllen Sie die Lücken mit demjenigen Wort, das Ihrer Meinung nach am ehesten in Ihrer Alltagssprache gebraucht wird. Dafür können Sie eine

(oder mehrere) der Vorgaben wählen oder unter „Anderes, nämlich" eine treffendere Möglichkeit angeben. Wenn Sie diese Wendung nicht kennen, bitte die letzte Zeile ankreuzen."
Z.B. Frage 2:
„Wenn jemand von einer Situation überfordert und ratlos ist, *steht er da wie der ... am/vorm Berg*.
a. *Bock*
b. *Esel*
c. *Ochs*
d. Anderes, nämlich ...[Freifeld zur Eingabe]
e. Ich kenne diese Wendung nicht.".

17. Einleitungstext zu diesem Abschnitt:
„Bitte geben Sie die Bedeutung der folgenden Wendungen an. Wählen Sie wieder eine (oder mehrere) der Vorgaben oder geben Sie eine treffendere Umschreibung an. Wenn Sie die Bedeutung nicht kennen, bitte einfach die letzte Zeile ankreuzen. Wir wüssten auch gern, ob es sich Ihrer Meinung nach um eine Redewendung handelt, die nur in der Schweiz oder auch ausserhalb der Schweiz gebräuchlich ist."
Z.B. Frage 17:
„*das Feuer im Elsass sehen* bedeutet:
a. starke Schmerzen haben
b. zu viel Phantasie haben
c. sehr gute Augen haben
d. Kenne ich nur in anderer Form, nämlich: ... [Freifeld zur Eingabe].".

18. Ebenfalls zu Frage 17:
„Kommt diese Redewendung Ihrer Meinung nach
a. nur in der Schweiz vor?
b. auch ausserhalb der Schweiz vor?
c. weiss nicht.".

19. Es wurden nur Daten derjenigen Probanden verwendet, für die eine eindeutige Zuordnung zu einem der drei Vollzentren (oder Liechtenstein) möglich war (d.h. sie mussten den größten Teil ihres Lebens im betreffenden Land verbracht haben und dort auch sozialisiert worden sein).

20. Für die Kartenerstellung geht mein herzlicher Dank an Dr. Stefan Meier, Universität Basel.

21. Mehr als zwei Drittel der Informanten aus Baden-Württemberg hatten einen alemannischen Hintergrund, die übrigen machen diesbezüglich keine expliziten Angaben – es wird auch hier davon ausgegangen, dass der größere Teil aus den südlichen zwei Dritteln des Bundeslandes stammt und damit dem alemannischen Teil angehört.

22. 11 von 12 Informanten aus Bayern hatten einen bairischen Dialekthintergrund.

23. Österreich: 5 Probanden aus Vorarlberg, Oberösterreich, Kärnten und dem Burgenland; Liechtenstein: 7 Probanden.

24. Die Nennformschreibung folgt Korhonen (2001).
25. Als „(nahezu) unbekannt" wurden in dieser Untersuchung Phraseme mit einem Bekanntheitsgrad von bis zu 20% eingestuft. Dieser relativ hohe Schwellenwert sollte „zufällige" arealfremde Kenntnis, Raten und Falschangaben weitgehend neutralisieren. Häufig liegt der tatsächliche Bekanntheitsgrad deutlich unter 20%, im Fall von *dastehen wie der Esel am Berg* bspw. bei 5%.
26. Siehe Fußnote 9.
27. In der Befragung wurden vereinzelt Formen wie *das Feuer/die Sterne in Holland sehen* angegeben. Inwieweit es sich hierbei um gängige Varianten handelt, müsste gesondert untersucht werden. In den dieser Untersuchung zugrunde gelegten Wörterbüchern sind diese Formen nicht aufgeführt. Im Schweizerischen Idiotikon (1881– , Bd. 1, Spalte 942) finden sich hingegen die Varianten *Feuer z' Basel/im Schwarzwald/z' Bade* mit der Bedeutungserläuterung „i.S.v. in Folge eines Schlages oder Stosses an den Kopf subjektive Lichtempfindungen haben".
28. Ähnliches gilt auch für den phraseologischen falschen Freund *jmdm. die Stange halten*. In der Bedeutung „sich mit jmdm. messen" war das Phrasem nur in der Westschweiz und hier zwischen 21 und 60% der Informanten bekannt, in der östlichen Landeshälfte sowie in Österreich und Deutschland wurde nur die offensichtlich gemeindeutsche „jmdn. nicht im Stich lassen, ihm beistehen" abgegeben.
29. Neben den in Abbildung 9 aufgeführten waren dies: *Jetzt ist genug Heu (dr) unten.* („Jetzt ist aber genug."); *Das schleckt keine Geiss weg.* („Daran gibt es keinen Zweifel, es lässt sich nicht leugnen."); *Zupf/züpf dich.* („Hau ab."); *jmdm. nimmt es den Ärmel rein* („Jmd. ist von einer Sache begeistert."); *jmdm. die Stange halten* („sich mit jmdm. messen"); *mit abgesägten Hosen dastehen* („blossgestellt sein"); *die Finken klopfen* („sich rasch und heimlich entfernen").
30. Dieses Ergebnis widerspricht demjenigen von Di Paolo/Glaser (2006: 17), die bei einer Befragung von rund 300 Informanten feststellten, dass deutsche Teilnehmende sieben Helvetismen (Einzellexeme) häufiger als Helvetismen einstuften als Schweizer.
31. Berücksichtigt man die Ergebnisse verschiedener Studien, denen zufolge Informanten mit zunehmendem Alter mehr Phraseme kennen (siehe Fußnote 13), dann könnten ältere Informanten unter Umständen auch mehr Phraseme als Helvetismen einstufen, als es die Studierenden getan haben.
32. *Jmd. kann mir in die Schuhe blasen.*, das neben der Schweiz auch in Österreich, Baden-Württemberg und Bayern als bekannt angegeben wurde (siehe Abbildung 7), beispielsweise lag recht genau auf der Regressionsgeraden und nicht, wie im Fall einer Bestätigung der o.g. Hypothese zu erwarten gewesen wäre, deutlich darunter.
33. Zu ähnlichem Ergebnis kommen auch Burger (1998) und Scharloth (2004 und 2005).

Bibliografie

Ammon, Ulrich. 1986. Explikation der Begriffe ‚Standardvarietät' und ‚Standardsprache' auf normtheoretischer Grundlage. In Günter Holtus, Edgar Radtke (Hrsg.), *Sprachlicher Substandard*, 1–63. Tübingen: Niemeyer.

Ammon, Ulrich. 1995. *Die deutsche Sprache in Deutschland, Österreich und der Schweiz: Das Problem der nationalen Varietäten*. Berlin/New York: Walter de Gruyter.

Ammon, Ulrich, Hans Bickel, Jakob Ebner, Ruth Esterhammer, Markus Gasser, Lorenz Hofer, Birte Kellermeier-Rehbein, Heinrich Löffler, Doris Mangott, Hans Moser, Robert Schläpfer, Michael Schloßmacher, Regula Schmidlin & Günter Vallaster. 2004. *Variantenwörterbuch des Deutschen: Die Standardsprache in Österreich, der Schweiz und Deutschland sowie in Liechtenstein, Luxemburg, Ostbelgien und Südtirol*. Berlin: Walter de Gruyter.

Bandilla, Wolfgang. 1999. WWW-Umfragen – Eine alternative Datenerhebungstechnik für die empirische Sozialforschung? In Bernad Batinic, Andreas Werner, Lorenz Gräf & Wolfgang Bandilla (Hrsg.), *Online Research: Methoden, Anwendungen und Ergebnisse*, 9–19. Göttingen/Bern/Toronto/Seattle: Hogrefe.

Bickel, Hans. 2006. Das Internet als linguistisches Korpus. *Linguistik online* 28(3). 71–83.

Burger, Harald. 1995. Helvetismen in der Phraseologie. In Heinrich Löffler (Hrsg.), *Alemannische Dialektforschung: Bilanz und Perspektiven*, 13–25. Tübingen, Basel: Francke.

Burger, Harald. 1996. Zur Phraseologie des Schweizerdeutschen. In Jarmo Korhonen (Hrsg.), *Studien zur Phraseologie des Deutschen und des Finnischen II*, 461–488. Bochum: Brockmeyer.

Burger, Harald. 1998. Helvetismen in der Phraseologie – Vorkommen und stilistische Funktionen. In Dietrich Hartmann (Hrsg.), *„Das geht auf keine Kuhhaut". Arbeitsfelder der Phraseologie: Akten des Westfälischen Arbeitskreises Phraseologie/Parömiologie 1996 (Bochum)*, 49–80. Bochum: Brockmeyer.

Burger, Harald. 2007. *Phraseologie: Eine Einführung am Beispiel des Deutschen*. Berlin: Erich Schmidt Verlag.

Clyne, Michael George. 1984. *Language and society in the German-speaking countries*. Cambridge: Cambridge University Press.

Clyne, Michael George. 1992. *Pluricentric languages: Differing norms in different nations*. Berlin: Mouton de Gruyter.

Di Paolo, Maria Concetta & Elvira Glaser. 2006. Wie lassen sich Helvetismen erkennen? In Christa Dürscheid & Martin Businger (Hrsg.), *Schweizer Standarddeutsch: Beiträge zur Varietätenlinguistik*, 11–22. Tübingen: Gunter Narr.

Dudenredaktion (Hrsg.). 1984. *Die Grammatik*. Bearb. von Günter Drosdowski. Mannheim etc.: Dudenverlag. Bd. 4.

Dudenredaktion (Hrsg.). 1990. *Aussprachewörterbuch: Wörterbuch der deutschen Standardaussprache*. Bearb. von Max Mangold. Mannheim etc.: Dudenverlag. Bd. 6.

Dudenredaktion (Hrsg.). 1991. *Rechtschreibung der deutschen Sprache: auf der Grundlage der amtlichen Rechtschreibregeln.* Mannheim etc.: Dudenverlag. Bd. 1.

Dudenredaktion (Hrsg.). 1992. *Redewendungen und sprichwörtliche Redensarten: Wörterbuch der deutschen Idiomatik.* Bearb. von Günther Drosdowski und Werner Scholze-Stubenrecht. Mannheim etc.: Dudenverlag. Bd. 11.

Dudenredaktion (Hrsg.). 2008. *Redewendungen.* Bearb. von Werner Scholze-Stubenrecht. Mannheim etc.: Dudenverlag. Bd. 11.

Ebner, Jakob. 2009. *Wie sagt man in Österreich? Wörterbuch des österreichischen Deutsch.* Mannheim etc.: Dudenverlag.

Földes, Csaba. 1992. Zu den österreichischen Besonderheiten der deutschen Phraseologie. In Csaba Földes (Hrsg.), *Deutsche Phraseologie in Sprachsystem und Sprachverwendung,* 9–24, Wien: Praesens.

Földes, Csaba. 1996. *Deutsche Phraseologie kontrastiv – intra- und interlingale Zugänge.* Heidelberg: Groos.

Grzybek, Peter. 1991. Sinkendes Kulturgut? Eine empirische Pilotstudie zur Bekanntheit deutscher Sprichwörter. *Wirkendes Wort* 2. 239–264.

Haas, Walter. 1982. Die deutschsprachige Schweiz. In Jachen C Arquint, Iso Camartin, Walter Haas, Pierre Knecht, Ottavio Lurati, Florentin Lutz & Robert Schläpfer, *Die viersprachige Schweiz,* 71–160. Zürich, Köln: Benziger.

Haas, Walter. 2000. Die deutschsprachige Schweiz. In Hans Bickel & Robert Schläpfer (Hrsg.), *Die viersprachige Schweiz,* 57–138. Aarau et al.: Sauerländer.

Häcki Buhofer, Annelies. 1998. Kenntnis- und Gebrauchsunterschiede bei Phraseologismen des Binnendeutschen, des Schweizerhochdeutschen und des Schweizerdeutschen. In Wolfgang Eismann (Hrsg.), *Europhras 95 – Europäische Phraseologie im Vergleich: Gemeinsames Erbe und kulturelle Vielfalt,* 295–313. Bochum: Norbert Brockmeyer.

Häcki Buhofer, Annelies & Harald Burger. 1994. Phraseologismen im Urteil von Sprecherinnen und Sprechern. In Barbara Sandig (Hrsg.), *EUROPHRAS 92. Tendenzen der Phraseologieforschung,* 1–33. Bochum: Brockmeyer.

Hofer, Lorenz. 2003. Phraseologismen im Wörterbuch der nationalen Varianten der deutschen Standardsprache. In Harald Burger, Annelies Häcki Buhofer & Gertrud Gréciano (Hrsg.), *Flut von Texten – Vielfalt der Kulturen. Ascona 2001 zur Methodologie und Kulturspezifik der Phraseologie,* 479–490. Baltmannsweiler: Schneider.

Juska-Bacher, Britta. 2009. *Empirisch-kontrastive Phraseologie: Am Beispiel der Bekanntheit von Bruegels Niederländischen „Sprichwörtern" im Niederländischen, Deutschen und Schwedischen.* Baltmannsweiler: Schneider.

Juska-Bacher, Britta. 2010. SDS-Exploratoren und Online-Befragung – Lässt sich im Methodenmix ein Wandel in der Schweizer Dialektlandschaft nachweisen? In Helen Christen, Sibylle Germann, Nadia Montefiori, Walter Haas & Hans Ruef (Hrsg.), *Dialektologie: Wege in die Zukunft (Beihefte zur Zeitschrift für Dialektologie und Linguistik),* 279–293. Stuttgart: Steiner Verlag.

Koller, Werner. 1999. Nationale Sprach(en)kultur der Schweiz und die Frage der „nationalen Varietäten des Deutschen". In Andreas Gardt, Ulrike Haß-Zumkehr & Thorsten Roelcke (Hrsg.), *Sprachgeschichte als Kulturgeschichte,* 133–170. Berlin/New York: Walter de Gruyter.

Meyer, Kurt. 1989. *Wie sagt man in der Schweiz? Wörterbuch der schweizerischen Besonderheiten.* Mannheim: Bibliographisches Institut.

Meyer, Kurt. 2001. Die lexikalische Situation des Standarddeutschen in der Schweiz. In D. Alan Cruse, Franz Hundsnurscher, Michael Job & Peter Rolf Lutzeier (Hrsg.), *An international handbook on the nature and structure of words and vocabularies / Ein internationales Handbuch zur Natur und Struktur von Wörtern und Wortschätzen,* 1189–1196. Berlin/New York: Walter de Gruyter.

Meyer, Kurt. 2006. *Schweizer Wörterbuch: So sagen wir in der Schweiz.* Frauenfeld/Stuttgart/Wien: Huber.

von Peter Polenz. 1999. Deutsch als plurinationale Sprache im postnationalistischen Zeitalter. In Andreas Gardt, Ulrike Haß-Zumkehr & Thorsten Roelcke (Hrsg.), *Sprachgeschichte als Kulturgeschichte*, 115–132. Berlin/New York: Walter de Gruyter.

Reiffenstein, Ingo. 2001. Das Problem der nationalen Varietäten. Rezensionsaufsatz zu Ulrich Ammon: Die deutsche Sprache in Deutschland, Österreich und der Schweiz. Das Problem der nationalen Varietäten, Berlin, New York 1995. *ZfdPh* 120. 78–89.

Scharloth, Joachim. 2004. Zwischen Fremdsprache und nationaler Varietät: Untersuchungen zum Plurizentrizitätsbewusstsein der Deutschschweizer. In Rudolf Muhr (Hrsg.), *Standardvariationen und Sprachideologien in verschiedenen Sprachkulturen der Welt / Standard Variations and Language Ideologies in Different Language Cultures around the World,* Frankfurt am Main etc.: Lang. [Zugriff am 20 11 2010 unter http://www.inst.at/trans/15Nr/06_1/scharloth15.htm]

Scharloth, Joachim. 2005. Asymmetrische Plurizentrizität und Sprachbewusstsein. Einstellungen der Deutschschweizer zum Standarddeutschen. *Zeitschrift für Germanistische Linguistik* 33(2). 236–267.

Scheuringer, Hermann. 1990. *Sprachentwicklung in Bayern und Österreich. Eine Analyse des Substandardverhaltens der Städte Braunau am Inn (Österreich) und Simbach am Inn (Bayern) und ihres Umlandes.* Hamburg: Helmut Buske.

Scheuringer, Hermann. 1997. Sprachvarietäten in Österreich. In Gerhard Stickel (Hrsg.), *Varietäten des Deutschen: Regional- und Umgangssprachen,* 332–345. Berlin/New York: Walter de Gruyter.

Schifferle, Hans-Peter. 1995. *Dialektstrukturen in Grenzlandschaften. Untersuchungen zum Mundartwandel im nordöstlichen Aargau und im benachbarten südbadischen Raum Waldshut.* Bern etc.: Peter Lang.

Schmidlin, Regula. 2004. Nationale Varianten standarddeutscher Phraseologismen. In Christine Palm Meister (Hrsg.): *EUROPHRAS 2000: Internationale Tagung zur Phraseologie vom 15. – 18. Juni 2000 in Aske/Schweden*, 435–447. Tübingen: Stauffenburg.

Schmidlin, Regula. 2004a. Lexikographische Probleme bei phraseologischen Varianten. In Csaba Földes & Jan Wirrer (Hrsg.), *Phraseologismen als Gegenstand sprach- und kulturwissenschaftlicher Forschung. Akten der Europäischen Gesellschaft für Phraseologie (EUROPHRAS) und des Westfälischen Arbeitskreises „Phraseologie/Parömiologie" (Loccum 2002),* 377–391. Baltmannsweiler: Schneider.

Schmidlin, Regula. 2007. Phraseological expressions in German standard varieties. In Harald Burger, Dmitrij Dobrovol'skij, Peter Kühn & Neal R. Norrick (Hrsg.), *Phraseologie. Phraseology,* 551–562. Berlin, New York: Walter de Gruyter.

Schweizer Schülerduden. 1980, 1976. Wabern: Büchler. 2 Bde.

Seidelmann, Erich. 1983. Die Stadt Konstanz und die Sprachlandschaft am Bodensee. In Hugo Steger, Eugen Gabriel & Volker Schupp (Hrsg.), *Forschungsbericht Südwestdeutscher Sprachatlas,* 156–234. Marburg: Elwert.

Schweizerisches Idiotikon (1881–). Frauenfeld: Huber.

Siebs, Theodor. 1969. *Deutsche Aussprache: Reine und gemäßigte Hochlautung mit Aussprachewörterbuch.* Hrsg. von Helmut de Boor, Hugo Moser & Christian Winkler. Berlin: Walter de Gruyter.

Anhang 1
Auflistung der im Fragebogen abgefragten vermeintlichen
phraseologischen Helvetismen

Phraseme

weder Fisch noch Vogel sein
dastehen wie der Esel am Berg
das Kalb machen
bachab gehen
jmdm. die Kappe waschen
einen Ecken abhaben
durchs Band weg
Jetzt ist genug Heu (dr)unten.
Das schleckt keine Geiss weg.
das Feuer im Elsass sehen
Zupf/züpf dich!
jmdm. nimmt es den Ärmel rein
Jetzt jagt es den Zapfen ab!
jmdm. die Stange halten
mit abgesägten Hosen dastehen
die Finken klopfen
Jmd. kann mir in die Schuhe blasen
kein Büro aufmachen

Anhang 2
Die Herkunft der Informanten nach Kantonen bzw. Bundesländern

Land	Verwaltungseinheit	Anzahl	gesamt
Schweiz	Aargau	100	
	Appenzell Ausserrhoden	8	
	Appenzell Innerrhoden	1	
	Basel-Landschaft	95	
	Basel-Stadt	126	
	Bern	84	
	Freiburg	7	
	Glarus	1	
	Graubünden	10	
	Luzern	38	
	Nidwalden	2	
	Schaffhausen	9	
	Schwyz	24	
	Solothurn	57	
	St. Gallen	104	
	Thurgau	17	
	Uri	1	
	Wallis	14	
	Zug	17	
	Zürich	148	863
Deutschland	Baden-Württemberg	45	
	Bayern	12	
	übrige Bundesländer	49	106
Österreich			5
Liechtenstein			7

Contextually determined fixity and flexibility in "thing" sentence matrixes[1]

GERALD DELAHUNTY

Abstract

This paper describes the semantics and pragmatics of Thing sentences (TSs) and derives them from the sentence's lexis and syntax. It describes several rhetorical and discourse management uses of the form and argues that these arise because the TS clause is simultaneously presupposed and focused. It shows that TSs are realized as a set of formal variants appearing to manifest a range of fixity and flexibility: some may be produced either analytically or holistically, others only holistically. Data from the Corpus of Contemporary American English (COCA) and other sources shows that most TSs occur at the informal end of the register spectrum, in registers typically produced under time pressure, which is also where the less flexible variants tend to occur. The paper proposes a source and conditions for the creation of discourse management expressions like TSs and identifies linguistic elements from which they may be constructed and a diachronic trajectory for their origination, development, and extinction.

Keywords: copula; corpus; COCA; discourse organization; fixedness; formulaicity; phraseology; register; specificational; shell nouns; subordination; thing; thing sentence.

1. Introduction

This paper investigates, from a phraseological point of view, the variant forms, discourse uses, and register distribution of a sentence type I call "*Thing* sentences" (TSs). It is a part of a broader research project that seeks to identify the linguistic resources that speakers of a language use to create new linguistic devices for discourse organizational purposes, and to describe and explain the pragmatics of a number of the devices so created (Delahunty 2001, 2006, 2007, 2008, in prep). These devices include a range of non-canonical sentence types constructed from semantically minimal lexis such as the copula, pro-forms, "shell" nouns (Schmid 2000), and the subordination of the clause representing the primary information to be communicated by the sentence (Pusch 2006).

Thing sentences are a subtype of specificational copular sentence (Higgins 1976) whose subject head is *thing*, which is characteristically definite (Brenier and Michaelis 2005), and whose complement is a finite clause:

(1) *the thing is that Black and White America doesn't exist* (COCA ADADEMIC)

TSs allow several formal variants that differ in their internal organization and are differentially associated with factors such as style, register, and mode (Delahunty 2007, 2008, in prep). I refer to the variant described and exemplified just above as the "full TS." Other variants are created by omitting the definite article:

(2) Thing is that CDOEXM isn't supported from ASP.NET... (http://forums.asp.net/t/1219872.aspx)

Or the conjunction:

(3) The thing is, it actually works (http://www.beastwithin.org/users/wwwwolf/games/nwn/gametools/neverblender)

Or both the article and conjunction:

(4) Thing is, I do that most of the time anyway (http://www.kevinleitch.co.uk/wp/?feed=rss2)

Although I will argue that the internal organizing principles of these variants are different from those of the full TS, their meanings and pragmatic functions are identical, so I include them among the *Thing* sentences that are the focus of this paper. I refer to *(The) thing is (that)* as "the matrix," and the tensed S as "the (complement) clause."

Additionally, the copula may be doubled:

(5) The thing *is is* that we haven't told John yet (Tuggy 1996: 713. See also Massam 1999; McConvell 1988).

This is the variant that has attracted most research attention, as scholars attempted to account for *is is*. Because Brenier and Michaelis (2005) offer a compelling optimality based account for the double copula, viz., it is a correction of the mismatch between the intonation contour and syntax of the sentence, I do not address that issue in this paper.

There are also sentence types that are lexically and syntactically related to TSs. One of these has *thing* as subject head but with pre-modifiers and/or post-modifiers, e.g., *The important thing is ...; The first thing is ...; The thing about X is ....* Because of these modifiers, the semantics and therefore the pragmatics and discourse functions of these sentence types differ from those of TSs, e.g., they may order a sequence of (sub)topics, and so are not included in this paper. (See Delahunty and Velazquez-Castillo 2002 for a discussion of these and other related sentence types).

The complement of these copular sentences may also vary. It may be an NP:

(6) The thing is also money (http://www.ungei.org/infobycountry/247-1214.html)

Or a *to*-infinitive:

(7) The thing is to not be on the receiving end of fate, ... (http://www.hpl.hp,com/news/2002/jan-mar/ramani.html)

Because these have different semantics and discourse potentials from TSs (e.g., the NP complement is not propositional and the *to*-infinitival forms have an exhortative function lacking in TSs), I do not deal with them here.[2]

Discourse uses of *thing* also occur in a range of other expression types, e.g., *OK. Here's the thing* (Restasis TV ad), and *The thing is this:* (Sirr 2009: 34). These, too, must await future research, though Schmid (2000) discusses a number of them.

Thing sentences are a subtype of specificational copular sentence which allows a potentially infinite range of subjects. The head of these subjects is a noun whose semantic specificity may range from the very specific, such as *milagro/miracle*, in:

(8) El *milagro* es que estos pinos se mantengan.
The miracle is that these pines themselves maintain
The *miracle* is that these pines survived.
(Corpus Oral de Referencia del Español Contemporáneo)[3]

to the maximally general *thing* that we find in TSs. Like Schmid (2000), I believe that a crucial analytic distinction must be made between TSs and sentences with semantically richer subject heads: the noun in the non-TS type names a relationship, e.g., *implication*, between the complement clause and its context and thereby evokes a (cognitive) frame in which the relevant context and complement clause are related, whereas the semantics of *thing* is so non-specific that it cannot do this, with the consequence that the relationship between the TS clause and the context must be otherwise accounted for, as I demonstrate below. (See also Delahunty 2008 in prep; Delahunty and Velazquez-Castillo 2002; Francis 1994)

For the purposes of this paper, I have divided the TS variants into the five types in Table 1.

One goal of this paper is to show that the TS-type is situationally dependent. That is, it is an expression "with contextually restricted conditions of use" (Kuiper et al. 2007: 317: cited in Edmonds 2010a: 11) or is "appropriate to a situation of a certain kind which is appropriate relative to certain communicative ends" (Coulmas 1981: 16: cited in Edmonds 2010a: 24). Edmonds adds, "With respect to conventional expressions, it is predominantly

Table 1. *TS variants*

---

a. Full TSs: *The thing is that S* <*the thing is S*>[1]
b. *The thing is* + punctuation marker (typically a comma) without *that* <*the thing is,*>[2]
c. *The thing is* without *that* and without any punctuation marker <*the thing is*>
d. *Thing is* + punctuation marker without *that* <*thing is,*>
e. *Thing is* without any punctuation marker and without *that* <*thing is*>[3]

---

1 I use < > to demarcate a cited form from surrounding text, and especially to disambiguate a comma, thus distinguishing <*thing is,*> from <*thing is*>,.
2 For brevity's sake and because the comma is the most frequently occurring punctuation mark in my data, I use "comma" to represent all the punctuation that occurs between the TS matrix and clause.
3 The paradigmatically related sentences with subject heads other than *thing* exhibit corresponding variants with similar internal organization.

the association with a social (e.g., classroom discourse) and/or pragmatic (e.g., different speech acts or *conversational management*) situation that is of interest" (2010a: 24; emphasis added). Edmonds also says, "Concretely, this implies that an identical surface string may be a formula in certain communication situations but not in others" (p. 13). As I show, the TS is a device with a specific discourse, and typically, conversational function. Its formal variants have the same characteristic interpretation and functions, though they differ in their internal organization and apparent degrees of fixity, and are associated with different registers and modes of production, though the full version appears to be capable of either holistic or analytic production, depending on the specifics of the situation, as allowed for by Edmonds and the research she cites.

Full TSs are syntactically organized according to the grammar of English while the punctuated variants are the result of the intonational separation of the matrix from the clause, and the ellipses result from very general reductive processes, presumably facilitated by the situational dependence of the TS-type. Additionally, the distribution of these variants across registers is such that the fuller variants occur in registers typically produced under little time pressure but which require considerable attention to language and prescriptive correctness, whereas the most reduced, most fixed variants occur in registers typically produced under considerable time pressure but which require little attention to language and prescriptive correctness.

2. Data sources

The data for this paper comes from several sources: Mark Davies' Corpus of Contemporary American English (COCA), the World Wide Web using WebCorp (Bergh 2005), five Inspector Rebus novels by Ian Rankin, and occasional items from whatever I happened to be reading. The data consists of instances of the sentences along with as much of their context as needed for adequate interpretation, or as much as the concordancers allow. COCA consists of five subcorpora: ACADEMIC, MAGAZINE, FICTION, NEWSPAPER, and SPOKEN texts.[4]

It's important to be aware of the types of texts in each subcorpus. ACADEMIC includes texts from publications such as *American Scholar, Africa Today, World Affairs, Anthropology Quarterly, Style*, and many others, representing a range of texts, some more highly edited than others. Some include representations of speech.

FICTION includes texts from books and from magazines such as *The Atlantic Monthly* and *Literary Review*. Fiction, of course, characteristically includes representations of speech, typically intended to be a realistic if conventionalized representation of conversation or of interior monolog.

MAGAZINES includes texts from publications such as *Money, American Heritage, Rolling Stone, Prevention*, and *Newsweek*. This latter magazine has adopted an informal style to survive challenges from electronic news magazines.

NEWSPAPERS includes texts from *The New York Times, Associated Press, USA Today*, and the *San Francisco Chronicle*, representing a range of styles and including representations of speech.

SPOKEN consists of transcriptions of talk on TV news programs, including ABC 20/20, ABC Primetime, and CNN Crossfire. This register is rather different from casual conversation amongst friends. The speakers are professional newscasters, journalists, and commentators, so the linguistic style is often of texts written to be spoken, and as journalists are often conservative in their language attitudes, the style tends to be prescriptively normative.

3. Uses and rhetorical strategies

In this section, I briefly describe how TSs are used in discourse and the rhetorical strategies they instantiate. I also explain why TSs function in these ways by showing how their functions can be derived from their lexico-grammatical characteristics interacting with their contexts and general pragmatic principles, without recourse to construction-specific stipulations. I will then return to the main topics of the paper: the register distribution of the TS variants and an explanation of that distribution. (For more detailed argumentation, see Delahunty in prep.)

3.1. *What TSs mean*

As the TS is a sub-type of specificational sentence, it has a definite subject which represents a variable whose value is represented by the clause (Higgins 1976). In other words, the subject represents a description that the complement clause instantiates, or the subject characterizes the clause (Schmid 2000). Unlike semantically richer nouns, *thing* denotes merely COUNTABLE ENTITY and so does not specify how the proposition represented by the complement is to be related to its context (Delahunty and Velazquez-Castillo 2002; Schmid 2000).[5] As TS subjects are also characteristically singular (see Section 5), only a single value or instantiation is relevant.

Because the TS subject is definite, it licenses the presupposition that an identifiable entity exists, but as (*the*) *thing* has no situational referent, it is interpreted as the speaker's assumption that the hearer accepts the description it denotes and that a contextually relevant entity exists that satisfies that description, namely, the proposition denoted by the complement. Consequently, that proposition is backgrounded rather than asserted.

However, in addition to being presupposed, the complement clause is doubly focused, first, by virtue of its predicate position, which Lambrecht (1994) characterizes as the default focus position and, second, because it represents the value of the variable represented by the TS subject, it is an argument, which Lambrecht claims is a marked focus. The complement clause is thus both presupposed and markedly focused and thus introduced into the discourse as a new and especially significant member of the set of propositions to be taken for granted in the local discourse.

These apparently contradictory interpretations are used to indicate that the speaker is proposing that the audience take for granted the proposition represented by the TS clause and as the ground for subsequent utterances, replacing the proposition represented by an utterance prior to the TS which would otherwise have functioned as that ground. For example:

(9) When the barman slouched back with Rebus's change, Hogan greeted him by name.
"Okay, Malky?"
The young man frowned. "Do I know you?"
Hogan shrugged. "Thing is, *I* know *you*." He paused. "Still on the smack?" (Rankin 2003: 192)

Malky's "Do I know you?" should have been the basis for the next contribution to the discourse, e.g., a yes/no answer. Hogan's TS preempts this topical trajectory and substitutes his "*I* know *you*" as the basis for further conversation, as his "Still on the smack?" demonstrates. (Delahunty 2007, 2008, in prep provide more detailed arguments.)

3.2. *Uses and rhetorical effects*

The semantics and pragmatics of TSs allows them to be used for several rhetorical effects, of which I describe just three here (see Delahunty in prep for others). TSs may contradict a prior assumption:

(10) I imagine that the hour you are onstage each week is high-energy and exhausting. Do you have fun doing the show each week?

What's the funniest unexpected thing that's happened onstage during the run?...
The thing is that since the plays are done in random order and, since there is a lot of audience participation, the whole thing is rather unexpected. (Too Much Light Makes the Baby Go Blind)

In this example, the assumption – a presupposition presented as an element to be taken as common ground by the interlocutors – is that there exists a unique "funniest unexpected thing that happened onstage during the run," licensed by the definite article and superlative "funniest." This presupposition is implicitly contradicted and replaced by the proposition represented by the TS in the interviewee's reply. This is consistent with Carter and MacCarthy's (2006) contention that TSs represent problems and with Tuggy's (1996) contention that they represent "disconformity" with their contexts, a characterization endorsed by Schmid (2000).

TSs also affect topical development. Aijmer (2007: 43) claims that a TS "signals a new" topic or subtopic. However, none of my examples effects a shift from one topic to another, while all of them signal a shift from one subtopic to another, as illustrated by:

(11) just got this new 2003 voyager. *The thing is that, the other day it didn't start in the morning* (would not turn the engine). I try it again and would you believe it? No lights come on on the dashboard, won't turn the engine nothing is happening. Change the battery, check the fuses, etc etc. What is it with it? Could you help please? Ta very much. (http://www.faqs.org/qa/qa-3417.html)

This is from a website to which one writes about cars. The first sentence sets up minimal expectations about how the topic will develop. The TS marks the subtopical shift from the fact that the writer had just got a new Voyager to the (unexpected) fact that it wouldn't start. The TS clause provides very little information, and thereby makes relevant further information, in this case, a description of the car's symptoms, a list of things the owner did to remedy the problem, and a request for help. In fact, TSs often function as topic sentences – projecting the content and point of view of what follows them.

Hudson (1998: 143), citing Finell (1996), suggests that topic changing discourse markers also "soften potentially impolite changes." While I don't believe that TSs are discourse markers (yet), the TS in (10) politely shifts subtopic. Politeness theory (Brown and Levinson 1987) claims that redressive action frequently requires elaboration of the message. As the proposition represented by a TS clause is the sentence's message, we can view the matrix as elaboration which may indicate increased politeness. Politeness theory also claims that impersonalizing a message may indicate increased politeness. Because TSs represent their propositions as presupposed rather than asserted by the speaker, they are politely impersonal. All of these features can be seen in (10) above.

A TS may also function as a "pre-" (Terasaki [1976] 2004), that is, as an expression that prefigures an upcoming utterance and bids for the interactional space it needs. TSs are often informationally less than optimally relevant in their contexts but in such a way as to provide audiences with clues to the information the speaker would provide if granted the opportunity. For example:

(12) Mackenzie was shaking her head. "These records are up-to-date. The last rent money we received was only last week. It was paid by Mr. Baird."
"You're thinking he sublet?"
A broad smile lightened Mrs. Mackenzie's face. "Which is strictly forbidden by the tenancy agreement," she said.
"But people do it?"
"Of course they do. *The thing is, I decided to do some sleuthing myself...*" She sounded pleased with herself. Rebus leaned forward in his chair, warming to her.
"Do tell," he said.
"I checked with the city's other housing areas. There are several Robert Bairds on the list. Plus other forenames, all with the surname Baird." (Rankin 2005: 84)

Mackenzie uses her TS to bid for an extended next turn. The TS anticipates, "projects," to use Hopper & Thompson's (2008: 105–6) term, further talk by its producer, and Rebus' "Do tell" indicates that he accepts her bid and cedes interactional space for additional talk. This kind of topical projection is a characteristic rhetorical function of TSs.

4. Fixity/formulaicity

In this section, I examine TSs against a set of criteria that have been used by researchers to determine whether expressions are fixed on formulaic.

Edmonds (2010a, 2010b) provides a valuable review of the literature on fixity and distinguishes two major analytic points of view – the conventional and the psycholinguistic, though she recognizes that many researchers invoke both points of view. The former views fixed phrases as "sequences with a stable form that are used frequently by speakers in certain prescribed social situations," (Bardovi-Harlig 2009: 757). The latter views fixed phrases as "a sequence, continuous or discontinuous, of words or other elements, which is, or appears to be, prefabricated: that is, stored and retrieved whole from memory at time of use, rather than being subject to generation or analysis by the language grammar" (Wray 2002: 9). The data show that TS matrixes have a stable form with some variation and a specific meaning and pragmatics and are used for specific discourse management purposes. Though my data cannot address how TSs are stored, it is consistent with holistic storage of all variants and analytic generation of one in certain contexts.

The remainder of this section discusses researchers' claims that expressions consisting of more than one word may be fixed if speakers intuitively deem them so, if they are situationally dependent, in community-wide use, occur frequently, are semantically opaque, non-compositional, syntactically incoherent, less costly to produce, more fluently produced, invariable, of greater complexity than a speaker seems otherwise capable of, and extend the uses of the expression beyond those of adult or native speakers. These last two criteria are irrelevant here as my data cannot address them.

Full TSs certainly consist of more than a single word, though the <*thing is,*> variants, typically written as two words, may be produced as a single intonational unit, though not with word stress.

My intuition suggests that the TS variants represent a cline of fixity, with full TSs least fixed and <*thing is,*> most fixed; that is, the full TS variant may, on occasion, be generated analytically and on other occasions may be produced holistically, while the <*thing is,*> variant is always produced holistically. Wray (2002) is properly skeptical of the reliability of intuition, primarily because corpus findings show that we have poor intuitions about statistical tendencies.

The clearest examples of situationally dependent expressions may have no words in common, e.g. limericks and expressions of the class represented by *Is the pope Catholic?* (Moon 1998: 95). About these, Wray says, "With the absence of common lexical or morphological forms across the set members, the formulaicity resides in the context-structure interface rather than the form per se. This challenges the idea of a form-based criterion, for what, precisely, is being stored when all the words can be novel?" (Wray 2002: 32). Applying this to TSs, we might say that they are one of a number, whose size we cannot determine, of ways in which a speaker may communicate or indicate disagreement with some proposition in the relevant prior discourse along with the intention to propose an alternative proposition as the common ground for the continuation of the discourse. For example, to "Can I have this transferred to my phone?" one might answer, "Well, the connection's not working," or "What on earth for?" or "The thing is that it's not my phone you're calling from." (modified from London-Lund Corpus). That is, at the point at which a TS occurs, the normal requirements of the interaction require a contribution to the discourse with certain characteristics, and the TS is one of indefinitely many ways in which these requirements may be met. That the speaker chooses a TS rather than one of the alternatives suggests that the TS is the best choice among those alternatives for their purposes at that point, or it was the least costly form to produce, and the least costly form is acceptable in the context and is compatible with the speaker's "abilities and preferences" (Wilson & Sperber 2004: 612). This suggests that TSs, as a type, are situationally dependent; that is, regardless of whether they are formally fixed, they perform a specific pragmatic function, viz., indicating that the complement clause is both presupposed and marked, with consequential discourse effects.

TSs are in community wide use – the expression is known to all or most of the members of the speech community. The variants occur in a broad range of COCA texts, in Scottish fiction, in the Wellington Corpus of New Zealand English, in blogs and other online texts, and native speakers, at least as represented by the US university students I have discussed them with, recognize the form and can roughly characterize how they use it.

On the basis of their frequency, Biber et al. (1999: 992) identify lexical bundles as "word combinations" that occur "at least ten times per million words in a register" and "must be spread across at least five different texts in the register." They identify *but the thing is* as a four-word bundle that occurs in conversation, though they are silent on the other variants, presumably because these did not meet their frequency requirements. My data collection techniques do not allow me to determine how frequently TSs occur per some benchmark number of words, though they do allow me to say how many actual TSs, and which variants, occurred in the first 100 *thing is* hits in each of the five registers in COCA (see Table 2 below).[7]

Wray (2002) is skeptical about the reliability of frequency counts in determining fixity, as these may be undercut by intuition-based decisions about which expressions are worth counting, the size of the corpus, and the difficulty of determining the boundaries of the target expression. And we do find that expressions that are clearly fixed, e.g., semantically opaque idioms, occur very infrequently (Moon 1998: 79), so clearly, frequency and fixity are logically separate. And because holistic storage is a characteristic of an individual idiolect and corpora are (typically) composed of texts produced by many individuals, frequent corpus occurrence of an expression can only be suggestive of its fixity; other criteria must be invoked to demonstrate it. However, if we took Wray's skepticism about frequency to its extreme, we would have to abandon a useful heuristic for identifying potentially fixed expressions. In any case, a search for *thing is* yielded only 50 TSs out of the first 100 hits for each of COCA's textual categories, while in the five Rankin novels (approx. 2000 pages), I found only 24, and my WebCorp search yielded only 36.

Regarding the compositionality of fixed expressions, Wray remarks (2002: 33) that, "[a]t the heart of this approach is the observation that a sequence of words, once it is formulaic, is subject to detachment from the effects of the live grammar and lexicon. The string is no longer required to be grammatically regular or semantically logical. Sequences become frozen, or fossilized, and as a result often retain words or grammatical forms that are no longer current in the language." To apply this to TSs, we must ask, "What is included in the live grammar and lexicon?" As we have seen, full TSs are semantically transparent, compositional, and grammatically coherent, and so need not be fixed. However, a COCA search for the grammatical variants *thing was, thing will be, thing is not, things are*, and *things were* returned few or no instances (see Section 5) indicating that speakers do not make use of the full range of grammatical alternatives made available by the grammar, suggesting that they are not "unrestrictedly constructed" (Mel'čuk 1998: 26).[8]

Additionally, one might question whether variants without *the* are transparent, and whether variants without *the* or *that* are grammatically coherent. The determination depends upon whether processes such as the omission of *the* and *that* are part of the "live grammar" of the language. Clearly, reductions may be the result of very general processes. *That* deletion is not limited to TSs and is generally regarded as a grammatical rule (e.g., as a "structural matter" by Quirk et al. 1985: 900; see also Huddleston and Pullum 2002: 949–954). According to Biber at al. (1998: 681), *that* omission is rare in academic prose, most frequent in news, and favored by the verbs *think* and *say*, which are like *thing* in being semantically quite non-specific. Dor (2005) claims that *that* deletion indicates increased speaker commitment to the truth of the proposition represented by the clause, a formulation that is consistent with the sense of presupposition associated with TS complements that I showed in Section 3.1.

The deletion is also not limited to TSs. In the Rankin data I found several other head nouns without *the*, e.g., *word is, fact is, bugger is, trouble is, story is*, as well as the plural *chances are*, functioning as the subjects of specificational sentences. Quirk et al. (1985) treat *the* deletion primarily as a "grammatical feature" (p. 1511 Note [b]), but also as "situational ellipsis" (p. 899), whereby words "that normally occur before the onset of a tonic unit …, and hence have weak stress and low pitch" may be omitted by "reductive process[es] on the phonological, rather than on the grammatical level" (p. 896, esp. Note [b]). According to Quirk et al. (1985: 883–890), reductions such as those displayed by TSs must be recoverable verbatim, a characteristic which would be facilitated by the situational dependence of TSs. (See also Biber et al. 1999: sections 3.7.5 and 14.3.5.1.) Carter and McCarthy (2006: 186–187) merely say that "articles considered obligatory in formal speech and especially in writing may be unnecessary in informal speech when the referent is obvious." To informal speech we can add informal writing, or perhaps more accurately, writing that indexes aspects of speech, especially its reduced need for explicitness. (Huddleston and Pullum 2002 seem not to deal with this issue.)

Regardless of how we understand these elisions, the elements of TSs that may be delimited by punctuation and which seem to function as units relative to the complement, <*the thing is that,*>, <*the thing is,*>, <*thing is,*> are not phrases and therefore not generatable by the grammar, suggesting that they may be fixed by Wray's criterion.

Written data is far from ideal in addressing whether TSs are produced with greater fluency and speed and with less internal disruption by restarts and hesitation phenomena than non-fixed expressions. Nonetheless, TS matrixes, especially the reduced ones delimited by punctuation, seem to fit the criterion of uninterruptability.

Wray (2002: 34) says that very few fixed items are "entirely fixed," and researchers allow for some variation in otherwise fixed expressions, including "open slots." While the specificational relationship between the subject and the complement is invariant, we can represent the TS variants with the formula: *(the) thing is/was (that) S.*

However, a formula of this kind is inadequate as a representation of the TS variants: it implies that the elements are organized only as a linear sequence and that the variants are related to each other merely by changes in tense and the optional omission of *the* and/or *that*, when in fact, the variants represent at least two different internal organizing principles.

According to Wray (2002: 37), Jespersen ([1924] 1976: 83), "sees stress as a key defining feature of formulaic sequences. Because a sequence is 'felt and handled as a unit,' he argues, it is not possible to pause between the component words or to stress them in an unaccustomed way." While I have seen no evidence that <*thing is,*> may be interrupted, the punctuation that may occur in all TS variants appears to be the written indication of the intonational separation of the TS matrix from its complement clause, as well as tonic stress and intonation on *is*.

Because they may be fully syntactic and compositional, the full TS forms should be most likely to occur in registers that allow for and expect considerable attention to language, manifested in greater explicitness, while the other variants should tend to occur in registers expecting less attention to language and less explicitness. This is consistent with Halliday's (1987) claim that written language tends to be syntactically organized, whereas spoken language tends to be intonationally organized. As the intonational TS variants occur in written registers as well as spoken ones, they are typical of speech – and speech-like – registers.

Jespersen's observation and my analysis are also consistent with Hopper & Thompson's (2008: 99) claim that in English *wh*-cleft and extrapositive sentences, "[p]rosodically, each clause typically forms its own prosodic unit, the first ending with a 'continuing' terminal pitch contour." In this context "clause" refers to expressions which in formal spoken and written texts would be "reformulated" as a complete clause but are incompletely clausal in speech.

We have arrived at the tentative conclusion that TSs may be fixed at two levels. The first level is that the expression type is a situationally dependent specificational copular sentence; the second is that the TS variants represent the operation of contextually determined reductions and reorganization, presumably facilitated by the situational dependence of the expression type, and manifesting a cline of fixity from full TSs to <*thing is,*>. I turn next to a discussion of the distribution of the TS variants across registers.

5. Register distribution of TS variants

From a Hallidayan (1987) point of view, the TS variants, with their vague lexis, intonational rather than syntactic organization, and rightward placement of important information should occur primarily in speech(-like) registers. We should also expect the TS variants, ranging from full forms <*the thing is that S*> via increasing reductions and intonalization to the most reduced form <*thing is,*>, to correlate with registers ranging from those composed under least time pressure and in which the greatest degree of surface correctness and the broadest lexical range are expected, through registers composed under increasing time pressure with decreasing expectations of surface correctness and lexical diversity, to those registers composed under the greatest degree of time pressure and with the lowest expectation of surface correctness and lexical range. And this is in fact what we find.

I searched COCA for instances of the strings *thing is, thing is not, thing was, thing will be, things are, things were.* All of these searches returned instances which upon investigation were not TSs, though some returned actual TSs. I identified all the TSs in the first hundred hits from each sub-corpus, and categorized these according to the variants distinguished in Table 1, and compared the numbers of variants returned in each register.

The searches for *things are, things were, thing will be,* and *thing is not* returned no TSs in the first 100 hits. The notable non-occurrence of these TS variants indicates that speakers do not make use of the range of variants made possible by English grammar and lexis. The non-occurrence of the plural variants may be due to the uniqueness implicature associated with focusing, while the non-occurrence of the negative variants may be due to the fact that a TS complement is focused and typically new information which replaces an assumption derived from the prior context and which functions as the basis for following text, and so would appear to be incompatible with negation.

The search for *thing was* returned 2934 hits, but only five of the first 100 were TSs; none of these were full TSs, four were <*the thing was,*>, all from fictional narrative, and one was <*thing was,*>, from a first person fictional narrative. The infrequency of past tense TSs – merely 10% of the number of present tense TSs – may be due to the two factors. First, because of the semantic vagueness of their matrix clauses, TSs are more likely to occur in speech(-like) contexts, especially in conversation, in which the present tense predominates (see Figure 6.1 in Biber et al. 1999: 456). Second, TSs comment on an aspect of their contexts, a meta-communicative act, which is most likely to occur in speech(-like) registers and especially in conversation, which Biber et al. (1999: 1045–1047) characterize as "interactive," and thus to favor the present tense. The infrequency of past tense forms and the non-occurrence of the other possibilities may be taken to indicate that TSs are grammatically limited, and thus evidence of fixity, though we should also take into account that the forms might simply be incompatible with the discourse functions of TSs.

Because the past tense variants are so infrequent and their distribution is so entirely consistent with that of the corresponding present tense ones, it provides no information not available from the distribution of the present tense variants, and so I omit it from the discussion the register distribution of TS variants.

A COCA search for *thing is* yielded only 50 in the first 100 hits. Table 2 shows how the variants distribute across the registers.

Table 2. *COCA distribution of TS variants*

	FICT	SPOK	NEWS	MAGS	ACAD	TOTALS
Thing is hits	1554	5319	1676	1540	473	10562
Actual TSs < 1st 100 hits	18	12	11	6	3	50
%age of TSs in register	36%	24%	22%	12%	6%	100%
Full TSs <*the thing is that S*>	5.6%	33%	9.1%	none	67%	14.5%
<*the thing is,*>	67%	50%	64%	100%	none	58%
<*the thing is*>	11%	16.7%	18.2%	none	33%	19.1%
<*thing is,*>	11%	none	9.1%	none	none	9.1%
<*thing is*>	5.6%	none	none	none	none	7.3%

The decline in the frequency of TSs from FICTION to ACADEMIC clearly shows a distribution skewed toward the casual, speech, and speech-like end of the register spectrum: there are six times as many TSs in FICTION as in ACADEMIC (18 vs. 3). The TOTALS column shows that reduced variants occur almost six times as often as the full variants (85.5% vs. 14.5%), and that the main reduced variant is <*the thing is,*> (58%).

In FICTION we find the broadest range of variants, of which only one 5.6% is full, while the vast majority (78%) are punctuated and therefore show signs of intonational organization, suggesting a degree of fixity.

SPOKEN had 12 TSs, of which 33% (4) were full, 50% (6) were punctuated, and none were <*thing is,*> or <*thing is*>.

We should expect NEWSPAPERS to share features with ACADEMIC and SPOKEN, given that COCA's SPOKEN is represented primarily by professional TV news personalities. We find that NEWSPAPERS and SPOKEN have very similar rates of TS occurrence: 22% and 24% respectively. In NEWSPAPERS, 9.1% (1) are full and 73.1% were punctuated, and none were <*thing is*>.[9]

In MAGAZINES we should expect a distribution like that in FICTION and NEWSPAPERS. However, 100% (6) of the TSs found in MAGAZINES are the <*the thing is,*> variant, and 83% (5) are in first person narratives and/or informal contexts.[10]

ACADEMIC texts had only 3 TSs; of these 2 (67%) were full TSs and one (33%) was <*the thing is,*>, which was transcribed from speech. In another, more homogeneous academic corpus of one million words of business, civil engineering, and environmental sciences journal articles (Bond 2007), not a single TS occurred. Clearly, TSs occur very rarely in academic texts and we can tentatively conclude that when they do occur in those texts, they do so in their full form, unless there is a local reason not to.

The TSs collected from the Rankin novels and by using WebCorp (Bergh 2005) also display the kinds of reductions and skewed register distribution found in COCA. Table 3 shows that every Rankin TS is reduced and occurs in dialog.

All of the TSs found in the Rankin novels occur in dialog and none are full TSs. 25% (5) are <*the thing is,*> and 75% (15) are the further reduced <*thing is,*>. As all are punctuated, they show signs of intonational organization, suggestive of relative fixity.

The TS variants returned by a WebCorp search for the string *thing is* are presented in Table 4.

Table 3. *TSs in five Ian Rankin novels**

Thing sentences	20	
	DIALOG	OTHER
<the thing is that S>	none (0%)	none
<the thing is,>	5 (25%)	none
<the thing is>	none	none
<thing is,>	15 (75%)	none
<thing is>	none	none

* Four instance of <*thing was*> occurred in the Rankin novels; one occurred in dialog and the other three occurred in free indirect speech, which is "constructed dialogue" according to Tannen 1986 and "heteroglossic" according to Bakhtin 1981 [1953], both cited in Johnstone 2008: 60.

Table 4. *WebCorp examples**

Thing sentences	36
<the thing is that S>	8.3%
<the thing is,>	64%
<the thing is>	11.1%
<thing is,>	14%
<thing is>	2.8%

* The WebCorp search also returned two instances with doubled copula.

These are primarily from personal blogs and represent a very informal and highly involved style which include lots of contractions and elisions, as well as being minimally edited. It is notable, even remarkable, that 78% of these instances are punctuated, and therefore intonationalized, suggesting an oral substratum for this kind of writing.

From the data and discussion, we can derive three main observations. First, full TSs are typically unpunctuated, suggesting that they may, at least occasionally, be analytically generated with syntactic integration of matrix and clause.

Second, both full and reduced variants allow punctuation, though the latter far more frequently than the former, suggesting intonational organization of the matrix and hypotaxis of the clause (Halliday 1987).

Third, the non- or infrequent occurrences of past tense, plural, and negative variants suggest that TSs are not "unrestrictedly constructed" (Mel'čuk 1998: 26), though other, functional, accounts are available.

6. Discussion

Though full TSs seem to be syntactically organized and semantically compositional, they have specific pragmatic and discourse effects and so are situationally dependent. That several of their grammatically possible variants rarely or never occur suggests that TSs are fixed to some degree, a conclusion consistent with the intonational separation of the matrix from the clause, indicated by the frequent occurrence of punctuation. The situational dependence and fixity of the type allow for general patterns of reduction, which in turn are consistent with a register distribution that is skewed toward online, unplanned production, contexts that allow (or perhaps strongly prefer) forms that leave linguistic information implicit and are generally holistically produced.

TSs appear to be on a diachronic trajectory similar to that described by Hudson (1998). Her goal is to identify the trajectory of fixation and to uncover the forces that underlie it. She proposes that the trajectory is from "*ad hoc*" expressions (i.e., expressions typically produced in conformity with the lexico-grammar of the language) through fixed expressions to univerbations (see Chapter 6). She proposes that underlying this trajectory are the "fixing forces" (see Chapter 4): reduction in salience of the meaning, grammatical role, and cohesive relations of the expression.[11]

When we apply Hudson's criteria to TS subjects, we find that their meanings are non-salient: they have no clear reference, indeed no reference at all; even in full TSs, they lack some of the characteristics of subjects, most notably, they are not agentive and seem to be limited to singular number; and they have no salient cohesive (e.g., antecedent/anaphor) relations with other phrases in their contexts (Hudson 1998: 109).

Hudson proposes that univerbation results in words belonging to one or other of the classes recognized by the grammar of the language, primarily to the heterogeneous class of adverbs. At this point in their history, full TSs seem to be still produceable as "*ad hoc*" expressions, though the most reduced TS form, <*thing is,*>, appears to be fixed, perhaps close to the point of univerbation, possibly as a sentential adverb. In this respect, it would be similar to the expressions analyzed by Hopper and Thompson (2008), though they do not go so far as to classify them as adverbs.

At this point in its development, the most reduced TS variant, <*thing is,* >, seems not to be independent of the full variant: the latter can readily be reconstructed from it. However, the occurrence of reduced forms in publications such as *Newsweek* and of full forms with punctuation between *that* and the remainder of the clause (see Example 11 and fn. 8) suggest that the reduced forms may be beginning to become independent of the full forms and ready to colonize the more formal registers which now strongly prefer the full, unpunctuated forms. If they continue on this trajectory, they will begin to allow a greater range of expression types as complement, just as Hopper and Thompson (2008) demonstrate is the case for *wh*-clefts and extrapositives. At that point, the relationship between "matrix" and complement will become proceduralized, and thereafter may lose some of its current semantic and pragmatic characteristics, perhaps the presupposed status of the complement, leaving the matrix as a generic markedness marker, competing with other such markers such as the inferential *It is (that) S* form (Delahunty 2001; Delahunty & Calude 2011; Pusch 2006).

We might think of TSs and their variants as providing contextualization cues. Heller (2001: 258) quotes Auer (1992: 4) to the effect that "contextualization ... comprises all the activities by participants which make relevant, maintain, revise, cancel, ... any aspect of the context which, in turn, is responsible for the interpretation of an utterance in its particular locus of occurrence." Thinking about TSs in this way allows us to identify the proceduralization of variants of sentence types like the TS as one source of such discourse management devices.

As I noted in Section 4, the Rankin data includes a number of specificational sentences with subject head nouns other than *thing*, e.g., *story*, which also perform discourse management tasks. This suggests that the specificational sentence type is a prolific source for expression types that can be used for discourse management functions.

Because TS matrixes are composed of elements which individually occur frequently and have minimal semantic specificity, they should come readily to mind and thus facilitate discourse planning. Indeed, it makes good sense to create discourse structuring devices that require minimal processing so that attention may be primarily directed to the propositions the devices mark.

These remarks suggest a trajectory like the following for the creation of discourse management devices such as TSs:

1. Speakers recognize a discourse need, e.g., to revise, cancel, or contrast an assumption derivable from the prior context, and create a form out of appropriate available linguistic elements to address that need.
2. Speakers recognize the effectiveness and particular "fit" between the new form and its discourse effects.
3. The form becomes established as a preferred one for its purposes.
4. Efficiencies set in and the form is subject to general patterns of intonationalization and reduction: it is realized as a range of variants that are differentially distributed across registers. (This is as far as TSs seem to have come.)
5. The form becomes independent of its linguistic origins and colonizes registers from which it was originally barred.
6. Its uses generalize and it is subject to further phonological reduction.
7. It eventually succumbs to competition from new forms and is eliminated.

This sequence is the reverse of that proposed by Hopper and Thompson (2008), who propose that the most colloquial versions of *wh*-clefts and extrapositives precede the more formal version and that their full forms are reformulations of the originals.

7. Conclusion

I have described the semantic and pragmatic meanings of TSs and shown how they are determined by the sentence's lexis and syntax. I have also described several rhetorical uses to which the form may be put, and argued that these uses are due to the simultaneous presupposing and focusing of the TS clause. I have shown that TS variants represent a range of fixity and flexibility, in which some of the variants may be produced analytically or holistically, while others may be produced only holistically. I have shown that the register distribution of TSs as a type is skewed toward the informal end of the register spectrum, that is, to registers typically produced under time pressure, which is where the less flexible variants most frequently occur. I have proposed a set of conditions for the creation of discourse management expressions like TSs and identified some of the linguistic elements from which they may be constructed and a diachronic trajectory for their origination, development, and extinction.

Colorado State University, USA

Notes

Corresponce address: Gerald.Delahunty@colostate.edu

1. I am grateful to Andreea Calude, Inga Vassilieva, Karen Vogel, the participants in the Perpignan conference on "Fixed Phrases in English," and two reviewers for the *Yearbook* for their helpful comments on earlier drafts of this paper. Any errors that remain are mine alone.
2. Example (6) occurs in the text of an interview regarding the education of girls in Benin, the relevant parts of which are:
   Q: You grew up in Benin, … Why is it so hard for girls to go to school?
   A: *First,* … *Secondly,* … and *the third thing* is that … So it's those three major things.
   The thing is also money. Because school is not free. And when you're poor, you think about how much it's going to cost you, year after year, to put your child in school. And another reason also is the abuse of the girls in school ….
   Because the complement of the highlighted sentence is a NP rather than a clause, it does not represent a propositional level discourse entity, as TS clauses do, so the discourse roles of the two complement types must necessarily differ. This sentence also comes after a series of numbered sub-topics, indicated by "First," "Secondly," and "the third thing," which are summed up at the end of Q's first full paragraph as "those three major things." "The thing" of the highlighted sentence may simply have been triggered by the several occurrences of "thing" in the immediately prior text, or it may contrast with "major things," and indicate a less important topic, or it may simply introduce an afterthought. Though this sentence seems to function as a marker of a shift in subtopic, as TSs often do, it does not reject and replace or revise an assumption derived from the prior context as TSs characteristically do (see Section 3 below), and so must be distinguished from them.
   Example (7) also comes an interview.
   Q: You've been deeply involved in bringing the Internet to India. How did this come about?

A: A key thing in my life has been not just computer communication, but computer communication for developing countries...
We were driven by the unarticulated needs of the developing market...
Another issue was language. Most e-mail around the world is in English. India has about 500 dialects and 17 scripts. What is great about technology – the fact that it is making our lives better is only part of it – is that it's giving us the hope of changing our lives. *The thing is to not be on the receiving end of fate, but to have your hand on the wheel – I think that changes you.* People needed something where they could post materials in their own languages.

To-infinitives and *that*-clauses are alike in that each represents a proposition, the latter more completely than the former. However, they differ semantically. *That*-clauses, unless they include a modal expression to the contrary, are factual, whereas *to*-infinitives denote "potential" (Quirk et al. 1985: 836), or "potentiality" or "projection into the future" (Huddleston and Pullum 2002: 1241). These elements of the interpretation of *to*-infinitives underlie the deontic interpretation so clearly present in (7), but lacking in the TSs with which this paper is concerned. Additionally, (7) does not reject and replace or revise an assumption licensed by the prior context.

Nonetheless, in spite of the difficulty of constructing a coherent interpretation of this paragraph, this sentence effects a shift in the trajectory of the topic, just as TSs and similar sentences with NP (and perhaps other) complements do, perhaps because of "The thing is ..." Clearly we are still at the initial stages of developing an understanding of the uses of *thing*.

3. This Spanish example shows that these sentence types occur in languages other than English, though the translation equivalents are not always discourse equivalent (Delahunty and Velazquez-Castillo 2002).
4. A reviewer for the *Yearbook* asked why I used COCA rather than BNC. COCA is a large (450 million words) balanced corpus consisting of the subcorpora I describe above (in this and other respects it is similar to the LSWE corpus used by Biber and his associates in the preparation of their *Longman Grammar of Spoken and Written English* [see pp. 29–35]), and as the spoken/written contrast seemed to be most significant in understanding the register distribution of TSs, COCA, with the limitations I describe in Section 2, being easily accessible and useable – and free – I opted for it.
5. A reviewer for the *Yearbook* asked that I amplify my assertion that "*thing* denotes merely COUNTABLE ENTITY." The first synonym in the first definition of *thing* in the American Heritage Dictionary (4th edition) is "An entity, ... " (p. 1797), whose countability is clearly indicated by the indefinite article, cf. *stuff*. I gloss *thing* as COUNTABLE ENTITY to indicate that it is the most semantically general countable noun in the language, with the possible exception of *entity*.
The reviewer also asked whether "my denotate [in the reviewer's example from BNC] relate[s] to 'things' (plural, sic!) or something else? If it is the

latter, please explain." The reviewer's BNC example is, "it was strange then, all these things were happening, and the thing was, sometimes you didn't hear about them until much later." First, the clause in which *things* occurs is not a TS and without further context, I can only assume that *things* in this extract functions as a general noun (Halliday and Hasan 1976: ch. 6) referring to events – i.e., "things that were happening." Halliday and Hasan characterize general nouns as "a borderline case between a lexical item ... and a grammatical item ..." (p. 274). Second, because *thing* in the reviewer's example does occur in a TS, it functions very differently from *things*. It is part of a semantically minimal definite description which, by virtue of its function as the subject of a specificational sentence, denotes but does not refer. It is akin to the *it* of meteorological sentences, *there* of existential sentences, and other expressions which on some occasions are referential, and on others serve just some grammatical, metalinguistic, or discourse function. We might view *thing* as the nominal analog of "light verbs" whose role in collocations is addressed in Mel'čuk (1998: 31).

6. This is the only example I have found with a comma between *that* and the clause, suggesting that the matrix and clause even of full TSs may be intonationally rather than syntactically integrated.

7. Andreea Calude (p.c.) found one TS in the written and 60 TSs in the spoken subcorpora of the Wellington Corpus. Each subcorpus is one million words and the written instance is from fictional dialog. This cross-register distribution is similar to that in COCA, as I discuss below.

8. Regarding my claim that full TSs are fully consistent with the grammar, lexis, and semantics of English and therefore may be produced analytically rather than holistically, a reviewer for the *Yearbook* says, "it cannot be claimed that expressions which do not contain 'words or grammatical forms that are no longer current in the language' are not fixed or less fixed and less "frozen" than irregular expressions." This amounts to the claim that any expression may be fixed, even if it is entirely regular, grammatically, semantically, pragmatically, and discoursally. I agree that this is possible. The reviewer also claims that "All TSs are constructions, regardless [of] their grammatical regularity." If s/he is using "constructions" in its broadest sense, as merely a grammatical form, then, of course, s/he is (tautologically) correct. If s/he is using the term as it is used in Construction Grammar, then s/he implies that TSs have linguistic and/or discourse properties that cannot be accounted for solely on the basis of their lexis, syntax, and semantics (cf. Mel'čuk's 1998: 30 quasi-phrasemes or quasi-idioms); however, I've shown that this is not the case for full TSs. If by "constructions," s/he merely intends that full TSs are fixed or formulaic to some degree, then the burden of proof is on those who would claim that an expression such as a full TS which superficially appears to be "unrestrictedly constructed" (cf. Mel'čuk 1998: 27) is fixed, and the discussion of the criteria for determining fixity in Section 4 shows just how

difficult it is to support such a claim. The rare or non-occurrence of grammatically possible variants is just such evidence

9. *The thing is* without a comma or *that* seems to be intermediate between the full and more reduced and intonationally organized forms. It seems to be favored in moderately formal circumstances.
10. *Newsweek* 10/18/10 p. 32, in an article on the puppet president of Chechnya, has *Trouble is, it's not always easy to see much difference*, perhaps reflecting the magazine's efforts to compete in a more colloquial market.
11. Hudson (1998: 91–93) argues, following Hopper & Traugott (1993: 7), that this trajectory differs from that of grammaticalization, whereby words belonging to the major lexical or content classes become grammatical words, which become clitics, which become inflectional affixes.

References

Aijmer, Karin. 2007. The interface between discourse and grammar: The fact is that. In Agnes Celle & Ruth Hart (eds.), *Connectives as discourse landmarks*, 31–46. Amsterdam: John Benjamins.

Auer, Peter. 1992. Introduction: John Gumperz' approach to contextualization. In Peter Auer & Aldo di Luzio (eds.), *The contextualization of language*, 1–37. Amsterdam: John Benjamins.

Bakhtin, Mikhail M. 1981[1953]. *The dialogic imagination* (ed. M. Holquist, tr. C. Emerson and M. Holquist). Austin: University of Texas Press.

Bardovi-Harlig, Kathleen. 2009. Conventional expressions as a pragmalinguistic resource: Recognition and production of conventional expressions in L2 pragmatics. *Language Learning* 59. 755–795.

Bergh, Gunnar. 2005. Min(d)ing the English language data on the Web: What can Google tell us? *ICAME Journal* 29. 25–46.

Biber, Douglas, Stig Johansson, Geoffrey Leech, Susan Conrad & Edward Finegan. 1999. *Longman grammar of spoken and written English*. Essex: Longman.

Bond, Laurel. 2007. *Metaphors in context: Domains and lemmas as indicators of disciplinary differences in conceptualizations of "Reality."* Fort Collins, Colorado: Colorado State University MA thesis.

Brenier, Jason M. & Laura A. Michaelis. 2005. Optimization via syntactic amalgam: Syntax-prosody mismatch and copula doubling. *Corpus Linguistics and Linguistic Theory* 1(1). 45–88.

Brown, Penelope & Stephen Levinson. 1987. *Politeness: Some universals in language usage*. New York: Cambridge University Press.

Carter, Ronald & Michael McCarthy. 2006. *Cambridge grammar of English*. New York: Cambridge University Press.

Calude, Andreea & Gerald Delahunty. 2011. Inferentials in spoken English. *Pragmatics*. 21(3). 307–340.

Coulmas, Florian. 1981. Introduction: Conversational routine. In Florian Coulmas (ed.), *Conversational routines: Explorations in standardized communication situations and prepatterned speech*, 1–17. The Hague: Mouton de Gruyter.
Delahunty, Gerald. 2001. Discourse functions of inferential sentences. *Linguistics* 39. 517–545.
Delahunty, Gerald. 2006. A relevance-theoretic analysis of *Not that* sentences. *Pragmatics* 16(2/3). 213–245.
Delahunty, Gerald. 2007. A relevance-theoretic analysis of a lexico-syntactic pragmatic marker: *The thing is that S*. Paper presented at Hawaii International Conference on Arts and Humanities, 8 January.
Delahunty, Gerald. 2008. What *Thing* sentences can tell us about register and mode. Paper presented at First North American Workshop on Pragmatics. Glendon College, York University, Toronto, Canada, 3–5 October.
Delahunty, Gerald. In prep. An analysis of *The thing is that* sentences.
Delahunty, Gerald & Maura Velazquez-Castillo. 2002. *The X is that S*: A lexico-grammatical device for local discourse management. In James F. Lee, Kimberley L. Geeslin & J. Clancy Clements (eds.), *Structure, meaning, and acquisition in Spanish*, 46–64. Somerville, MA: Cascadilla Press.
Dor, Daniel. 2005. Toward a semantic account of *that*-deletion in English. *Linguistics* 43(2). 345–382.
Edmonds, Amanda. 2010a. *On the representation of conventional expressions in L1-English and L2-French*. Bloomington, Indiana: Indiana University dissertation.
Edmonds, Amanda. 2010b. Formulaic language and its many terms, definitions, and identification criteria. Paper presented at the International Conference on Fixed Phrases in English, Perpignan, France, 22–23 October.
Finnell, A. 1996. *Discourse markers and topic change: A case study in historical pragmatics*. Cambridge, UK: University of Cambridge dissertation.
Francis, Gill. 1994. Labelling discourse: An aspect of nominal-group lexical cohesion. In Malcolm Coulthard (ed.), *Advances in written text analysis*, 83–101. London: Routledge.
Halliday, M.A.K. 1987. Spoken and written modes of meaning. In Rosalind Horowitz and S. Jay Samuels (eds.), *Comprehending oral and written language*, 55–82. San Diego: Academic Press.
Halliday, M.A.K. & Ruqaiya Hasan. 1976. *Cohesion in English*. London: Longman.
Heller, Monica. 2001. Discourse and interaction. In Deborah Schiffrin, Deborah Tannen & Heidi E. Hamilton (eds.), *The handbook of discourse analysis*, 250–264. Malden, MA: Blackwell.
Higgins, Francis R. 1976. *The pseudo-cleft construction in English*. Bloomington, Indiana: Indiana University Linguistics Club.
Hopper, Paul & Sandra A. Thompson. 2008. Projectability and clause combining in interaction. In Ritva Laury (ed.), *Crosslinguistic studies of clause combining: The multifunctionality of conjunctions*, 99–123. Amsterdam: John Benjamins.

Hopper, Paul & Elizabeth C. Traugott. 1993. *Grammaticalization*. Cambridge, UK: Cambridge University Press.
Huddleston, Rodney & Geoffrey Pullum. 2002. *The Cambridge grammar of the English language*. New York: Cambridge University Press.
Hudson, Jean. 1998. *Perspectives on fixedness: Applied and theoretical*. Lund: Lund University Press.
Jespersen, Otto. 1976 [1926]. Living grammar. In *The philosophy of grammar*, 17–29. London: George Allen and Unwin. Reprinted in Diane D. Bornstein (ed.), *Readings in the theory of grammar*. 82–93. Cambridge, MA: Winthrop Publishers.
Johnstone, Barbara. 2008. *Discourse analysis*, 2nd edn. Malden, MA: Blackwell.
Kuiper, Koenraad, Marie-Elaine van Egmond, Gerard Kempen & Simone Sprenger. 2007. Slipping on superlemmas: Multi-word lexical items in speech production. *The Mental Lexicon* 2. 313–357.
Lambrecht, Knud. 1994. *Information structure and sentence form*. Cambridge, UK: Cambridge University Press.
Massam, Diane. 1999. *Thing is* constructions: The thing is, is what's the right analysis? *English Language and Linguistics* 3(2). 335–352.
McConvell, Patrick. 1988. To be or double be? Current changes in the English copula. *Australian Journal of Linguistics* 8. 287–305.
Mel'čuk, Igor. 1998. Collocation and lexical function. In Anthony P. Cowie (ed.), *Phraseology: Theory, analysis, and applications*, 23–53. Oxford: Clarendon Press.
Moon, Rosamund. 1998. Frequencies and forms of phrasal lexemes in English. In Anthony P. Cowie (ed.), *Phraseology: Theory, analysis, and applications*, 79–100. Oxford: Clarendon Press.
Pusch, Claus. 2006. Marqueurs discursifs et subordination syntaxique: La construction inférentielle en français et dans d'autres langues romanes. In M. Drescher & B. Frank-Job (eds.), *Les marqueurs discursifs dans les langues Romanes: Approches théoriques et méthodologiques*, 173–188. Frankfurt: Peter Lang.
Quirk, Randolph, Sidney Greenbaum, Geoffrey Leech & Jan Sartvik. 1985. *A comprehensive grammar of the English language*. Essex, UK: Longman.
Rankin, Ian. 2003. *Resurrection men*. Boston: Little, Brown, and Company.
Rankin, Ian. 2005. *Fleshmarket alley*. New York: Time Warner.
Schmid, Hans-Jörg. 2000. *English abstract nouns as conceptual shells: From corpus to cognition*. Berlin: Mouton de Gruyter.
Sirr, Peter. 2009. The thing is. In *The thing is*. Loughcrew, Ireland: The Gallery Press.
Tannen, Deborah. 1986. Introducing constructed dialogue in Greek and American conversational narratives. In Florian Coulmas (ed.), *Direct and indirect speech*, 311–32. New York: Mouton de Gruyter.
Terasaki, Alene K. 2004 [1976]. Pre-announcement sequences in conversation. In Gene H. Lerner (ed.), *Conversation analysis: Studies from the first generation*, 171–224. Amsterdam: John Benjamins.

Tuggy, David. 1996. The thing is is that people talk that way. The question is is Why? In Eugene H. Casad (ed.), *Cognitive linguistics in the redwoods: The expansion of a new paradigm in linguistics*, 713–752. Berlin: Mouton de Gruyter.

Wilson, Deirdre & Dan Sperber. 2004. Relevance theory. In Laurence R. Horn and Gregory Ward (eds.), *The handbook of pragmatics*, 607–632. Malden, MA: Blackwell.

Wray, Alison. 2002. *Formulaic language and the lexicon*. New York: Cambridge University Press.

A phraseological approach to film dialogue: Film stylistics revisited

MARIA FREDDI

Abstract

The paper takes film dialogue as a test case for a corpus-driven investigation of phraseology. The analysis is mainly based on three strands of research, both linguistic and translational. These are: corpus work comparing contemporary film and television dialogue with natural conversation, research on translational routines in audiovisual translation (dubbese) and the phraseological approach to language. However, in order to focus on the formulaic features of English original film dialogue, the translational perspective is backgrounded. The study is corpus-driven in that formulae of filmic speech are extracted from the corpus on the basis of their frequency. Furthermore, the sequences thus found are compared to general reference corpora of British and American English in order to explore their distribution and functions. The results are shown to be relevant to a stylistic appraisal of scripted film dialogue as well as to an understanding of some methodological issues associated with corpus-driven studies of phraseology in general.

Keywords: film dialogue; formulaic expressions; corpus-driven phraseology; film stylistics.

1. Background

Recent findings on the similarities between contemporary film and television dialogue and real-life unscripted conversations, together with research on translational routines in audiovisual translation, serve as a background to the present analysis of formulaic language in film dialogue. In particular, through systematic comparisons between the typical features of spontaneous conversation and television dialogue, Quaglio (2008, 2009a, 2009b) has shown how

TV dialogue tends to capture and reproduce the linguistic characteristics of authentic face-to-face conversations. Among the features he analysed are: first- and second-person pronouns, discourse markers (including *okay*, *well*, *you know*), intensifying adverbs (like *so* in *This is so not like him*, or *totally* in *I totally like it*), hedges (*kind of, sort of*), emphatics (e.g., *just*), slang terms, vocatives and familiarisers (e.g. *guys*), etc. These were studied in the very popular sit-com *Friends* and in natural conversation, and, although the two kinds of talk present different distributional profiles, they can be explained in terms of functional and situational differences. For example, features of emotional language are found to be consistently more frequent in *Friends* than in the conversation corpus, due to the dramatic nature of the dialogue. However, as Quaglio has observed, markers of vagueness are consistently higher in conversation as too much vague language leads to incomprehensibility on the part of the viewers. In the same way, the limited range of conversation topics and settings in televised dialogue is also found to affect the distribution patterns. He concludes that, on the whole, most of the linguistic features of naturally occurring conversation are shared by the sit-com corpus, thus making scripted speech a valuable substitute for spontaneous spoken data in foreign language classrooms (Quaglio 2009a: 149).

Within the scope of audiovisual translation, particularly film dubbing, researchers have investigated the formulaic nature of dubbed language. This has been described as a series of semantic and structural calques found to occur repeatedly across films, hence the term "translational routines" (Pavesi 2005: 48) and the sometimes derogatory term "dubbese". There is a long list of routine translations, in both Italian and Spanish dubbed dialogue (see Pavesi (2005, 2008) on the English-Italian language pair and Romero Fresco (2006, 2009) on the English-Spanish pair), ranging from single items such as *absolutely*-'assolutamente', *sure*-'sicuro', to multiword units like *you know something?*-'la sai una cosa?', *forget about it*-'scordatelo', etc. Such expression patterns have been described as colloquial speech conveying the spontaneity of everyday language which, as a result of the translation process, tends to generate calques – e.g. vocatives and response forms in Italian dubbed language, as shown by Pavesi (2005, 2008, 2009); and discourse markers and intensifiers in the Spanish dubbed dialogue analysed by Romero Fresco (2009). According to the studies cited, therefore, it is the speech-like idiomatic quality of original scripted dialogue that most leaks into film translation, often making it sound unnatural and artificial. This perspective on translated film dialogue can be coupled with studies on the predictability of textual occurrences and frequencies as associated with particular scenes and scene types in a variety of original film dialogue. Specifically, Taylor (2004, 2006, 2008) describes the language of standardized exchanges such as service encounters, telephone conversations and other ritual moves involving greetings and leave-takings, and shows how a lot of the dialogue taking place on the screen is predictable. In the same way, in describing the features of scripted dialogue, Chaume (2001, 2004: 168) talks about "prefabricated orality", a concept that indicates the carefully planned and controlled nature of this kind of spoken discourse at each level of language, from prosodic to syntactic to lexico-semantic. The notion has been recently reprised by Baños-Piñero & Chaume (2009) in relation to audiovisual translation issues.

In conclusion, even though the concept of naturalness, as described in relation to spontaneous spoken data (cf. among others, Warren 2006), does not entirely pertain to onscreen scripted dialogue, the kinds of conversational resources that are found to accompany real-life interactions do, however, occur in filmic speech. These concern the interpersonal dimension of dialogue as well as the micro-level of discourse organisation and its cohesive potential – elements of hearer feedback including backchannels and non-minimal responses, speaker hesitations and repeats, interjections and discourse markers are all present in screen dialogue and their frequency and functions have been pointed out (see also Taylor 1999, 2008). Comprehensibility and reduction of processing effort on the part of the viewers as well as the overarching dramatic or humorous purposes of much film and TV dialogue can help explain the distributional differences observed when compared with unscripted speech. What is worth investigating further is the generalizability of these findings towards a reappraisal of film stylistics from a linguistic and phraseological perspective.[1] In order to do so, the process of enquiry is reversed. In fact, instead of taking available descriptions of the grammar and pragmatics of conversation to check one more time how they fit film dialogue and whether the same features are present and to what extent, the present investigation embarks on a frequency-driven analysis of filmic speech aimed at finding out the phraseological profile of the latter, i.e. at identifying frequent formulae to see how typical they are of the kind of orality represented by the sample under examination.

2. A phraseological approach: clusters

Predictions regarding systematic variations in language use in different communicative situations (what is commonly termed register variation) are supported by the phraseological approach. We are referring mainly to the theory of phraseology as developed by John Sinclair through the "idiom principle" (Sinclair 1991). That is to say, to the idea that the unit of meaning is no longer the single word. Rather, "words tend to go together and make meanings by their combinations" (Sinclair 2004a [1996]: 29). This tendency goes beyond simple collocations and idioms in the traditional sense, which is strictly associated with semantic opacity and non-compositionality, lexico-syntactic fixedness and institutionalisation. It is pervasive and concerns a wide range of multi-word combinations, as shown by corpus data. It is indeed corpus linguistic research with its systematic analysis of repeated usage in large sets of concordances that has brought to the fore the key role of phraseological expressions in language. As pointed out by Granger and Meunier in their (2008) introduction to an interdisciplinary volume on phraseology, before the advent of corpus linguistics, only the most fixed and opaque multi-word combinations offered themselves as an object of study. Now, however, a much wider variety of expressions displaying both lexico-syntactic variability and semantic compositionality are being investigated. Obviously, this has implications for both automated language processing and language pedagogy (see Sinclair (2004b) and the volume on phraseology in foreign language learning edited by Meunier and Granger in 2008). In fact, the new unit of meaning, the "lexical item", is the result of words repeatedly co-selecting each other in a corpus, with co-selection involving collocational and colligational patterns, semantic preference and semantic prosody (Sinclair 2004a [1998]). In Sinclair's latest contribution, this notion has been reconceptualised as "Meaning Shift Unit". An MSU is an extended unit of meaning corresponding to a shift in the ambient meaning (Sinclair in press). Although this is an abstract category, it is supported by frequency observations on recurrent chunks in a corpus variously called "clusters" (Scott 2004), "n-grams" (e.g. Fletcher 2007), "lexical bundles" (Biber et al. 1999), to name but a few of the terms used in the literature.

Clusters are defined as groups of words which are found repeatedly together in each other's company, in sequence.[2] They are "repeated strings which may have little or no psychological reality for speakers" (Scott and Tribble 2006: 19), but which "give insights into important aspects of the phraseology used by writers in specific contexts" (Scott and Tribble 2006: 132). Lexical bundles are frequent multi-word sequences which vary according to the register examined. Their structural and functional characteristics are found to be different in speech and writing, thus they provide a good indicator of register variation (Biber and Conrad 1999; Biber, Conrad & Cortes 2004). They are identified on the basis of their frequency in a "radically" corpus-driven fashion and therefore they are neither necessarily complete structural units nor perceptually salient (Biber 2009: 283). In sum, clusters or bundles are uninterrupted sequences of words found to occur repeatedly in a corpus. Also, in both accounts there is a focus on style and register variation: different styles and registers are characterised by different distributions of clusters, as these are indicative of "preferred ways of saying things" (cf. Altenberg 1998).[3] A frequency-driven approach like this goes well with a broad pragmatic concept of idiomaticity, which is typical of discourse-functional approaches (see Moon 1998; and more recently Corrigan et al. 2009). In the present paper, clusters as generated by a software for text analysis, namely *Wordsmith Tools version 4.0* (Scott 2004), offer the operational basis on which to ground an analysis of the phraseology of contemporary filmic speech. The corpus and the methodology used are illustrated in the next section.

3. Data and methodology

In order to investigate the formulaicity of contemporary filmic speech, two sample corpora have been used. One is the original component of the *Pavia Corpus of Film Dialogue*, a parallel corpus comprising both British and American films and their Italian dubbed versions. The other is a small addition compiled *ad hoc* by the author of this paper according to the same sampling criteria and conceived of as a further test case for the findings based on the former. The movies sampled in the PCFD at the time of writing cover the time span 1995–2004 and are all defined as "conversational" films, i.e. portraying interactions of different kinds, all characterised by face-to-face conversation in contemporary settings (on naturalistic drama see also the discussion in Richardson 2010). As a guarantee of their status and diffusion within the cultures that produced and consumed them, they were successful both with the critics and the general public (Freddi & Pavesi 2009). The sampling cuts across rigid film genre distinctions, ranging from the social cinematography of Ken Loach and Mike Leigh to romantic comedies such as *Notting Hill* and *Bend it Like Beckham*. There are no costume films nor musicals, but action movies such as *Ocean's Eleven* and thrillers like *One Hour Photo* are included. The second dataset consists of four extra movies chosen according to the same sampling criteria as above: two American (*Lost in Translation* and *Michael Clayton*) and two British (*Snatch* and *Love Actually*). The time span covered is roughly the same except for the slight update represented by *Michael Clayton*, and the genres match those in the PCFD.

Both *Lost in Translation* and *Love Actually* are romantic comedies, like, for example, *Notting Hill* and *Sliding Doors* are in the PCFD; *Snatch* is a heist film, very much like its PCFD American counterpart represented by the *Ocean's* saga; while *Michael Clayton* is a lawyer movie like *Erin Brockovich* in the other corpus. At the time of writing, the PCFD runs about 23 hours of film in each language (there are 12 films altogether) totalling almost 118,000 words of original dialogue and slightly fewer words in the translations-adaptations (almost 112,000). The second dataset consists of only 4 films, the total size of the corpus being roughly 60,000 words between the two languages, thus adding almost another 8 hours of film for each version.[4]

For the purposes of the present study, the translational component of each corpus is used only as background data, as issues of film translation go beyond our scope. It should also be noted that the text in the corpus is the orthographic transcription of the actual lines uttered by the characters on screen. In other words, the version included in the corpus differs greatly from the available scripts in terms of features of spokenness often added by actors when they are shooting, such as hesitations, repeats, false starts and interruptions, overlaps, etc. (see on this Taylor 2004: 79–80). Since the speech-like and colloquial nature of conversation in scripted dialogue is of interest to the present investigation, only a careful transcription of the final product could be used as the object of study. We do not know as yet which features of conversation will be captured by the clusters list, but, as they affect the frequency counts, they might be part of some repeated sequences relevant to the phraseological profile of the corpus, so a different picture would emerge if they were left out.

The two corpora are processed using the concordance software for text analysis *Wordsmith Tools v. 4.0*, which is also used to create clusters lists. The initial analysis is therefore frequency-driven in that it is the clusters rather than previous accounts of the grammar of conversation that offer an initial description of the sample of filmic speech in question (differently from the literature expounded in Section 1). The same procedure is adopted for both the PCFD and the additional dataset to see if results corroborate each other. The formulae thus identified are subsequently compared with available reference corpora of spoken British and American English (the spoken components of the British National Corpus and the Corpus of Contemporary American English) in order to explore differences and similarities in the distributions. Finally, the functions of the various formulae are identified and discussed also in relation to their being present in the large general corpora of spoken British and American English. It is claimed that a data-driven approach points to functional differences and register-specific usage.

4. Film phrases: distributions and functions

4.1. *4-word clusters in film dialogue*

Figure 1 offers a graphic representation of the top 25 frequencies in the PCFD. This allows the visualization of the flattening out of the frequency distribution with the curve becoming asymptotic. For this reason, a cut-off point is established on the eleventh cluster in the list.

In Table 1, a list is given of the top 11 clusters with raw frequency, normalized frequency per hundred thousand words, and the number of films (texts) in which they are found to occur. The last information, which is displayed in the right-most column, gives a clue as to how clusters are distributed across the films in the corpus – sometimes called "dispersion" (Scott and Tribble 2006: 29) – and should be kept in mind for the comparative phase of the discussion. At this stage, it should be noticed that the 11 most common clusters in the PCFD contain the pronouns *you* or *I*, or both, which are the most frequent words in the corpus. This comes as no surprise given the dialogic nature of the text-type under consideration and is in line with Quaglio's findings on two of the most frequent lexical bundles in the sit-com *Friends*, namely *I can't believe you* and *Thank you so much*, both containing *I* (elided in thanks) and *you*. According to Quaglio, this is

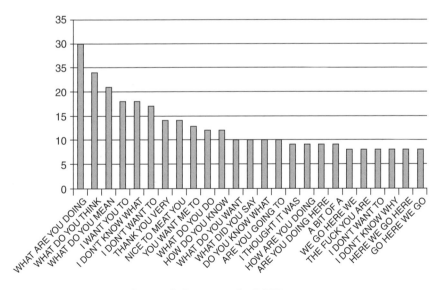

Figure 1. *Frequency of 4-word clusters in the PCFD*

Table 1. *Top 11 clusters in the PCFD*

N	Cluster	Freq.	PHT	Texts
1	WHAT ARE YOU DOING	30	25	11
2	WHAT DO YOU THINK	24	20	9
3	WHAT DO YOU MEAN	21	18	11
4	I WANT YOU TO	18	15	9
5	I DON'T KNOW WHAT	18	15	6
6	I DON'T WANT TO	17	14	7
7	THANK YOU VERY MUCH	14	12	8
8	NICE TO MEET YOU	14	12	6
9	YOU WANT ME TO	13	11	8
10	WHAT DO YOU DO	12	10	6
11	HOW DO YOU KNOW	12	10	6

evidence for the involved nature of the exchange and is even more so when compared to other kinds of conversational data (Quaglio 2009a: 100).

Why 4-word clusters? There is indeed a problem with the horizon of the multi-word sequences which are searched for in a corpus. Obviously, the longer the span we set, the fewer the clusters we obtain. In previous research, 3-word clusters have been looked at (Freddi in press), which contained fragments of *what*-questions (see the top 3 and no. 10 in Table 1). They displayed the interrogative pronoun followed by subject-verb inversion or a potentially intervening swearword (e.g. WHAT ARE YOU, WHAT DO YOU, WHAT THE HELL, etc.). However, 3-word clusters come up with a lot of overlap, which is hard to filter out (the list contained sequences such as WHAT ARE YOU and ARE YOU DOING, or WHAT DO YOU and DO YOU MEAN, DO YOU THINK, DO YOU WANT, etc.). Therefore, 4-word clusters have been chosen here in order to avoid the overlap of the 3-word clusters and to obtain a higher number of independent chunks. Also, a string of 4 words in a cluster makes it comparable to previous research on clusters and register variation done by Biber et al. (1999) and Biber and Conrad (1999). See the discussion in Section 4.2.

The same search was done on the smaller dataset; the same clusters appear on top of the list although there is a skew effect observable in the frequencies due to the presence of one film in particular, *Love Actually*, which is longer than the others and has songs containing refrains. This brings us back to data sampling and transcription practices. On the one hand, an excessively small sample is more sensitive to the presence of a single film. On the other, songs could be left out in principle, but it was decided not to do so when they constituted an inherent part of the plot and were linked to the characters' lines, as in this case. The data has been ordered according to dispersion (i.e. the number of films in which the clusters were found) to avoid this problem. Notice the steep decrease: only the top 3 clusters are found in at least 75% of the corpus (Table 2). However, the interpersonal routine *Nice to meet you* (rank no. 4), already found as prominent in the PCFD, and other *what*-questions (nos. 5, 7) or chunks thereof (no. 11) are also in the list. With rank no. 12, clusters come from just the one film mentioned above and are no longer worth considering.

Table 2. *Top clusters in test dataset sorted according to dispersion*

N	Cluster	Freq.	%	Texts	%
1	WHAT ARE YOU DOING	8	0,02	4	100,00
2	WHAT DO YOU THINK	7	0,02	3	75,00
3	YOU WANT ME TO	5	0,02	3	75,00
4	NICE TO MEET YOU	10	0,03	2	50,00
5	WHAT DO YOU WANT	8	0,02	2	50,00
6	I DON'T KNOW WHAT	7	0,02	2	50,00
7	WHAT DO YOU MEAN	7	0,02	2	50,00
8	ARE YOU DOING HERE	6	0,02	2	50,00
9	I CAN TELL YOU	5	0,02	2	50,00
10	I DON'T KNOW I	5	0,02	2	50,00
11	WHAT THE HELL IS	5	0,02	2	50,00
12	FEEL IT IN MY	11	0,03	1	25,00
13	I FEEL IT IN	8	0,02	1	25,00
14	ALL I WANT FOR	7	0,02	1	25,00
15	I WANT FOR CHRISTMAS	7	0,02	1	25,00
16	IT IN MY TOES	6	0,02	1	25,00
17	LOVE LOVE LOVE LOVE	6	0,02	1	25,00

4.2. Film clusters and the BNC

In this section, the results of the comparisons drawn between the film corpus and the BNC are presented and discussed. Firstly, the clusters from the PCFD are compared to the BNC spoken, particularly face-to-face spontaneous conversations. Secondly, the BNC spoken without any genre restriction is used. The results are displayed in the following histograms in order to facilitate the visualisation of the distributions. However, to avoid misinterpreting the results, a word of caution is in order concerning the text-types sampled in the spoken BNC.

The corpus contains approximately 100 million words of text, 90% written and 10% spoken, divided into various sub-genres. The spoken component includes 10 million words from 1970 to 1994 between demographically sampled and context-governed data (respectively 4 and 6 milion words). The corpus is a closed sample, i.e. not updated with fresh material. The demographic sampling reflects the sociolinguistic variation of the speakers according to age, sex, occupation and geographical provenance within the UK, while context-governed sampling identifies the different kinds of interactions taking place, including business meetings, trade unions meetings, academic lectures, TV or radio news, political speeches, parliamentary proceedings, radio phone-ins, etc. A comparative view of 4-word clusters in the three corpora is given in Figure 2 below.

The frequency of the top 4 clusters in the PCFD (the black bar) is significantly different from the BNC distribution, both for the face-to-face conversations (the white bar) and for the overall spoken corpus (the grey bar). The difference is such that even without calculating a test for statistical significance, we can hypothesise that register-specificity and functional specialisation explain the high frequency of the top 4 clusters (namely, the *what*-questions and the directive *I want you to*). It should also be remembered that they have been found to occur in almost all films throughout the PCFD as well as in the additional dataset. Particularly, the very high frequency of the top cluster *what are you doing* can be explained by recalling the principle of conflict as constitutive of screenwriting (cf. among others Aimeri 2007; Seger 2009). Characters take action on screen and their actions are challenged by other characters who will therefore address them

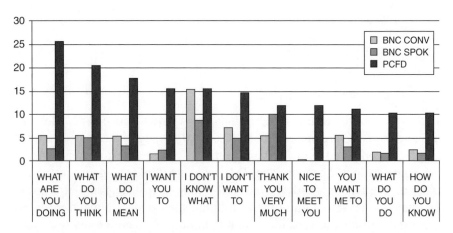

Figure 2. *4-word clusters: comparative view 1*

directly and ask *what are you doing?* or *what are you doing here?* These are very common in the film corpus, as is visible from the concordance lines (cf. Section 4.4). The question becomes an almost fixed formula whose purpose is not only the exchange of information, as in real-life situations, but also what can be termed, following Kozloff (2000: 33), the "anchorage of the diegesis", i.e. it is part of the main narrative. In contrast, in the kinds of conversations sampled in the BNC, the people are less likely to be doing something, possibly because of the way the data are recorded. In fact, the speakers are carrying around a tape-recorder, without, actually, doing much (e.g. in informal conversations, chatting and after-dinner talking). This is also because of the types of interactions, especially in the context-governed part of the corpus, as the smaller proportion of the grey bar shows.

The clusters *I don't know what* and *I don't want to*, occupying ranks 5 and 6 respectively in the PCFD, are much closer to the BNC frequencies, especially when compared to conversation. Interestingly, 5 and 6 not only fit the general pattern of a large number of bundles in conversation, which, as stated by Biber et al. (1999: 991), "are constructed from a pronominal subject followed by a verb phrase plus the start of a complement" (cf. the clusters *I don't know what, I don't know how, I don't want to, I don't think so*, etc. from the *Longman Corpus of Conversation*), but are the two most common 4-word clusters found by Biber and Conrad (1999: 183) and Biber et al. (1999: 994) to be typical of conversation when compared to written academic prose. In Biber *et al.*'s corpus they both occur over 100 times per million words (i.e. over 10 times PHT), which again is comparable to the BNC conversations frequencies in Figure 2. The function of both clusters is to introduce the speaker's stance relative to the information that follows, which is perhaps why their use is as widespread across all kinds of conversational data considered, whether scripted or unscripted.

Very little has been observed to be typical of filmic speech in the remaining clusters. An exception is presented by no. 8 *nice to meet you*, which was found to occur only 5 times in the overall spoken BNC, 4 of which occurred in the face-to-face conversations, and also possibly no. 9, where the directive *you want me to* is part of a larger interrogative sequence and is symmetrical to the other directive *I want you to* in rank no. 4. The high incidence of the greeting formula *nice to meet you* is probably due to the different kinds of situations portrayed in films. People are introduced to each other for the first time much more often in films than in the kind of real-life conversations sampled in the reference corpora. Quaglio (2009a: 35) reports the same, noticing how greeting exchanges are extremely frequent in the *Friends* corpus because of the structure of the scenes, which often commence with characters arriving in places and meeting one another (although not for the first time). It should also be noted that clusters in ranks 8, 10 and 11 were only found in 50% of the movies in the corpus. Therefore, whether they are typical or not can hardly be assessed in relation to a reference corpus.

4.3. Film clusters and the COCA

The data can also be compared to the COCA, given that half the movies in the film corpus are American productions. Again, knowledge of the sampling criteria followed by the COCA compiler when choosing the texts to include in the corpus is necessary to better interpret the results of the comparisons.

The corpus contains more than 410 million words of text and is equally divided among spoken, fiction, popular magazines, newspapers, and academic texts (five sections). It includes 20 million words each year from 1990 to 2010 and it is updated once or twice a year (the most recent texts are from Summer 2010). However, the sampling of the spoken component differs from the BNC. The spoken COCA comprises approximately 87 million words, it contains only transcripts of conversations from TV and radio programmes, such as, *All Things Considered*, *Newshour*, *Good Morning America* (broadcast by ABC), *The Today Show* (NBC), *60 Minutes* (CBS), *The Larry King Show* (CNN), etc. Leaving aside a discussion of whether this kind of data is in fact unscripted and representative of non-media varieties of spoken American English, its nature should be kept in mind when drawing the comparisons. Conversely and unlike the BNC, the fiction section in the COCA contains a relevant proportion of movie scripts (almost 12 million words). According to the compiler of the COCA, since movies are written by a screenwriter, they do not represent actual, unscripted speech and therefore are considered written, not spoken data (cf. the COCA site). In addition, and related to this, characters' names are not separated out from the lines, so part of the 12 million words of the movies sub-section includes that information as well. This is different from how we calculated the total number of running words in the PCFD and in the test dataset for that matter, where we only took the lines leaving out the characters and setting information. This rules out a comparison between the PCFD on the one hand and the COCA movie sub-section on the other. The difference in size between the two samples is indeed too big – 117,000 tokens vs. 11,700,000 words – , that is to say the COCA movie sub-section is a hundred times bigger than the PCFD and even with the small addition of the 4 films from the test dataset, things would not change significantly.

A phraseological approach to film dialogue 149

So, the comparison that is worth drawing seems to be the one between the overall spoken section of the COCA (ca. 87 million words) and the movie sub-section in the COCA (ca. 11,700,000 words) by checking the frequency distributions of the clusters extracted from the PCFD. The results are shown in the next figure (see Figure 3).

The comparison shows that clusters nos 1 (*what are you doing*), 4, 9 (the directive chunks *I want you to* and *you want me to*) and possibly no. 3 (*what do you mean*) can be considered typical of movies (represented by the black bar), while the same cannot be said of no. 2 *what do you think* for which the frequencies are higher in the spoken section (the white bar) than in the movies. This might be due to the kinds of texts that are sampled in the COCA spoken section, mainly TV and radio interviews in which interviewers ask interviewees about their opinions on the various issues debated (*What do you think about/of...?*), and seek further explanation (*what do you mean...?*). The clarifying function is more distinctive of the types of interactions sampled in the spoken COCA and less typical of movies.

Furthermore, clusters nos 5 and 6 are as frequent in the overall spoken section as in the movies, replicating the same situation as with the BNC-PCFD comparison (see Figure 2). A slightly different trend from the BNC-PCFD is observable in cluster no. 7 *thank you very much*. This is practically absent from the COCA movie sub-section and significantly higher than the other clusters in natural spoken data. In contrast, when compared to the overall spoken BNC, *thank you very much* was higher in the PCFD, although not

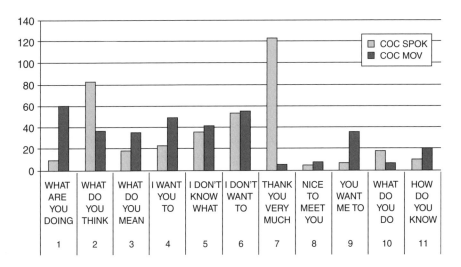

Figure 3. *4-word clusters: comparative view 2*

significantly so. Again, the very high frequency of this routine in the COCA spoken section might be linked to the recurrence of certain set situations and communicative moves in the data sampled in the corpus, like when the host of a TV or radio programme thanks his/her guest interviewee. Additionally, no. 8, the greeting formula, has very few occurrences in both the spoken COCA and in the movies (unlike the PCFD). No. 9, the directive *you want me to*, is higher in the movies than in the spoken data, very much like the previous comparison between the PCFD and the BNC and thus adding evidence to its being characteristic of film dialogue. Nos. 10 and 11 are not considered relevant because of their sparsity in the original data, namely in the PCFD, where they were only associated with half or fewer than half of the films in the corpus.

4.4. The functions of film phrases: film stylistics revisited

If we check the concordances for each cluster in order to observe them in context, we see that there are sequences of two kinds. On the one hand, *what*-questions like *What are you doing?* and *What are you doing here?* are found throughout the film corpus. On the other hand, fixed expressions with a specific conversational-interpersonal function also seem to be quantitatively prominent and diffuse, see, for example, *Thank you very much*, *Nice to meet you*, *How are you doing?*

The first group is of particular interest as it comprises often confrontational questions, signalling that some kind of conflict is going on between the two characters involved in the exchange. Sometimes they are "enriched" by expletives, a mark of emotionally-loaded language, as in *What the hell/the fuck are you doing here?*. Notably, a problem with extracting clusters in the way we have done here, that is on the basis of the frequency of contiguous word-forms in a given span, is that they do not show the amount of lexical variation within the unchanging structural combination (see also Biber 2009). This is why the concordance helps to see sequences interrupted by a swearword and variations on the interrogative patterns *What do you think?* and *What do you mean?* like, for example, *What do you want?* (also frequent in the film corpus, but less so, see Figure 1). The same can be said of *What are you talking about?*, which indeed counts as a 5-word cluster, and other questions like *What's going on?*, *What is it with you?*, *What's wrong with you?*, etc., which are not frequent enough to count as cluster if considered individually, but taken together express an attitude of conflict.[5] This is in line with Van Lancker-Sidtis and Rallon's observation that conventional or formulaic expressions "are generally laced with attitudinal or emotional innuendos" (2004: 208). Besides, they maintain their prototypical function and explicitating purpose of prompting the missing bit of information, which is functional to the advancement of the plot. In the first example, Jamie (played by British actor Colin Firth) gets back home where he left his malingering wife, finds his brother unexpectedly there and utters the line *What the hell are you doing here?*, expressing surprise if not conflict. The question sets off a scene which ends in Jamie's finding out that his wife is cheating on him:

(1) from *Love Actually*
Jamie is back home
JAMIE Hello! What the hell are you doing here?
JAMIE'S BROTHER Oh, I just popped over to borrow some old CDs.
JAMIE The lady of the house let you in, did she?
JAMIE'S BROTHER Yeah.
JAMIE Lovely, obliging girl.
JAMIE'S BROTHER Yeah.
JAMIE I-I just thought I'd pop back from the reception to see if she's better.
JAMIE'S BROTHER Oh.
JAMIE Listen, erm, I've been thinking. I think perhaps we ought to take mum out for her birthday on Friday. What do you think? I just feel we've been bad sons this year.
JAMIE'S BROTHER Okay, sounds fine. A bit boring but fine.
JAMIE'S WIFE (VOICE) Hurry up big boy! I'm naked and I want you at least twice before Jamie gets home!

More examples of the sequence *What are you doing?* from the PCFD are given in Table 3. It is interesting to note the use of the vocative *man* and the tag *eh* both reinforcing the interpersonal dimension of the interrogative (lines 33 and 136, both from *Billy Elliot*) and the insult accompanying the question in *Ae Fond Kiss* (line 233). The translations have been left in, as they explicitate the fixed and argumentlike quality of the situation through the marked verb 'combinare' instead of the unmarked 'fare'-*do*, and the addition of the weak connective 'ma' (Eng. *but*) in turn-initial position. These questions very often do not even expect an answer. As they signal conflict or at least tension between two characters in the flow of conversation, they are emptied of their actual propositional content, i.e. asking for information, and become a sort of speech act of criticising or expressing

Table 3. Concordances of *What are you doing?* from the PCFD

Film	Line No.	Language	Character	Text	Translator
Ae Fond Kiss	105	English	TAHARA	What are you doing?	
Ae Fond Kiss	105	Italian	TAHARA	Cosa stai combinando?	Depaolis Federica
Ae Fond Kiss	233	English	DANNY	What are you doing? You stupid bastard.	
Ae Fond Kiss	233	Italian	DANNY	Ma guarda che hai combinato!	Depaolis Federica
Ae Fond Kiss	278	English	HAMMID	What are you doing later on? No, let's go!	
Ae Fond Kiss	278	Italian	HAMMID	Che cosa fate dopo?	Depaolis Federica
Ae Fond Kiss	287	English	CASIM	What are you doing here?	
Ae Fond Kiss	287	Italian	CASIM	Che ci fai tu qui?	Depaolis Federica
Ae Fond Kiss	300	English	CASIM	What are you doing?	
Ae Fond Kiss	300	Italian	CASIM	Che cosa stai facendo?	Depaolis Federica
Bend it like Beckham	29	English	FRIEND 1	Yeah. What are you doing here man? You haven't left everything to the last minute man, have you?	
Bend it like Beckham	29	Italian	FRIEND 1	Ciao, sposina! Che ci fai qui, non avrai rimandato tutto all'ultimo momento, vero?	Caporello Elettra
Bend it like Beckham	846	English	JULES	What are you doing?	
Bend it like Beckham	846	Italian	JULES	Ma che state facendo?	Caporello Elettra

A phraseological approach to film dialogue 153

Film	#	Language	Character	Dialogue	
Bend it like Beckham	900	English	JESS	Tony, what are you doing?!	
Bend it like Beckham	900	Italian	JESS	Tony! Tony, ma che vuoi fare?	Caporello Elettra
Bend it like Beckham	1004	English	JESS	What are you doing here?	
Bend it like Beckham	1004	Italian	JESS	Come mai sei qui?	Caporello Elettra
Billy Elliot	33	English	GEORGE WATSON	(…) This is man-to-man combat, not a bloody tea dance. What are you doing, man? Hit him! He's just pi	
Billy Elliot	33	Italian	GEORGE WATSON	(…) È un combattimento corpo a corpo, non un tè danzante! Dove accidenti vai? Colpiscilo! Chris ti prende	Cosolo Carlo
Billy Elliot	87	English	DAD	What are you doing going around like creeping Jesus?	
Billy Elliot	87	Italian	DAD	Che stai facendo che ti aggiri come un ladro?	Cosolo Carlo
Billy Elliot	91	English	DAD	What are you doing?	
Billy Elliot	91	Italian	DAD	Che stai facendo?	Cosolo Carlo
Billy Elliot	136	English	TONY	Got enough food there, scab? What are you doing, eh?	
Billy Elliot	136	Italian	TONY	Hai preso abbastanza da mangiare, crumiro? Che stai facendo? eh?	Cosolo Carlo
Billy Elliot	251	English	BILLY	What are you doing?	
Billy Elliot	251	Italian	BILLY	Che stai facendo?	Cosolo Carlo
Billy Elliot	445	English	BILLY	What are you doing?	

(*Continued*)

Table 3. *Continued*

Film	Line No.	Language	Character	Text	Translator
Billy Elliot	445	Italian	BILLY	Cosa stai facendo?	Cosolo Carlo
Crash	26	English	KIM LEE	(...) You fuck you too! Fuck you too! So, what are you doing, are you gonna arrest me?	
Crash	26	Italian	KIM LEE	(...) Lei fatto incidente e lei ola paga pe' lipalale mia macchina! Lei no amelicana! Lei mexcana! Ffanculo Mexico! Ffanculo somblelo!	Ottoni Filippo
Dead Man Walking	344	English	SISTER HELEN	(...) So he's on his deathbed and a friend comes to visit and he sees him reading the Bible. The friend says "W.C., you don't believe in God, what are you doing reading the Bible?" and Fields says	
Dead Man Walking	344	Italian	SISTER HELEN	(...) Insomma sta sul letto di morte, un amico va a trovarlo e vede che legge la Bibbia, allora gli chiede: "W.C. tu non credi in Dio, ma che fai leggi la Bibbia?" E Fields dice (...)	Bertini Lorena
Dead Man Walking	834	English	MATTHEW PONCELET	Hey, you know what I'm doing. What are you doing?	
Dead Man Walking	834	Italian	MATTHEW PONCELET	Lo sai. Tu che stai facendo?	Bertini Lorena
Erin Brockovich	168	English	ERIN	What are you doing making all that goddamn noise?	
Erin Brockovich	168	Italian	ERIN	Come vi salta in mente di fare tutto questo casino?	Mete Marco

A phraseological approach to film dialogue   155

Film	Line	Language	Character	Dialogue	Translator
Erin Brockovich	416	English	ERIN	Ooh… It's some slim pickings here, baby. Maybe that's Ed McMahon. Let's go see. Wow. Oh… wrong Ed. What are you doing here?	Mete Marco
Erin Brockovich	416	Italian	ERIN	E con che le pago? Oh… Qui la vedo magra, piccina mia… Ah… Potrebbe essere Eddie Murphy, andiamo a vedere… Ah, l'Eddie sbagliato. Che ci fai qui?	
Finding Forrester	404	English	JAMAL	What are you doing?	Caporello Elettra
Finding Forrester	404	Italian	JAMAL	Ma che sta facendo?	
Notting Hill	364	English	BELLA	Quickly, quickly, quickly. Talk very, very quickly. What what are you doing here with Anna Scott?	Vairano Francesco
Notting Hill	364	Italian	BELLA	Presto, presto, presto. Parla più in fretta che puoi. Che cosa ci fai qui con Anna Scott?	
Ocean's Eleven	95	English	BARRY	I'm out what are you doing?	Mete Marco
Ocean's Eleven	95	Italian	BARRY	Ma che fai?	
Ocean's Eleven	593	English	TESS	What are you doing here?	Mete Marco
Ocean's Eleven	593	Italian	TESS	Che ci fai qui?	
Ocean's Eleven	644	English	MR BENEDICT	What are you doing?	Mete Marco
Ocean's Eleven	644	Italian	MR BENEDICT	E che cosa fa?	

disagreement. This function is also visible in *What are you doing making all that goddamn noise?* (line 168 from *Erin Brockovich*, but also 87 from *Billy Elliot*) where the construct with the gerund adds to the function of the question. Clearly, the meaning of the question is not always confrontational, as, for example, in line 278 from *Ae Fond Kiss*, where it is a real question expecting an answer (cf. *What are you doing later on?*).

The same *what*-questions can be searched for in the spoken components of the reference corpora used in the previous Sections (cf. 4.2 and 4.3) to check their distribution and functions therein. To illustrate this, let us take the string WHAT DO YOU MEAN in the spoken BNC. The search returned 336 hits in 165 different texts (with a frequency of 32.28 instances per million words, cf. also Figure 2). The following examples highlight its use in dialogic contexts to frame the interlocutor's own words on which some clarification is asked for. See example (2) from a radio broadcast phone-in:

(2) HUV 72
What do you mean you tried for two days?

In the extracts in (3), taken from demographically sampled conversations, the framing function is made explicit by the transcribers' choice to separate the reporting from the reported part with a comma:

(3) KB7 4064
What do you mean, left the table?
KB7 4451
What do you mean, been conning you?
KB7 6063
What do you mean, nothing?

Interestingly, the last concordance line in example (3) was also found in the film corpus, where the notation used to indicate a piece of reported speech is the double quotes. The meaning of the question could be glossed as "taking up the interlocutor's words to either rebut or challenge them", cf. (4) from the film *Finding Forrester*:

(4) TERREL What do you mean "nothing"? This getting in the way of your plans or something?

If we look at the list of collocates of WHAT DO YOU MEAN in the spoken component of the BNC, the most statistically significant collocate is the question mark, as in *What do you mean?* making up a whole turn, which is also frequent in the two film corpora. On the other hand, the second most frequent collocate to the right in BNC spoken is the preposition *by* (as in *what do you mean by...*) whose use, however, seems to be restricted to institutionalised discourse types such as lectures, business meetings and the like. There is no such usage in the film corpus, showing that it belongs to more formal contexts.

The second group of routine expressions represents the verbal accompaniment of highly ritualised acts of daily experience. Their relevance to film dialogue vs. natural conversation has already been discussed in relation to what Quaglio (2009a: 135) has termed "movement", that is the characters walking into a place and exchanging greetings with other characters like in ordinary encounters. This, in particular, explains the high incidence of *Nice to meet you* and *How are you doing?* in the films (cf. Figure 1). Following Van Lancker-Sidtis and Rallon's categorisation, both groups would be classified as speech formulae, that is "the expressions used in conversational interaction" (2004: 209). Among the examples the authors give are *See you later!*, *Let's call it a day* and *You don't say!* and in their analysis of conversational dialogue in the screenplay *Some Like it Hot* speech formulae constitute by far the highest number of formulaic expression types (and highest number of repetitions per type). Although their analysis is not frequency-driven, many of the speech phrases they find in the screenplay are similar to our findings: thanks and apologies are frequent, and a variety of *what*-questions occur repeatedly (including *What's the matter?*, *What's going on here?*, *What do you think you are doing?*, *What are you talking about?*, etc.). Also, the authors draw attention to the fact that formulaic expressions often occur in a context of confrontation and disagreement and concede that disagreement is part of the texture of the screenplay they chose to analyse (2004: 220).

In conclusion, frequent phrases work on a double level:

i) *diegetic*, i.e. internal to the fictional world of narrated situations and events. They have a plot-advancing function and contribute to the representation of conflict,

and

ii) *conversational-interpersonal*, i.e. mimicking the spontaneity of natural conversation as linked to the interpersonal sphere of dialogic interactions.

This double function can be linked to two fundamental purposes of film dialogue as formulated by Kozloff in her (2000) study of dialogue in film.

These are the anchorage of the diegesis and characters and the "verbal wallpaper" of ordinary conversational activities (Kozloff 2000: 47). The frequent *what*-questions identified under i) are verbal acts whose purpose is the anchoring of the narrative; they help to carry on the action while signalling some sort of challenge between two characters in the flow of conversation. The conversational routines in ii) are part of the mannerism of film as a realistic construct.

5. Conclusions

The description proposed in the present study on the phraseology of contemporary filmic speech is first and foremost frequency-based in that recurrent sequences of words in a film corpus (PCFD) have served as the starting point for the research. Furthermore, in order to make a comparison between spontaneous conversation and film dialogue and look into register-specific usage, the clusters thus identified have been compared to general spoken corpora, namely the spoken components of the BNC and the COCA. The comparisons have identified very few clusters which are typical of the register under examination, i.e. scripted film dialogue, most of them being common to natural spoken data. As for the methodological issues involved in using clusters as a tool for identifying phrases of film dialogue, one should note that clusters do not allow for variations on a pattern. In order to overcome this problem, the distributional patterns have been further checked against the concordances from the PCFD. The analysis has foregrounded chunks of speech functioning on two levels, namely diegetic and conversational. The former has been explained as triggering off the advancement of the situations and events internal to the fictional world narrated by film (the interrogative pattern); in this respect it reflects the register-specificity of formulae in film dialogue. The latter has been understood as functioning in real life conversation mainly interpersonally, therefore, it is said of formulae which are mimetic of natural conversation in English. This takes us back to film theory and the development of both the diegetic and mimetic dimensions of film, which works simultaneously as a telling, a narration or verbal activity, and a showing, a mimesis. Dialogue, as one of the codes in the complex semiotic environment of film, has been shown to function both narrationally and mimetically, also in virtue of its formulaicity. In this regard, the study corroborates previous observations on the predictability of filmic speech as expressed by Taylor (2004, 2008) and resonates with Eikhenbaum's concept of "divination" on the part of the film viewer:

Cinema demands of the viewer a certain special technique for divination, and this technique will of course become more complex as the art of film-making develops. Directors already make frequent use of symbols and metaphors, the meaning of which depends directly on current verbal metaphors. Film viewing is accompanied by a continual process of internal speech. We have already grown accustomed to a whole series of typical patterns of film-language; the smallest innovation in this sphere strikes us no less forcibly than the appearance of a new word in language. To treat film as an absolutely non-verbal art is impossible.

(Eikhenbaum 1974: 14)

In conclusion, the phraseological approach used here allows a reconsideration of film stylistics, a reconsideration which focuses on the language used in films and highlights its role as integral to the other semiotic codes (esp. images and montage).

Notes

Correspondence address: maria.freddi@unipv.it

1. I use "film stylistics" as a homage to Eikhenbaum's (1974) seminal paper on film as a form of art.
2. In the *Wordsmith Tools* handbook we read "each n-word cluster will be stored, if it reaches n words in length, up to a punctuation boundary, marked by semicolon, comma, full-stop, exclamation and question marks".
3. For a discussion of recurrent word-combinations as "preferred ways of saying things" as in Altenberg (1998), see Granger and Paquot (2008); Corrigan et al. (2009: xiv) talk about restricted distributions and formulae as "true hallmarks of style". On phraseology and style, see also some of the contributions in the two volumes by Burger et al. (2007).
4. For details concerning each film, runtime and number of running words, see Freddi and Pavesi (2009: 99) and Freddi (in press).
5. Contracted forms like *what's* as opposed to *what is* do of course represent a problem for the automatic computation of clusters but because contractions are frequent in conversation, they should be taken into account when analyzing clusters.

References

Aimeri, Luca. 2007. *Manuale di sceneggiatura cinematografica: Teoria e pratica*. Torino: Utet.

Altenberg, Bengt. 1998. On the phraseology of spoken English: The evidence of recurrent word combinations. In Anthony P. Cowie (ed.), *Phraseology*, 101–122. Oxford: Oxford University Press.

Baños-Piñero, Rocio & Frederic Chaume. 2009. Prefabricated orality: A challenge in audiovisual translation. *inTRAlinea Special Issue on The Translation of Dialects in Multimedia*. Online at: http://www.intralinea.it/specials/dialectrans/eng_more.php?id=761_0_49_0_M (accessed 30 April 2011).

Biber, Douglas. 2009. A corpus-driven approach to formulaic language in English: Multiword patterns in speech and writing. *International Journal of Corpus Linguistics* 14(3). 275–311.

Biber, Douglas, Stig Johansson, Geoffrey Leech, Susan Conrad & Edward Finegan. 1999. *Longman grammar of spoken and written English*. London: Longman.

Biber, Douglas & Susan Conrad. 1999. Lexical bundles in conversation and academic prose. In Hilde Hasselgard & Signe Oksefjell (eds.), *Out of corpora: Studies in honour of Stig Johansson*, 181–190. Amsterdam/Atlanta: Rodopi.

Biber, Douglas, Susan Conrad & Vivian Cortes. 2004. If you look at...: Lexical bundles in university teaching and textbooks. *Applied Linguistics*. 25(3). 371–405.

Burger, Harald, Dobrovol'skij Dmitrij, Peter Kühn & Neal R. Norrick (eds.). 2007a. *Phraseology: An international handbook of contemporary research. Vol. 1*. Berlin: de Gruyter.

Burger, Harald, Dobrovol'skij Dmitrij, Peter Kühn & Neal R. Norrick (eds.). 2007b. *Phraseology: An international handbook of contemporary research. Vol. 2*. Berlin: de Gruyter.

Chaume, Frederic. 2001. La pretendida oralidad de los textos audiovisuales y sus implicaciones en traduccion. In Rosa Agost & Frederic Chaume (eds.), *La Traducción en los Medios Audiovisuales*, 77–87. Castelló de la Plana: Publicacions de la Universitat Jaume I.

Chaume, Frederic. 2004. *Cine y Traduccion*. Madrid: Catedra.

Corrigan, Roberta, Edith A. Moravcsik, Hamid Ouali & Kathleen M. Wheatly. 2009. Introduction: Approaches to the study of formulae. In *Formulaic language. Vol. 1 Distribution and historical change*, xi–xxiv. Amsterdam/Philadelphia: Benjamins.

Eikhenbaum, Boris. 1974. Problems of film stylistics. *Screen* 15(3). 7–34.

Fletcher, William. 2007. *kfNgram*. Online at: http://kwicfinder.com/kfNgram/kfNgramHelp.html (accessed 30 April 2011).

Freddi, Maria. in press. What AVT can make of corpora: Some findings from the Pavia Corpus of Film Dialogue. In Mary Carroll, Pilar Orero & Aline Remael (eds.), *Media for all: Quality made to measure, (Approaches to Translation Studies.)* Amsterdam: Rodopi.

Freddi, Maria & Maria Pavesi (eds.). 2009. *Analysing audiovisual dialogue: Linguistic and translational insights*. Bologna: Clueb.

Granger, Sylviane & Fanny Meunieur. 2008. Introduction: The many faces of phraseology. In Sylviane Granger & Fanny Meunier (eds.), *Phraseology: An interdisciplinary perspective,* xix–xxviii. Amsterdam/Philadelphia: Benjamins.

Granger, Sylviane & Magali Paquot. 2008. Disentangling the phraseological web. In Sylviane Granger & Fanny Meunier (eds.), *Phraseology: An interdisciplinary perspective*, 27–49. Amsterdam/Philadelphia: Benjamins.

Kozloff, Sarah. 2000. *Overhearing film dialogue*. Berkeley/Los Angeles: University of California Press.

Meunier, Fanny & Sylviane Granger (eds.). 2008. *Phraseology in foreign language learning and teaching*. Amsterdam/Philadelphia: Benjamins.

Moon, Rosamund. 1998. *Fixed expressions and idioms in English: A corpus-based approach*. Oxford: Clarendon.

Pavesi, Maria. 2005. *La traduzione filmica: Aspetti del parlato doppiato dall'inglese all'italiano*. Roma: Carocci.

Pavesi, Maria. 2008. Spoken language in film dubbing: Target language norms, interference and translational routines. In Delia Chiaro, Christine Heiss & Chiara Bucaria (eds.), *Between text and image: Updating research in screen translation*, 79–99. Amsterdam/Philadelphia: Benjamins.

Pavesi, Maria. 2009. Dubbing English into Italian: A closer look at the translation of spoken language. In Jorge Díaz-Cintas (ed.), *New trends in audiovisual translation*, 197–209. Bristol: Multilingual Matters.

Quaglio, Paulo. 2008. Television dialogue and natural conversation: Linguistic similarities and functional differences. In Annelie Ädel & Randi Reppen (eds.), *Corpora and discourse: The challenges of different settings*, 198–210. Amsterdam/Philadelphia: Benjamins.

Quaglio, Paulo. 2009a. *Television dialogue: The sitcom* Friends *vs. natural conversation*. Amsterdam/Philadelphia: Benjamins.

Quaglio, Paulo. 2009b. Vague language in the situation comedy *Friends* vs. natural conversation. In Maria Freddi & Maria Pavesi (eds.), *Analysing audiovisual dialogue: Linguistic and translational insights*, 75–91. Bologna: Clueb.

Richardson, Kay. 2010. *Television dramatic dialogue: A sociolinguistic study*. Oxford: Oxford University Press.

Romero Fresco, Pablo. 2006. Spanish dubbese: A case of (un)idiomatic *Friends*. *The Journal of Specialized Translation* 6. 134–151. Online at: http://www.jostrans.org/issue06/art_romero_fresco.php (accessed 30 April 2011).

Romero Fresco, Pablo. 2009. Naturalness in the Spanish dubbing language: A case of not-so-close *Friends*. *Meta* 54(1). 49–72.

Scott, Mike. 2004. *Wordsmith Tools, v. 4*. Oxford: Oxford University Computing Unit.

Scott, Mike & Christopher Tribble. 2006. *Textual patterns: Key words and corpus analysis in language education*. Amsterdam/Philadelphia: Benjamins.

Seger, Linda. 2009. *Come scrivere una grande sceneggiatura*. Roma: Dino Audino Editore (It. Transl. of *Making a good script great*. 2nd ed. Hollywood, CA: Samuel French Trade).

Sinclair, John. 1991. *Corpus, concordance, collocation*. Oxford: Oxford University Press.

Sinclair, John. 1996. The search for units of meaning. *Textus* 9(1). 75–106. Reprinted as chap. 2 of *Trust the text: Language, corpus and discourse*, 24–48. London: Routledge.
Sinclair, John. 1998. The lexical item. In Edda Weigand (ed.), *Contrastive lexical semantics*, 1–24. Amsterdam/Philadelphia: Benjamins. Reprinted as chap. 8 of *Trust the text: Language, corpus and discourse*, 131–148. London: Routledge.
Sinclair, John. 2004a. *Trust the text: Language, corpus and discourse*. London: Routledge.
Sinclair, John. 2004b. *How to use corpora in language teaching*. Amsterdam/Philadelphia: Benjamins.
Sinclair, John. in press. *Essential corpus linguistics*. Elena Tognini Bonelli (ed.) London: Routledge.
Taylor, Christopher. 1999. Look who's talking: An analysis of film dialogue as a variety of spoken discourse. In Linda Lombardo, Louann Haarman, John Morley & Christopher Taylor (eds.), *Massed medias: Linguistic tools for interpreting media discourse*, 247–278. Milano: Led.
Taylor, Christopher. 2004. The language of film: Corpora and statistics in the search for authenticity. *Notting Hill* (1998) – A case study. *Miscelanea* 30, 71–86. Zaragoza: Departamento de Filologia Inglesa y Alemanna, Universidad de Zaragoza.
Taylor, Christopher. 2006. *I knew he'd say that! A consideration of the predictability of language use in film*. MuTra 2006 – Audiovisual Translation Scenarios, EU-High-Level Scientific Conference Series. Online at: http://www.euroconferences.info/proceedings/2006_Proceedings/2006_Taylor_Christopher.pdf (accessed 30 April 2011).
Taylor, Christopher. 2008. Predictability in film language: Corpus-assisted research. In Carol Taylor-Torsello, Katherine Ackerley & Erik Castello (eds.), *Corpora for university language teachers*, 167–180. Berlin/Bern: Peter Lang.
Van Lancker-Sidtis, Diana & Gail Rallon. 2004. Tracking the incidence of formulaic expressions in everyday speech: Methods for classification and verification. *Language and Communication* 24(3). 207–240.
Warren, Martin. 2006. *Features of naturalness in conversation*. Amsterdam/Philadelphia: Benjamins.

Whoop her up, hit it, go it alone: The role of the personal pronoun in the fossilization process

LAURE GARDELLE

Abstract

The present study looks into verbal phrasemes with a verb + it *pattern, which have received little attention beyond the well-established fact that the pronoun there loses some of its referentiality. It focuses more specifically on the role and morphological features of the pronoun in those phrasemes. A corpus-based study shows that the* verb + it *pattern licenses a number of prototypically intransitive verbs; it is argued that this capacity of the transitive pattern to override individual argument realisations is related to the prototypical semantics associated with the syntactic function of direct object. The study also seeks to determine why personal pronouns are the only type of pronoun licensed in those phrases. They are shown to be the default pronouns in terms of procedural information. Another issue is that of gender: a few phrasemes license alternation between the neuter and the feminine in several varieties of nonstandard English.*

Keywords: gender; personal pronoun; syntactic overriding; transitive pattern; "verb + it" constructions; verbal phrasemes.

1. Introduction

Studies in English phraseology have given considerable attention to what Huddleston & Pullum (2002: 273) term "verbal idioms", that is, to lexicalized predicates whose major element is a verb. Research interests, to name just a few, range from syntax and morphology (as in Chafe 1968; Jackendoff 1975 or Marantz 1984) to semantics (see for instance Newmeyer 1974, Bennett 1996; Goldberg 2006), typological differences (as in Fillmore et al. 1988; Nunberg & Sag 1994, Cowie 1994, or Fellbaum 2007), pragmatics (for example, Naciscione 2010), automatic retrieval in texts (such as Pankhurst 2001), or acquisition and natural language processing (see for instance Abel 2003) – for more detailed references and a discussion of the various areas of research, see Burger et al. (2007).

One aspect, however, has up to now been very little studied; the specificities of the personal pronoun in verbal phrasemes with a *verb + it* pattern. This is partly due to the data used in analyses, which typically display a *verb + full NP* pattern – as in *hit the deck, pull strings* or *pay the devil his due*. The present study therefore looks specifically at verbal phrasemes that show a *verb + pronoun (+ adverbial particle or adjective)* pattern, such as *hit it* or *go it alone*, and focuses on the pronoun in this pattern.

In the narrow sense of the word, these verbal phrasemes are not idioms (Croft 1986), or at least not "pure idioms" (Cowie 1994). An idiom is semantically non-compositional and morphologically inflexible. The verbal phrasemes under study do form semantic units and are more than just collocations, but, as the present article shows, they allow for a partly compositional analysis. In addition, although *go it alone*, for instance, cannot be altered in any way, most of the phrasemes have to compete with other forms – for instance, *hit it / hit the road*. Consequently, they are less idioms than constructions, that is, units of syntactic representation that are not just the combination of the isolated meanings of their components, but which have their own syntactic and semantic properties (Croft & Cruse 2004: 237; Fried & Östman 2004: 12). From here on, therefore, they will be termed "verbal constructions", in a narrow acception of the word (Fried & Östman 2004: 1), or "phrasemes".

In order to allow for reliable analyses and statistics, the study is based on a corpus made up of all the lexicalised constructions showing a *verb + pronoun (+ adverbial particle or adjective)* pattern registered in the OED (2009), with the addition of data collected from Svartengren (1927) and Gardelle (2006) for nonstandard or very informal English. This yields a total of 62 different phrasemes.

What is well established today about the objective personal pronoun in verbal constructions is that it does not have an identifiable referent in context; for instance, Huddleston & Pullum (2002: 1481) state that, "*it* appears with no identifiable meaning in a large number of generally colloquial idioms". Hence a clear-cut contrast between the following utterances:

(1) She said she was going to pack her bag and leave it in the entrance.
(2) She said she was going to pack her bag and beat it back to Tennessee.

(1) is a prototypical case of anaphora in a free sequence: the pronoun *it* is co-referential with its textual antecedent *her bag* and gives access to a salient, clearly identifiable referent. In (2), on the other hand, *beat it* is a verbal construction, the whole of which denotes the idea of leaving. The pronoun *it* still appears to have an element of referentiality there: it is possible to substitute a full NP for it (*beat the road, beat her way*). It does not have an antecedent, however, and cannot be replaced *freely* by an NP: *beat the way, *beat her route, for instance, are impossible. Moreover, when using the pronoun, the speaker may not have thought out the referent precisely as being the *way* back. In some constructions, as in (3), it is even totally impossible to substitute any NP for the pronoun:

(3)   Defence sources told the *Jerusalem Post* they were considering going it alone in a strike on Iran.

It would be ungrammatical, for instance, to use **going the project alone* or **going their way alone*. It should be added that even when a full NP can be substituted for the pronoun, the NP and the pronoun are not simply co-referential. For example, while the phrase *whoop her up* shows a singular pronoun, the only full NP that can be substituted is plural: *whoop things up*. Even in the case of *beat it / beat one's way*, the OED indicates that the two constructions are not simply synonymous, but that they carry different connotations: *beat one's way* is used especially for someone travelling "by illicit means".

These few examples raise several questions. First, from a syntactic point of view, (3) stands out, in that while it has a typically intransitive verb, it shows a personal pronoun in the syntactic position of direct object. This is not an isolated case, although it does not appear to have been noted in previous studies; it concerns 24 constructions out of the 62 under study. This capacity of some syntactic patterns to override the individual argument structures of verbs is not restricted to verbal constructions; it is also the case with some resultative structures, such as *he sang the baby to sleep*, or in isolated patterns such as *look me in the face*. But why does the *verb + object* pattern prevail in no less than 24 verbal constructions? Why does it concern only the *verb + pronoun* pattern, and not verbal phrasemes with full NPs? Is the personal pronoun a true direct object there? Finally, are there any constraints on this overriding, or could any intransitive verb potentially enter the pattern one day?

A closer look at the morphology of the pronoun in verbal constructions also raises several questions. First, as the few examples given so far show, it is always a personal pronoun – and not a demonstrative, for instance. This fact, which has been taken for granted in studies, needs to be accounted for; why is the procedural information coded by a personal pronoun more adapted to verbal constructions than that of a demonstrative? Another issue is that of pronominal gender. All the examples given in the OED show the neuter, but in nonstandard American and Canadian English, at least 5 verbal constructions show an alternation between the neuter and the feminine: *hit it/her up* (get started), *whoop it/her up* (keep up the excitement, for instance at a party), *touch it/her off* (fire a weapon), *get it/her made* (succeed in life), all of which were found in authentic utterances, and *go it/her alone* (the feminine was found in Steinbeck's *Grapes of Wrath* (1939: 443). Such alternations confirm that the pronoun is still felt to be somewhat referential; in those varieties of English, the feminine is never used for dummy pronouns, for example in extraposed constructions or cleft structures.[1] The alternations also raise the question of the criterion for gender use in those constructions; is it similar to "free" uses of the pronoun?

In order to answer these questions, Section 1 looks specifically at verbal constructions that display prototypically intransitive verbs, since they reveal a number of phenomena. The findings are then extended to constructions that contain prototypically transitive verbs. Section 3 addresses more theoretical considerations about the morphological characteristics of the pronoun in *verb + pronoun* constructions.

2. Verbal constructions involving prototypically intransitive verbs

Prototypically intransitive verbs, as stated in the introduction, were found in 24 different phrasemes of the corpus. They fall into four categories:

1. verbs indicating the institution with which the event is achieved: *hotel it*, defined by the OED as 'stay at a hotel'; similarly *inn it, camp it* and *pub it*. For instance one reads:

    (4) Could I ask a question please. This summer will be my first time in France with the van, and I too am staying in Des Quatre Vents for my first week. How do people manage with regard to security on the sites. When you <u>hotel it</u>, you have safes or security boxes, but how do you store your valuables safely in a caravan when you go out for the day? Or do sites typically have safety deposit boxes that you can hire?

2. verbs expressing the means of transport thanks to which the event is achieved: *train it*, which can be glossed as "go by train", as in (5):

(5) From Aberdeen to Edinburgh we <u>trained it</u> by easy stages.

Other examples include *boat it, bus it, cab it, coach it, foot it, oar it, sledge it* and *tube it*.
3. verbs expressing the attitude with which the event is achieved, for instance *lord it*, defined by the OED as "behave in a lordly manner, assume airs of grandeurs". *Lord it* is used chiefly with *over* + NP, as in the following utterance:

(6) Direct my steps according to your word, and let no iniquity <u>lord it</u> over me.

The other verbs of the corpus in this category are *coquet it* (now obsolete), *king it, queen it, brave it, flaunt it* and *trip it* (in the sense of moving lightly and nimbly).
4. other prototypically intransitive verbs: *go*, in *go it* (do something recklessly), *go it alone* (act alone) and *go it blind* (plunge into a course of action without regarding the consequences), and *sleep*, with the phrase *sleep it rough* (sleep in the street).

Most of the verbs in the first three categories are historically derived from nouns (17 out of 20), but all of them are true, well-established intransitive verbs. Their use as verbs, therefore, is not restricted to the idiomatic *verb + it* pattern.

For 22 out of the 24 constructions cited above,[2] the *verb + it* pattern is in competition with the verb used intransitively. For instance, beside *hotel it*, one finds the verb *hotel*, as in (7):

(7) Why anyone would want to <u>hotel</u> is beyond me though.

The definition given by the OED is similar for the two variants: stay at a hotel. Similarly, one finds *camp Ø, boat Ø, foot Ø* (obsolete, in the sense of "move one's foot"), *brave Ø* (now obsolete), *sleep Ø rough* and so on. This alternation between intransitive and transitive constructions raises two questions: which pattern appeared first diachronically, and what is the choice criterion? From a diachronic point of view, the occurrences collected by the OED suggest that the *verb + it* construction is more recent

168 *Laure Gardelle*

than the intransitive use of those verbs. For verbs in categories 1 to 3, in at least 16 cases out of 19,[3] the word was first used as a noun, then converted to an intransitive verb, and then used in the *verb + it* pattern. The *it* variant appeared typically about 15 to 20 years later than the intransitive use (at least in known sources): for instance, *boat Ø* is dated back to 1673, while *boat it* is first recorded in 1687.[4] The data also show that the *prototypically intransitive verb + it* pattern is not a recent one; it was used at least from the 16th century for *foot it* (1576) and *trip it* (1579), from the 17th for *boat it* (1687) and *coach it* (c. 1632), from the 19th for *bus it* (1838), *cab it* (1860) and *train it* (1888), and from the early 20th century for *tube it* (1902). It is therefore a productive pattern, which integrates new verbs as they enter the language in the wake of technological inventions. There are no occurrences of *car (it)*, possibly because the verb *drive* already provides the meaning. As for verbs of category 4, *go it* and *go Ø* phrases are not in competition, and as the OED does not record *sleep it rough*, no comparison of the intransitive and *it* patterns is possible.

Regarding choice criteria, the two structures are so close that only 2 utterances could be found in which one could not be substituted for the other; both concern the verb *hotel* (utterances 8 and 9):

(8) (personal description) I love hoteling (*<u>hoteling it</u>*), shopping, music, movies and poetry.

The structural parallelism alone (one word for each complement) does not explain the use of the intransitive pattern: the variant **I love hoteling it, listening to music, watching movies* is not acceptable either. Rather, *hoteling Ø* only denotes the type of accommodation, whereas with *it*, the notion of a patient would be added – in other words, the idea of an element, even though not a clearly identified one, to which the way of achieving the event (*hoteling*) is applied. This point of view is incompatible with the purely generic perspective of the extract, which lists a series of tastes. This utterance, therefore, is different from (8'):

(8') When I go on holiday, I love <u>hoteling it</u>.

Here, *hoteling it* is acceptable despite the generic perspective because the co-text (*when I go on holiday*) delimitates a frame for the event, so that the situation[5] denoted by the verb (*hoteling*) can be felt to apply to an element. *Hoteling Ø* would have been possible as well, but would only have foregrounded the type of accommodation. In other words, *hoteling Ø* can be glossed as "staying in hotels", while *hoteling it* is closer to "achieving (the trip) using hotels".

The other utterance that yields a different interpretation according to which variant is used is (9):

(9) (Gary Stout) Having been to Le Mans for a few years, sleeping outside, in a tent, in a car, a caravan, I suppose a hotel is out of the question near the circuit, booking at this later date. Any ideas? Many thanks, still wet from 2001. – (reply from the administrator) Our Le Mans resident contributor, Gilles, will be along in a minute to advise. Watch this space. Why anyone would want to <u>hotel</u> is beyond me though....

(9') (...) Why anyone would want to <u>hotel it</u> is beyond me though....

The reference would be different according to the variant used: in (9), *hotel* is the notion in general, the means of accommodation, not specifically applied to anything. Conversely, in (9') it is applied to trips to Le Mans only; again, it is the co-text that serves to delimitate the frame within which *hotel* is felt to be applied.

It can be concluded from these few analyses, therefore, that the intransitive pattern denotes just the [situation], whereas the *verb + it* pattern denotes [situation] + [element affected]. Although that element cannot be clearly identified, the action is still felt to be applied to something. This distinction applies to all the utterances in the corpus, including those in which both variants are acceptable. For instance in (10):

(10) Well all is said and done now. Tomorrow the instance will reset. So if those few want to <u>camp it</u> again tonight, so be it... life and the game will still go on!

(10') Well all is said and done now. Tomorrow the instance will reset. So if those few want to <u>camp</u> again tonight, so be it... life and the game will still go on!

Camp it can be subdivided into [sleep under a tent] + [applied to an element] (the night), while *camp Ø* would only give the type of accommodation ([sleep under a tent]). Both are possible because the co-text again provides a delimitating frame (*tonight*), but the difference between the two variants is one of degree of foregrounding of the idea that the situation applies to an element. The same analysis applies to (11):

(11) So exhausted were the men from the effect of the previous day's ride that all <u>trained</u> from Winchester to Farnham.
(11') So exhausted were the men from the effect of the previous day's ride that all <u>trained it</u> from Winchester to Farnham.

In (11), *train Ø* is preferred because the focus is on the means of transportation only: *train* stands in contrast with *ride*. *Trained it* would have been possible, as *from Winchester to Farnham* delimits an element to which the mode of transport can be applied, but it would have foregrounded the idea of achieving a journey. Due to that focus, *it* would be less appropriate for (11) than it is in (12), in which the speaker details a pre-planned stage in his trip:

(12) From Aberdeen to Edinburgh we <u>trained it</u> by easy stages.

Here again, *from Aberdeen to Edinburgh* delimits the element that was achieved, and *train* denotes the manner. *Trained it* can be glossed as "did the journey by train", whereas *trained Ø* would merely have denoted "took the train".

These analyses enable us to answer several questions. One concerns the syntactic function of the pronoun; can it be a direct object when it is used with a prototypically intransitive verb? The OED is rather inconclusive in that respect: indications about the verbs range from "intransitive with *it*" (for *tree it* and *trip it*), "intransitive – mostly with *it*" (e.g. *king / queen it*) to "intransitive (and constr. *to brave it*)" (*brave it*), "quasi-transitive with *it*" (*flaunt it*) and "transitive" (*hotel it*). There does not seem to be any logical criterion for such differences in the treatment of the pronoun. I would suggest rather that because *it* is felt to denote a patient, it is syntactically a direct object in all the constructions under study: the syntactic function of direct object is the one that is prototypically associated with the semantic role of patient. The phraseme therefore derives part of its semantics from what Construction Grammar calls the "argument structure construction" [$_{VP}$ V + OBJ] (Gries 2008: 8). In that respect, *camp it*, for instance, is little different from a prototypical transitive construction such as *leave the bag*. This predicate, too, can be divided into [situation] + [element affected]. The only difference between *it* in verbal constructions and the NP in *leave the bag* is that the former is not a *prototypical* direct object. For instance, it fails the passive (*it can be camped, **it is slept rough by people* and so on). But this restriction holds, too, for many verbal constructions with clearly transitive patterns. For instance, *beat one's way* cannot yield *her way to

Tennessee was beaten. The constraints on direct object behaviour have to do with reference and not with syntactic function. The direct object is not an argument in verbal constructions (Kleiber 1994: 88; Simatos 1996: 78).

Let us now consider the origin of the *verb + it* pattern for prototypically intransitive verbs. What makes it powerful enough to override the individual argument realizations of those verbs? The OED suggests that the *verb + it* pattern might be derived from the proform *do it*, "There may have been some influence from *do it* as a substitute, not only for any transitive verb and its object, but for an intransitive verb of action, as in 'he tried to swim, but could not do it', where *it* is the action in question." (2009, online edition, entry "it"). There is evidently a link since the proform *do it*, too, divides the event into [situation] + [element affected], as evidenced by (13):

(13) I did it – graduated nursing school 2009!

In this example, *did* indicates that there was an action and *it* instantiates the patient, in other words, the idea that the "doing" bore on something (which is then developed as *graduate nursing school 2009*). It seems unlikely, however, that the sole proform *do it* should be powerful enough to allow for the argument realizations of intransitive verbs to be overridden. Rather, I propose that the ultimate source is a more abstract one, the transitive pattern itself – in other words, the prototypical semantics associated with the syntactic function of direct object. The proform *do it* would then be just one manifestation of the semantics generated by default by the transitive pattern.

As a consequence, there are constraints on the semantics of the verbs that could theoretically enter the *verb + it* pattern. For instance, one could never find **the sea glistened it* or *she glowed it. The denotation of the verb must contribute to the achievement of the event, as in prototypical transitive patterns, which is not the case with verbs such as *glisten* and *glow*. Conversely, it must be noted that there is an element of arbitrariness in the language. Among verbs of category 1, for instance, *camp it* is less frequent than *camp*, whereas *hotel it* is more common than *hotel*, and there does not seem to be any semantic explanation in context for this difference in frequency.

We now turn to *verb + it* constructions involving prototypically transitive verbs, to see whether the findings for intransitive verbs can be extended to them.

3. Verbal constructions involving prototypically transitive verbs

The corpus shows 38 different constructions of this type. For 36 of them, the alternation is between a *verb + it* structure (as in [14]) and a *verb + NP* pattern, in which the object can be a free NP (15) or one constrained by a phraseme (16):[6]

(14) chance it [=take risks], carry it [=win]
(15) Don't chance a general insurance broker, use a professions specialist.
(16) carry the day

Only two constructions in the corpus do not allow a free NP to be substituted for *it*: *have it away* and *have it off*, in the sense of *have sex*.

As with intransitive verbs, the *it* pattern appears to be more recent than the *verb + free complement* sequence.[7] For most, the OED shows a gap of several decades (e.g. *chance sth* 1859 / *chance it* 1870), sometimes several centuries (e.g. *fight sth* 1300 / *fight it* 1769). One verb, *whoop up*, does not show any gap (*sth* 1884, *it* 1885), but again, the findings can only be based on written sources and might therefore be unreliable.

The semantics of the verbs in these constructions are extremely varied, but as with prototypically intransitive verbs used in the *verb + it* pattern, all are dynamic predicates – for instance *chance it, blow it* or *push it*.[8] As regards the semantics of the construction as a whole, one difference with prototypically intransitive verbs is the frequency of polysemous phrasemes. Out of the 38 *transitive vb + it* phrases in the corpus, no less than 10 (i.e. over a quarter) are or have been polysemous. More specifically, 6 have 2 possible meanings. For instance, *push it* can mean either "press one's claim strongly" or "go too far", while *have it away* means either "escape from prison" or "have sex". 4 have at least 4 meanings: *hit it* (4 meanings), *make it* (4), *make it up* (4) and *have it* (6). For example, *make it up* may mean "compensate", "make up one's mind / agree to", "get married" or "be reconciled". The most polysemous phrase, *have it*, has a rather poorly informative verb, which probably enables more extensive applications and hence more polysemy.

As regards syntax, the constructions do not all show the same degree of flexibility. 32 out of the 38 can be inserted freely in a sentence, like the constructions involving prototypically intransitive verbs. For instance, *blow it* can be inserted in the past (*they blew it*), in the imperative (*don't blow it*), after a modal auxiliary (*he will blow it*), in a question (*are we going to blow it?*), ... Only 6 belong to a larger structure that is more or less fossilized. 4 can only be used in the imperative (*come off it, confound it, damn it* and *hang it*). 1 has to be used with a negation (*push it: you shouldn't push it, don't push it*), and 1 is restricted to two constructions (*do it* conveying exasperation: *that does it / that did it*).

Turning to semantics, it remains to be determined why a speaker would use a *verb + it* construction rather than a *verb + NP* sequence with those transitive verbs. Indeed, in both cases, due to the transitive pattern, the *verb + object* sequence can be subdivided into [situation] + [element affected]. Again, the criterion is one of foregrounding. Because a personal pronoun does not give lexical information, it enables to foreground the semes of the verb, as is confirmed by a comparison between (17) and (18):

(17) Sethill, CEO of Frontier Silicon <u>whooped up</u> the benefits of his company's new product.
(18) (headline) Fun in the Sun – Revellers <u>whooped it up</u> one last time as a star-studded line-up brought the curtain down on the festival of fun that was T in the Park.

In (17), by using a free complement, the speaker indicates what is actually whooped up, which is therefore as important as the whooping up. Conversely, with the *verb + it* pattern (18), all that remains is the action (*whoop up*) and the idea that something was affected by it (*it*), thus foregrounding the action itself. This contrast applies to all the utterances in the corpus. Two other subsidiary reasons might be added for a minority of cases. One, which concerns only three phrases in the corpus, has to do with the sex taboo; hence a pronoun is used instead of an explicit NP in *make it* (for *make love*), *have it away* and *have it off (with sb)*. The other reason is specific to the verb *fight*:

(19) The senate dispatched their ambassadors to Alaric, desiring him to give them leave to <u>fight it</u> with him in the open field.

While *fight Ø* denotes an atelic event, with no hint as to how long it is to be performed, *fight it* applies the fighting to something, yielding a telic interpretation which can be glossed as "solve the problem by fighting".

Now that the properties of the two types of *verb + it* constructions have been studied, a few theoretical considerations as to the morphology of the pronoun can be addressed.

4. Morphological characteristics of the personal pronouns in *verb + it* constructions

The first characteristic to be accounted for is that of class. As noted in the introduction, the objective pronouns used in verbal constructions are all personal pronouns. This constraint is related to the procedural information that they encode. Following Cornish (1999: 259) and Rotgé and Lapaire (2004: 30), Gardelle (2010: 92) showed that personal pronouns are the default thematic pronouns. They merely indicate mental contact, in other words, giving the gender and number information is felt to be sufficient for the hearer to access the referent, or at least, in the case of our verbal constructions, to consider that what is being talked about is not problematic. All other pronouns carry more information: *this / that* imply an additional pointing towards the referent, the possessives add a relation to someone's sphere, relative pronouns indicate subordination, and interrogative pronouns encode an information deficit to be filled by the addressee. Personal pronouns are therefore the most appropriate pronouns for lexicalized phrases; speakers feel that they know what they are talking about, although they cannot point where the referent is to be accessed. Within the paradigm of personal pronouns, *it* is the default form, singular is the default number, and neuter is the default gender – the label *neuter* translates as "neither one nor the other", neither masculine nor feminine. It is therefore the form that most conveniently applies to an inanimate element which, besides, is not clearly identifiable. Interestingly, in French, for example, it is also a personal pronoun that is used in *verb + pronoun* constructions, for instance *elle l'a emporté sur son concurrent* or *il se la ramène*.

Another issue is that of gender. As stated in the introduction, because a referent is still felt to exist, gender alternation is found in some verbal constructions in nonstandard American and Canadian English. The alternation is between the neuter and the feminine, and chiefly concerns phrasemes with prototypically transitive verbs: *hit it / her up* (set off), *whoop it / her up* (maintain or arouse excitement / enthusiasm), *touch it / her off* (fire a weapon) and *get it / her made* (succeed in life). In addition to these, Steinbeck once uses *go her alone* in *The Grapes of Wrath* (1995 [1939]), although no authentic occurrence of this construction could be found. The question is whether the criteria for gender use in those phrasemes are the same as in free uses of the personal pronoun. In nonstandard English, use of the feminine signals that the referent is raised above the prototypical set of inanimates in order to signal an emotional involvement or a particular importance of the referent to the speaker (Gardelle forthcoming). This criterion holds for verbal constructions as well; for instance in (20), one reads:

(20) [thanks to] everyone from norman wells who treated us so fine. they sure know how to whoop her up. glenda and ken from ft.good hope, as always...

The adverb *sure* signals emotional involvement. *It* would have been possible instead of *her*, but seems to bring the enthusiasm one step below. As a consequence, gender alternation is restricted to verbs whose semantics allow such added closeness on the part of the speaker, either as a result of enthusiasm, exasperation or admiration. However, the use of the feminine is restricted by language register and region of use; *her* in verbal constructions was judged typical of "uneducated Americans", especially of southern rural areas, by American informants (Gardelle 2006: 483–489). That is why one finds instances of *whoop it up*, with the neuter pronoun, in utterances which, like (20), contain the adverb *sure* and convey obvious enthusiasm:

(21) Can you even remember the days BK (Before Kids) when you could just do whatever you wanted and did ? And now when you have time to yourself you get stuff done (scrapbooking, cleaning, videos, etc.) ? That's so funny... I remember I spent something like 8 hours watching biographies of Great Britain's Royal Family, LOL... / Woohoo ! We sure know how to whoop it up, LOL ! Hugs, V.

As a conclusion, all uses of a *verb* + *it* pattern are motivated by a single pattern of perception of the event. That event is viewed as a situation (in the sense of what is denoted by the verb) affecting an element, although that element is not specifically identifiable. In other words, different constructions reflect different modes of perception, as evidenced by verbs such as *fight*, which license three different argument realisations: *fight Ø* foregrounds the sole action, *fight it* applies the action to an unidentified element, while *fight sth* presents the action and the patient as equally important.

It has been proposed here that because the transitive pattern is a fundamental one in the mapping of semantic relations, it has led to overriding of the syntactic possibilities of individual verbs, on condition that the object *it* be not clearly referential. Thus, a typically intransitive verb that licenses idiomatic *it* cannot take an NP complement (as was noted, for instance, with *go it alone*: **go the project alone*, …). This fact would tend to suggest that the pronoun, far from being a "light" version of an NP, is in fact more fundamental in the grammar of the language than NPs. This conception of the pronoun, already put forward by Peirce (1893–1913) and, more recently, by Blanche-Benveniste et al. (1987), would need further exploration. More research is also needed to determine the extent of the influence of syntactic patterns on semantic interpretations in cases of overriding. The present study focused on intransitive verbs in phrasemes, but the phenomenon also occurs in non-lexicalized predicates with nouns that are borrowed without lexicalised class conversion to instantiate a verbal function. For instance, in 2010 commercials in Britain, no less than two brands used the process in their slogans: "Don't just book it. Thomas Cook it." (Thomas Cook), and "Find it… Get it… Argos it." (Argos).

Ecole Normale Supérieure de Lyon, France

Notes

Correspondence address: laure.gardelle@ens-lyon.fr

1. Gender alternation also occurs in some idioms with pronouns in subject position, such as *there she / it blows* in American and Canadian English, or *she/it's apples, she/it'll be jake* in Australian English.
2. The only two exceptions in the corpus are *go it alone* and *go it blind*, which are not quasi-synonymous with *go alone* and *go blind*.
3. There are three possible exceptions:
   – for *coach*, both variants are recorded around the same date (*coach Ø* 1630/ *coach it* c. 1632;).
   – for *bus* and *coquet*, the *it* variant was found in older documents than the intransitive use: *bus it* 1838 / *bus Ø* 1889; *coquet it* 1701 / *coquet Ø* 1792.
   It is difficult to determine, however, whether these are actually exceptions, or whether the data is restricted by the documents to which we have access today.
4. For *oar* and *trip*, however, the *it* variant is suggested to have appeared several centuries after the intransitive use (*oar Ø* 1616 / *oar it* 1894, *trip Ø* 1386 / *trip it* 1579).
5. "Situation" is meant here as what is denoted by the verb, and therefore as a hyperonym for actions, states, …, whereas "event" is understood as what is denoted by the whole clause.
6. In addition, three verbs out of the 36 also license an intransitive pattern: *fight* (*fight Ø / fight it / fight sth*), *move* (*move Ø / move it / move sth*), and *make up*

(*make up Ø / make it up / make sth up*, as in *make up lost ground*). For these, it is difficult to determine which construction is the initial one. According to the OED, the intransitive constructions are the oldest for *fight* (*fight Ø* c. 900, *fight sth* 1300, *fight it* 1769) and *move* (*move Ø* 1275, *move sth* 1382; *move it* is not mentioned), but not for *make up* (*make sth up* 1472, *make up Ø* 1711 and *make it up* 1860). What these data show, however, is that the *verb+ it* pattern is the most recent.
7. The only possible exception is *carry it* (in the sense of "win"), dated 1580 whereas the first occurrence of *carry sth* is recorded in 1607 and *carry the day* in 1685; this order might be linked to the limited sources of language use to which we have access today.
8. The only verb that is not truly dynamic is *have*, which merely denotes localisation; but in the context of the idioms, it implies acquiring a situation, and therefore can be considered as having a dynamic interpretation.

References

Abel, Beate. 2003. English idioms in the first language and second language lexicon: A dual representation approach. *Second Language Research* 19. 329–358.

Bennett, Paul. 1996. Compositionnalité et figement des locutions: étude comparative du français et de l'anglais. In Pierre Fiala, Pierre Lafon & Marie-France Piguet (eds.), *La locution, entre lexique, syntaxe et pragmatique: identification en corpus, traitement, apprentissage*, 11–17. Paris: Klinsieck.

Blanche-Benveniste, Claire, José Deulofeu, Jean Stefanini & Karel Van der Eynde. 1987. *Pronom et syntaxe: L'approche pronominale et son application en français*. 2nd edn. Paris: SELAF.

Burger, Harald, Dmitrij Dobrovol'skij, Peter Kühn & Neal R. Norrick. 2007. *Phraseology: An international handbook of contemporary research*. Berlin: Walter de Gruyter.

Chafe, Wallace. 1968. Idiomaticity as an anomaly within the Chomskyan paradigm. *Foundations of Language* 4. 109–127.

Cornish, Francis. 1999. *Anaphora, discourse and understanding*. Oxford: Oxford UP.

Cowie, Anthony P. 1994. Phraseology. In R.E. Asher (ed.), *The encyclopedia of language and linguistics*, 3168–3171. Oxford: Oxford UP.

Croft, William. 1986. *Lexical semantics*. Cambridge: Cambridge UP.

Croft, William & D. Alan Cruse. 2004. *Cognitive linguistics*. Cambridge: Cambridge UP.

Fellbaum, Christiane (ed.). 2007. *Idioms and collocations: Corpus-based linguistic and lexicographic studies*. London: Continuum.

Fillmore, Charles J., Kay Paul & Mary Catherine O'Connor. 1988. Regularity and idiomaticity in grammatical constructions: The case of let alone. *Language* 64. 501–38.

Fried, Mirjam & Jan-Ola Östman (eds.). 2004. *Construction grammar in a cross-language perspective*. Amsterdam: John Benjamins.

Gardelle, Laure. 2006. *Le genre en anglais moderne (XVIe siècle à nos jours): Le système des pronoms*. Paris: Paris IV-Sorbonne, doctoral dissertation.

Gardelle, Laure. 2010. Article défini, pronoms personnels de 3e personne et démonstratifs: Approche comparée de l'accès à la référence. *Anglophonia* 26. 92–104.

Gardelle, Laure. Forthcoming. The contribution of pronominal gender to the representation of hybrid linguistic identity. In Vanessa Guignery (ed.), *Hybridity: Forms and figures in literature and the visual arts*.

Goldberg, Adele E. 2006. *Constructions at work: The nature of generalization in language*. Oxford: Oxford UP.

Gries, Stefan Th. 2008. Phraseology and linguistic theory: A brief survey. In Sylviane Granger & Fanny Meunier (eds.), *Phraseology: An interdisciplinary perspective*, 3–25. Amsterdam: John Benjamins.

Huddleston, Rodney & Geoffrey K. Pullum. 2002. *The Cambridge grammar of the English language*. Cambridge: Cambridge UP.

Jackendoff, Ray S. 1975. Morphological and semantic regularities in the lexicon. *Language* 51. 639–671.

Kleiber, Georges. 1994. *Anaphores et pronoms*. Paris: Duculot.

Marantz, Alec P. 1984. *On the nature of grammatical relations*. Cambridge, Mass.: MIT Press.

Naciscione, Anita. 2010. *Stylistic use of phraseological units in discourse*. Amsterdam: John Benjamins.

Newmeyer, Frederick. 1974. The regularity of idiom behavior. *Lingua* 34. 327–42.

Nunberg, Geoffrey, Ivan A. Sag & Thomas Wasow. 1994. Idioms. *Language* 70 (3). 491–538.

Oxford English dictionary online edition. 2009. Oxford: Oxford UP. http://www.oed.com/ (accessed 2011 January).

Pankhurst, Rachel. 2001. Les unités verbales polylexicales: problèmes de repérage en traitement automatique. In Francis Tollis (ed.), *La locution et la périphrase du lexique à la grammaire. Actes des journées d'étude sur la locution organisées à l'université de Pau les 16 et 17 octobre 1998*, 55–63. Paris: L'Harmattan.

Peirce, Charles Sanders. 1998 [1893–1913]. *The essential Peirce: Selected philosophical writings Vol. 2. Peirce Edition Project (ed.)*. Bloomington: Indiana UP.

Rotgé, Wilfrid & Jean-Rémi Lapaire. 2004. *Réussir le commentaire grammatical de textes*. Paris: Ellipses.

Simatos, Isabelle. 1996. Référence et argumentalité du GN dans les locutions verbales. In Pierre Fiala, Pierre Lafon & Marie-France Piguet (eds.), *La locution, entre lexique, syntaxe et pragmatique: Identification en corpus, traitement, apprentissage*, 77–102. Paris: Klinsieck.

Steinbeck, John. 1995 [1939]. *The grapes of wrath*. London: Mandarine.

Svartengren, T. Hilding. 1927. The feminine gender for inanimate things in Anglo-American. *American Speech* 3. 83–113.

Book reviews

Hrisztalina Hrisztova-Gotthard: *Vom gedruckten Sprichwörterbuch zur interaktiven Sprichwortdatenbank.* Bern, Berlin, Bruxelles, Frankfurt am Main, New York, Oxford & Wien: Peter Lang, 2010. 247 pp. ISBN 978-3-0343-0523-5.

Hrisztova-Gotthard studied in Sofia, Bulgaria, followed by a research fellowship in Basel, Switzerland, and a doctorate in Pécs, Hungary. In her dissertation, *Vom gedruckten Sprichwörterbuch zur interaktiven Sprichwortdatenbank* (*From printed proverb dictionary to interactive proverb database*), she addresses phraseologists' common complaint about the poor representation of phrasemes in printed dictionaries. To resolve the issue, she proposes the use of interactive databases, making suggestions for the design of a multilingual version in Bulgarian, Hungarian, and German.

Contemporary lexicographers must decide whether or not to embrace the digital age. In the author's view, digital versions offer advantages on three levels, at least. First, since digital databases provide (almost) unlimited space to store significantly higher amounts of lexicographic information than traditional print dictionaries, they allow the inclusion of links to research papers, for instance. Next, they can be updated, modified, and expanded at any time to remain current and up-to-date. Finally, provided that adequate links are inserted, they make rapid access to a wide range of data possible. These aspects make digital databases attractive not only as reference tools but also for research.

Hrisztova-Gotthard's thesis opens with an introduction (Chapter 1) and ends with a conclusion (Chapter 6). The main body is structured into four parts. It contains a discussion of terminology in Chapter 2 where the author defines the terms "proverb" and "proverb dictionary" by making a distinction between proverbs and related phraseological units. This is followed by a chapter presenting several analyses of different monolingual and plurilingual proverb dictionaries and proverb collections to establish criteria for the structure and function of the multilingual proverb database.

Chapter 3 begins with a brief overview of the history of paremiography in German, Bulgarian and Hungarian from the 16th century to the present. This is followed by analyses of one current monolingual proverb dictionary in each of these languages (Dudenredaktion 2007, Tóthné Litovkina 2005, Stojkova 2007) and a number of multilingual dictionaries. To establish their advantages and shortcomings, Hrisztova-Gotthard discusses macro-structural, micro-structural, and medio-structural criteria. Proverb definition, classification, selection and configuration, as well as external retrieval structures are employed for the macro-structural analysis. Micro-structural aspects involve the content and structure of the dictionary articles, whereas the reference system covers the medio-structural dimension. Many of the issues mentioned here can be resolved by the use of digital databases. In terms of macro-structure, such databases provide sufficient space for definitions and selection criteria of data items, as well as for links to research and results from empirical paremiology. Provided that the data are annotated properly, they can be structured and displayed according to a wide range of criteria. In other words, users can search for all components alphabetically, but also for other criteria such as geographic reach, thematic fields, and so forth. By constrast, multilingual print proverb dictionaries have had to accept, in particular, a trade-off between the number of proverbs and the amount of information about them. Thus, digital databases have the unarguable advantage of virtually unlimited space, which permits the inclusion of traditionally neglected information, such as variants of proverbs and rate of familiarity. Moreover, digital references allow rapid access to data. The final part of Chapter 3 is concerned with computer-assisted paremiography. It introduces a couple of digital proverb databases, such as Matti Kuusi and Outi Lauhakangas' internet-based *International Type System of Proverbs* (http://lauhakan.home.cern.ch/lauhakan/cerp.html), and on-line proverb databases (e.g. http://www.afriprov.org/). Several more recent and equally relevant databases would also have to be mentioned here: e.g. the pentalingual *SprichWort-Plattform* (2008–2010, http://www.ids-mannheim.de/lexik/SprichWort/), created alongside this dissertation and on-line since 2010; *EPHRAS* (2004–2006, http://www.ephras.org/), a preliminary tetralingual project; or *sprichwoerter.net* (http://www.sprichwoerter.net/), a popular trilingual compilation.

The interactive database is described in Chapter 4. It first compiles the structural and functional criteria for multilingual proverb databases.

Hrisztova-Gotthard opts for a "maximalist" approach to the input of lexicographically relevant information to ensure the availability of copious data on proverbs in various languages (e.g. synchronous, diachronous, and diatopic variants, regional usage, stylistic register, frequency, interpretations, origin) as well as thematic classifications and combinations. The author mentions retrieval options that such databases should provide, not only for complete proverbs but also for their components (and inflectional forms), thematic categories, synonyms, antonyms and equivalents. This requires comprehensive data that are comparable across various languages, and also demands for highly time-consuming annotations of the proverb compilations. Data would originate from extant dictionaries and research literature. It is extremely unlikely, however, that direct interlingual comparison of data will be possible due to striking differences in terms of data basis and information content.

The presentation of the interactive database is followed by Chapter 5, which offers a few selected technological suggestions on how the theoretical considerations above might be realized. The author provides a few ideas on the technical implementation such as data tokenization or use of Unicode to record data from various different languages (leaving the rest in the hands of the database architect). She also suggests the time-consuming procedure of manual lemmatization to overcome the language-specificity of lemmatizers. Ontology is to guide the lexical-semantic categorization of lemmata.

Hrisztova-Gotthard's dissertation is concerned with the highly topical issue of lexicography, which offers many new opportunities at the shift from classical printed dictionaries to digital databases. Her analysis of a number of relevant proverb dictionaries provides an interesting insight into the paremiographic standards of three linguistic traditions, from which she condenses the criteria for a multi-lingual proverb database, trying to express these new possibilities at the macro-, micro- and meso-structural levels. As suggested by the subtitle of the thesis, *On a linguistic and lexicographic concept for multilingual proverb databases*, the book is of major interest to scholars who are about to establish a (multilingual) phraseological database. However, with regard to the concrete implementation of such a far-reaching project, the problem of the provenance of comparable material remains unresolved. So far, printed dictionaries have been the primary source of digital databases. In the future, it will be essential to access new pools of lexicographic information – (comparable) corpus and survey data – in order for such databases to provide significantly more added value than a mere accumulation of existing dictionary information. This will make them of even greater interest as a basis for research, and it will permit the more detailed study of equivalence relations.

BRITTA JUSKA-BACHER
Correspondence address: britta.juska-bacher@unibas.ch

References

Dudenredaktion (ed.). 2007. *Das große Buch der Zitate und Redewendungen*. Mannheim/Leipzig/Wien/Zürich: Duden.
Tóthné Litovkina, Anna. 2005. *Magyar közmond'st'r. Közmond'sok értelmező szótára példakkal szemléltetve*. Budapest: Tinta.
Stojkova, Stefana. 2007. *Balgarski poslovici i pogovorki*. Sofia: IK Kolibri.

Harald Burger: *Phraseologie. Eine Einführung am Beispiel des Deutschen*, 4., neu bearbeitete Auflage (Grundlagen der Germanistik 36). Berlin: Erich Schmidt, 2010. 239 pp. ISBN 978-3-503-12204-2 (Pb.).

In 1998, Harald Burger first published his introduction to phraseology, which has served as a reference book to many a researcher and student ever since. Aiming at constantly improving *Phraseologie. Eine Einführung am Beispiel des Deutschen*, he has now presented its fourth edition already. In the foreword Burger clearly defines the standards his work is supposed to establish: he stresses the need to introduce terminology, as well as criteria of analysis and categorization, on the one hand, and to provide an account of the actual use of phraseological units in spoken and written language, on the other. He also promises to provide a balance between academic scholarship and readability, in addition to illustrating the theoretical discussion with authentic examples.

The first chapter of the book is dedicated to presenting the main characteristics of phraseological units, namely polylexicality, fixedness, and idiomaticity. The author goes into detail about various aspects of fixedness, also showing that it only constitutes a relative characteristic, since phraseological units do allow for various kinds of intentional and unintentional variation. Burger emphasizes that idiomaticity is optional and applies only to the very heart of phraseology – idioms.

Chapter 2 introduces a possible classification of phraseological units. It ranges from giving a basic categorization to presenting specific types of multi-word units, such as binominals, fixed comparisons or winged words.

In doing so, the author largely relies on the terminology used in Burger et al. (1982), but claims that he has updated it where necessary.

The next two chapters deal with semantic issues, which constitute the main focus of Burger's introduction. Superbly, the author works his way through the often confusing terminology involving the semantics of phraseological units. Anyone eager to understand, say, the difference between *Motiviertheit* ('motivatedness'), *Motivierung* ('motivation') and *Motivierbarkeit* ('motivatability') (Chapter 3) or between *Bildlichkeit* ('imagery') and *Bildhaftigkeit* ('figurativity') (Chapter 4), will undoubtedly benefit from consulting these elaborations. Chapter 4 – *Idiom und Metapher* – focuses on a cognitive perspective concerning the motivation of phraseological units, mainly with regard to Conceptual Metaphor Theory (Lakoff and Johnson 1980). However, Burger warns the reader against an overestimation of cognitive factors in the description of source domains, claiming that a large number of idioms cannot be explained in terms of the very global system of conceptual metaphors. The chapter closes with a description of the differences between metaphoric idioms and single-word metaphors.

Burger then continues by taking a closer look at proverbs, which he positions within the field of phraseology. In this detailed fifth chapter, the author not only comments on the basic characteristics of proverbs and on the similarities and differences between proverbs and other types of phraseological units, but also on the change of function that they have experienced over the centuries. He clearly denies the widespread opinion that proverbs are on the verge of dying out and illustrates how current ways of using them (modifications, anti-proverbs, etc.) keep them alive enduringly.

Chapter 6 presents a detailed discussion of diachronic aspects pf phraseology. The author highlights three possible ways in which diachrony can become relevant to the language user: first of all, when users come across a completely unfamiliar multi-word expression and want its meaning defined; secondly, when they are intrigued by the image underlying a specific phraseological unit and wish to find out more about its etymological source and development; and thirdly, when language users are going through an old text and are confronted with an expression that somehow seems familiar to them, but whose meaning or usage does not correspond to its current one. It is this problem in particular that Burger expands upon, He shows that while a considerable number of German phraseological units have remained stable over the centuries, an even larger proportion has undergone formal or semantic changes, whereas only a few have disappeared entirely.

The seventh chapter is a fairly heterogeneous compilation of considerations revolving around the topic 'phraseologisms in texts'. It starts off with a short passage on where they are usually placed in a text and then briefly addresses the issue of phraseology and cohesion before taking a closer look at modification. Burger lists three forms of modification, dependent on whether form and/or meaning are concerned. The presumption is made that mainly phraseological units with two levels, i.e. with a literal and a phraseological reading, undergo modification. This, however, is clearly open to debate, as on-going studies on modifications carried out by this reviewer suggest the contrary. What follows is a description of the use of phraseological units in specific text genres: in television scripts, in specialized texts, and in children's books.

In his eighth chapter, the author criticizes the way phraseological units are still treated within modern dictionaries. He states that, even though phraseography has clearly pointed out its claims to lexicography, none of the current general dictionaries has sufficiently taken them into account. Burger lists the questions that dictionary users might have in mind when they consult such compilations to find information about phraseological units: How do they find out that they are actually dealing with a phraseological unit?, Under which lemma do they find a specific multi-word expression?, What does it mean?, etc. Burger illustrates convincingly how current dictionaries fail to answer these essential questions.

Phraseologie. Eine Einführung am Beispiel des Deutschen ends with a chapter on the regional differences within German phraseology. Burger – himself born in Germany, but today a Swiss citizen – shows that there is a need to distinguish between expressions that are solely used within Germany and those specific to Austria and German-speaking Switzerland on the one hand, and those which are used among speakers of all three countries on the other. He explains that this distinction is particularly important in connection with phraseography. But the author not only illustrates the regional differences that exist, notably by referring to his own data on Helvetisms, but he also comments on various sociolinguistic aspects of these differences as well as on the stylistic functions of Helvetisms.

In comparison to the third edition, only a few changes have been made. Although the layout is very similar, the new edition is a little more appealing, since a larger number of key expressions have been set in bold print and are therefore more eye-catching. What is more important is the fact that every chapter now ends with a short summary in a separate information box. This clearly enhances the book's readability, particularly for students who need a first orientation in phraseology. At the end of each chapter, Burger also gives suggestions for further reading, which is one of the major assets of the new edition, notably since the author has considered both the 'classics' dealing with the particular topics and the latest studies published in the diverse fields that he discusses. The current updates, despite being few in number, contribute to the general impression *Phraseologie* conveys to the reader: Burger has lived up to his own expectations in striking the right balance between scholarliness and readability. Explanations, descriptions, and arguments are always simple enough to assure comprehensibility, which makes the book a welcome aid for every seminar on phraseology. However, Burger spares us the simplistic approach and patronizing style of a potential 'Phraseology for Dummies' unfortunately found in many introductions to linguistic subfields. What is more, the author provides a very comprehensive insight into German phraseology, clearly going beyond what one would expect to be thoroughly treated in an introduction. This is particularly true for the last two chapters on phraseography and regional differences. Thus, the book excellently manages to present all the basic technical terms that the reader might come across on a first encounter with phraseology. It also shows where future research could make a valuable contribution and might consequently constitute a suitable starting point for current or prospective phraseologists. It can therefore be concluded that Burger's work is a pleasure to read – not only for the information it presents, but also because of its layout and accessible style.

Despite its superior quality, I would nevertheless like to make some suggestions for future editions. Although Burger includes some of the latest studies in the field of phraseology, cognitive theories are neglected throughout almost the entire book. Only Chapter 4.1 (*Die kognitive Perspektive*) briefly takes into account psycholinguistic and cognitive studies, mainly those by George Lakoff and Raymond W. Gibbs (see, e.g., Gibbs 1994; Lakoff 1987). However, the last decade or so has clearly shown that Cognitive Linguistics has much more to offer to phraseology than Lakoff & Johnson's 1980) approach to conceptual metaphor. For example, one could mention the application of Conceptual Integration Theory (Fauconnier & Turner 2002) in the analysis of phraseological modifications. In addition, some of the elaborations in the second part of the book could be more concise: it would seem advantageous for Burger to abandon some of his illustrative examples in a series or even some of his subchapters. This suggestion goes for passages such as in 7.3.3, where the use of phraseological units and their modifications in children's books are described in great detail, or for the subchapters in 6.2, where the description of phraseology in older texts amounts to a total of eighteen pages, which, in my view, is far more detailed than necessary for an introduction to phraseology.

Irrespective of the question whether one might agree with the author in all aspects, Burger's introduction to German phraseology is decisively an excellent example of how such a book can meet various needs. On the one hand, it manages to be a helpful and basic tool for beginners, while keeping its promise to be readable throughout. This is why it is, at least in my opinion, particularly apt as a course book for seminars. On the other hand, the scope of this book goes far beyond what one would expect from an introduction to phraseology, and this renders this monograph equally interesting and useful to the informed reader. In a great many respects the fourth edition of *Phraseologie. Eine Einführung am Beispiel des Deutschen* is therefore highly recommendable and deserves being assigned a prominent position on the bookshelf of anyone working in the field of German phraseology.

SYLVIA JAKI
Correspondence address: sylvia.jaki@lipp.lmu.de

References

Burger, Harald, Annelies Buhofer & Ambros Sialm. 1982. *Handbuch der Phraseologie*. Berlin: Walter de Gruyter.
Fauconnier, Gilles & Mark Turner. 2002. *The way we think: Conceptual blending and the mind's hidden complexities.* New York: Basic Books.
Gibbs, Raymond W. 1994. *The poetics of mind.* Cambridge: Cambridge University Press.
Lakoff, George. 1987. *Women, fire, and dangerous things: What categories reveal about the mind.* Chicago: University of Chicago Press.
Lakoff, George & Mark Johnson. 1980. *Metaphors we live by.* Chicago: University of Chicago Press.

Meng Ji: *Phraseology in corpus-based translation studies* (New Trends in Translation Studies 1). Bern, Berlin, Bruxelles, Frankfurt am Main, New York, Oxford & Wien: Peter Lang, 2010. 231 pp.
ISBN 978-3-03911-550-1 (Pb.).

The book *Phraseology in corpus-based translation studies* by Meng Ji was published as the first volume in Peter Lang's new series *New Trends in Translation Studies* edited by Jorge Díaz Cintas. The launch of this series confirms the consolidation of Translation Studies as an independent discipline with thriving research activity and it is heartening to see phraseology making its way to the very first volume.

Meng Ji's book is a stylistic study of two contemporary direct translations of *Don Quijote* into Mandarin Chinese. *Don Quijote*, which enjoys high popularity in China, has been studied as a political tract rather than an entertaining comedy (Zhang, quoted in Ji p. 7). Ji analyses the translations by Yang Jiang (1978) and Liu Jingsheng (1995), both of which were well-received but are separated by a span of almost 20 years and have a different status and *skopos*. Yang's translation was the first direct translation into Mandarin Chinese although several relay translations from French and English existed before. She is an acclaimed literary translator and an academic who translated mainly from English and French while her knowledge of Spanish was limited when she first approached the text. However, her translation is the most published Chinese version of *Don Quijote* and is included in school textbooks as a standard translation interestingly, in the period 1990–2001.

The first chapter explains the rationale for corpus construction and contains a thorough and honest discussion of technical problems with the segmentation and alignment of Chinese texts, offering some practical solutions which might be of use for researchers of ideographic languages. The author discusses the application of an adjusted segmentation tool which is both statistics-driven and lexis-supplemented due to the fact that Chinese sentences do not carry word delimiters and segmentation produces mismatches. The deficiencies of currently available corpus tools are particularly noticeable in the case of the alignment of unrelated languages as was the problem here with 17th-century Castilian and contemporary Mandarin Chinese. Even though both languages mainly use SVO-type sentences, they have different modification and subordination patterns. As a result, a complex subordinate Castilian sentence is usually split up into shorter sentences in Chinese. This requires arduous manual alignment with the one-to-multiple model.

Chapter 2 discusses data retrieval, problem-oriented annotation (using a pragmatic rather than a traditional approach) and classifies the four-character expressions chosen by the author as the object of study. The four-character expressions constitute a salient, complex, and heterogeneous phraseological category of rhetorical devices associated with stylistic elegance and formality, as well as "prosodic musicality, structural equilibrium or symmetry, and semantic succinctness of Chinese" (Xu, quoted in Ji p. 56). Ji identifies seven types of these expressions and classifies them into two big groups of compositional and non-compositional structures.

Compositional expressions are further divided into schematic ones (morphologically patterned words, syntactically schematic phrases, structurally symmetrical phrases, and semantically bipartite phrases) and non-schematic ones (shortened phrases) while non-compositional ones are divided into archaic and figurative idioms (p. 57). The discussion next focuses on idioms, which are used flexibly and are subject to syntactic and structural variation. Four-character expressions include 20–25% idioms, while approximately 90% of idioms are four-character expressions (p. 59), which adds to the complexity of this phraseological category. A surprising feature of this category of idioms is that a large number of them, the so-called archaic idioms, may not have a figurative interpretation and are not semantically transparent as they contain archaic function or content words or grammatical structures from Ancient Chinese. These structures are marked by syntactic underspecificity and the functional flexibility of content words. As for figurative idioms, they include metaphors, metonymies, similes, synecdoches, and hyperboles (p. 68). The main focus of the book is on such figurative and archaic idioms.

Next the author moves on to discuss quantifying style, stylometry, and corpus stylistics in literary studies. Ji argues that the existing studies by translation stylisticians show "limited versatility and a certain lack of sophistication in argumentation" by focusing mainly on function words, punctuation and syntactic information and neglecting lexis and phraseology (pp. 80–81). This is partly due to technical problems. Moreover, it is argued that the studies rarely move from descriptive data to inferential statistics. This may well be true. However, Ji does not document these points of critique. Hence, it is unclear whom she refers to. The literature review only comprises three pages and it would benefit from more detail. In general, the author discusses theoretical issues very perfunctorily, which I find to be a major shortcoming of the book (among its many virtues). Apart from a brief mention of Kenny's (2001) study into hapax legomena and normalisation (pp. 6 and 50) and a very selective list of research into translationese (p. 47), there is no overview of how phraseology has been treated in Translation Studies so far. For example, she does not address the issue of T-universals, i.e. the relation of textual fit between translated and non-translated language (Chesterman 2004: 7), which is a curious omission. In particular, one would expect some discussion of Tirkkonen-Condit's unique items hypothesis (2004: 177) and Mauranen's untypical collocation hypothesis (2006: 97), according to which translated language tends to be marked by distorted phraseological patterns and their unnatural distribution.

I also have some reservations about the title *Phraseology in corpus-based translation studies*, which, given the content of the book, is misleading. First of all, the author discusses only corpus-based literary Translation Studies, which, due to the lack of theoretical discussion, is not applicable to specialised Translation Study. Ji's focus is very narrow: she is interested in the analysis of style variation (or distinct stylistic profiles) related to the use of figurative and archaic language. Therefore, the use of a very broad label 'phraseology' in the title seems unfounded as the author does not discuss collocations or other less fixed patterns, which still remain one of the most under-researched categories in literary and specialised Translation Studies.

The third chapter identifies three major differences in the distribution of translated phraseological patterns due to personal stylistic preferences: Yang uses more morpho-syntactically patterned expressions (semantically bipartite phrases, morphologically patterned phrases, and structurally symmetrically phrases), whereas Liu tends to use more figurative language and archaic idioms. An interesting component of the analysis is an attempt to account for these differences by taking into consideration the time factor and recent changes of Chinese linguistic habits. Ji uses two comparable corpora, the *Lancaster Corpus of Mandarin Chinese* and the *UCLA Chinese Corpus*, to demonstrate shifts in idiom distribution across genres – namely, the growing use of idioms in fiction and their diminishing use in the official register and the news (p. 106). Liu's approach produces "a much more conventionalized version in the target language" (p. 111).

Chapter 4 shows two different strategies in bridging the cultural gap related to *Don Quijote*'s figurative language, the richness of which may be opaque to the target audience. Yang seems to opt for foreignisation with her more literal approach of word-by-word translation supplemented with footnotes. Liu's approach is evaluated as more creative and target-text-oriented, which in literary translation studies is usually referred to as domestication. Liu is less visible as a translator by assimilating idiomatic expressions into natural Chinese idioms and archaisms which also enrich the target text with local cultural connotations. As a result, Liu's strategy "brings about a flavour to the target text this is definitely more idiomatic and vivacious" (p. 127). This chapter contains an engaging discussion with ample illustrations of cross-cultural differences in the conceptualisation of moral integrity, philosophy of life, and emotions.

Having identified major stylistic traits, Ji applies corpus-linguistic statistical tools, such as a correlation test and a linear regression test, "to investigate the rationale" behind the different distribution of figurative and archaic idioms in the translations (p. 143). Yet this objective does not seem to be investigated; the author in fact focuses on the impact of similar source text devices and on testing the hypothesis of potential (over)reliance of Liu on the earlier translation by Yang (to find out that Liu's use of archaisms is distinct from that of Yang). As to the impact of ST (source text) devices, the author arrives at a rather obvious and predictable conclusion that a TT (target text) figurative expression is more likely to be triggered by a ST figurative rather than by a non-figurative expression. The tests however are quite useful in pinning down the differences in distribution of figurative and archaic idioms. The distribution of archaisms in Liu's translation is further elaborated in the next chapter with the application of context-motivated theory, Biber's (1994) quantitative study of register variation and Categorical Principal Component Analysis. Ji attempts to find the rationale behind the stylistic variation and analyses the cognitive dimension to find co-textual factors that may trigger style shifting.

Overall, the book is lucid and enjoyable to read. It provides ample explanations that help to follow the line of reasoning. Although Ji believes that "the significance of this corpus project for future studies will be precisely in the way technical and linguistic problems have been identified and pragmatically resolved" (p. 43), some of the solutions seem to be applicable to languages which have a similarly complex phraseological category as the Chinese four-character expressions. This category, as Ji acknowledges herself, reflects "a unique phrasal predilection of the Chinese people" (p. 76). Nevertheless, the book may be regarded as a promising attempt to integrate a number of approaches in order to develop an interdisciplinary corpus-based methodology to research style variation related to the use of figurative and archaic language in literary translation.

Łucja Biel
Correspondence address: anglb@ug.edu.pl

References

Biber, Douglas. 1994. *Sociolinguistic perspectives on register*. Oxford: Oxford University Press.
Chesterman, Andrew. 2004. Hypotheses about translation universals. In Gyde Hansen, Kirsten Malmkjær & Daniel Gile (eds.), *Claims, changes and challenges in translation studies: Selected contributions from the EST congress, Copenhagen 2001*, 1–13. Amsterdam & Philadelphia: John Benjamins.
Kenny, Dorothy. 2001. *Lexis and creativity in translation: A corpus-based study*. Manchester: St. Jerome.
Liu, Jingsheng. 1995. *Don Quijote de La Mancha*. Guang Xi: Li River Publisher.

Mauranen, Anna. 2006. Translation universals. In Keith Brown (ed.), *Encyclopedia of language and linguistics*, Vol. 13, 93–100. Oxford: Elsevier.
Tirkkonen-Condit, Sonja. 2004. Unique items – over- or under-represented in translated language? In Anna Mauranen & Pekka Kujamäki (eds.), *Translation universals: Do they exist?* 177–184. Amsterdam & Philadelphia: John Benjamins.
Yang, Jiang. 1978. *Don Quijote de la Mancha.* Beijing: People's Literature Publisher.

Christine Fourcaud: *Phraseologie und Sprachtransfer bei Arte-Info* (Im Medium fremder Sprachen und Kulturen 15). Bern, Berlin, Bruxelles, Frankfurt am Main, New York, Oxford & Wien: Peter Lang: Peter Lang, 2009. 451 pp. ISBN 978-3-631-56699-2.

This monograph presents the author's doctoral dissertation obtained from the *Universität des Saarlandes*, Germany. It investigates phraseology and language transfer in a bilingual TV programme of the French-German television channel *Arte*. The study breaks new ground with the analysis of the French and German phraseological units used in this TV programme. By focussing on the news programme *Arte-Info*, the author scrutinises a special text type that has not been investigated in a systematic way before. To do so, she established a large database of 1000 phraseological units extracted from the news broadcast during a period of four months, from October 1999 to January 2000. The phraseological units are analysed according to three parameters: text type specifics, discursive situatedness, and thematic fixedness. The study examines, inter alia, important questions such as: What discursive strategies have been applied by using phraseological units in this journalistic genre? and Which functions do these strategies have?

The book consists of five chapters. Chapter 1 (pp. 15–115) introduces the research object, describes the state-of-the-art in this research domain, and presents the methodology. The next three chapters are structured according to the three analytical dimensions outlined above. Chapter 2 (pp. 117–208) discusses the text type specifics in the four main sections of the analysed news programme: news headlines, news overview, introduction/ presentation, and reports. Chapter 3 (pp. 209–313) focuses on the discursive situatedness. The subjects of this chapter revolve around the practice of translation, the distribution of the phraseological units, the differences of phraseological usage in the German and French versions, as well as the text type differences. Chapter 4 (pp. 315–394) discusses the phenomenon of thematic fixedness, i.e. it explores the subjects that are rich in phraseological units, and compares them to the ones which are poor in them. Finally, Chapter 5 (pp. 395–403) draws a conclusion.

Chapter 1 provides a thorough overview of the actual state of research in the special fields of both 'phraseology and text' and 'interlingual phraseology'. Moreover, there are some important comments on translation research, text and discourse analysis, as well as media science. The author follows the definition of phraseology by Burger (2010), which is centred about the features of polylexicality, fixedness, and idiomaticity. Although she also takes neologisms into account, she abandons the often used definitional criterion of lexicalization. In addition, she only considers referential phraseological units, and excludes structural and communicative phrasemes, the two other main types of phrasemes according to Burger. Structural phrasemes, such as *in Bezug auf, sowohl – als auch*, are rarely thematised as phrasemes in the relevant literature. However, communicative phrasemes, including formulaic expressions (e.g., *Guten Morgen, ich meine*), could be important research objects in the investigation of television news programmes. Unfortunately, they are excluded from Fourcaud's analysis. The restriction of the research object to 'phraseology in the narrow sense' (as defined through polylexicality, fixedness, and idiomaticity) also prevents the author from including non-idiomatic collocations.

With regard to the research methodology, it is to be appreciated that the author employs several approaches: deductive and inductive methods as well as quantitative and qualitative analyses. After presenting the methodological considerations, the author then introduces and explains the three dimensions of analysis: text type specifics, discursive situatedness, and thematic fixedness.

Chapter 2 discusses the text type specifics of the phrasemes. In the news headlines, pictorial idiomatic and partially idiomatic verbal and nominal constructions such as *am Scheideweg stehen* or *dans tous ses états* predominate. The rhetorical possibility of employing phrasemes for pictorial remotivations that work on the level of connotation is to be emphasized here. Moreover, remotivations of phrasemes on the sound and the pictorial level increase the thematic expressiveness of headlines. By contrast, both the brevity and the concentrated nature of the news overviews do not favour the use of pictorial phrasemes and idioms, as the author states. As a result, in this text type one can find slightly idiomatic and mostly motivated phrasemes, e.g. *Euro-Zone* or *coup de frein*. In the presentation part of the programme, phrasemes are not applied in order to provide coherence, but they primarily perform an appeal function, which coincides with the pragmatic intention of introducing the programme. In the reports, the presence of interviews affects the increased presence of phrasemes like *bis an die Zähne bewaffnet sein* and *coup de théâtre*. They are also confirmed by the 'eyewitness character' of the reports.

Chapter 3 first discusses the influence of the translation practice on the distribution of the phraseological units. When interpreting, the interpreter adopts only phrasemes that are congruous with the basic information or those that have total equivalents in the target language. This strategy is pursued in order to make the topic of the presentation more simple and comprehensible. According to the study's results, translators are more creative than interpreters with regard to the usage of phraseological units. Deverbalisation induces the translator to produce pictorial translations. The author shows that non-pictorial phrasemes are translated with equivalents both in form and content, while semantically unmotivated expressions are reproduced with a higher degree of creativity. As to differences between language version and text type, the audio-visual rhetoric has to be emphasized. Fourcaud claims that the rhetorical strategies pursued in the programme would give the opportunity of remotivating the phrasemes. However, hardly any examples of remotivated phrasemes can be found in the corpus.

Text relation processes are described by applying the model of Gréciano (1987), who differentiates between synonym progression, antonym progression, and language game modification, as far as the text progression through phrasemes is concerned. The most frequent processes in the corpus are synonym and antonym progression. The less frequent occurrence of language game modification is due to the objective and factual form of presentation in the examined news programme. The comparison of two different text types in the German and French language versions for the same programme, i.e. having the same audio and image set, is a very instructive part of this chapter. The different *skopos* of the German and French film reports (*Filmberichte/commentaires*) is the reason for the higher density of full idiomatic phrasemes in *commentaires*. In contrast to the objectivity and factual nature of the German text type *Filmbericht*, the French text type *commentaire* is rather opinion-based and more entertaining. Hence, the latter permits the usage of more idioms. Furthermore, the high proportion of winged words in the interviews, which are part of the *Filmberichte/commentaries*, is striking. As can be seen from the examples discussed by the author, these authentic and understandable phraseme types with intertextual indications are placed as conclusions, as supports of claims, and as a strategy to spare the effort of argumentation.

Thematic fixedness constitutes the subject of Chapter 4. Phrasemes are mostly used in the context of emotionally charged topics (e.g. political scandals). The investigation, however, provides a surprising result. Analysing the programmes centred about EU policy – the eastward growth of the European Community in particular – it is shown that very few phrasemes can be found in the news on this topic. The author assumes that the editors refrain from employing phraseological units in favour of presenting reports without polemicised discussions. Another news topic investigated by the author is culture. In the cultural programme section, a great number of phrasemes occur. This is partly due to the soft-news character of these broadcasts. Comparing the German and French versions of the programme, German phrasemes are regularly transferred into French. This can most likely be explained by the fact that French reports are very sensitive to German phrasemes.

Fourcaud's monograph is an absolute novelty at the interface of text linguistics and phraseology. It covers new terrain because, to my knowledge, there are no other publications dealing with the phraseological and text linguistic aspects of bilingual German-French TV programmes, let alone studies that systematically take into account all the dimensions discussed in this book. The author draws three main conclusions from her research: first, the usage of phrasemes is text type specific; second, it is motivated by its discursive situatedness; and finally, it is thematically fixed. Diagrams and schemas help the reader to follow the author's arguments and discussions. Pictures of film sequences and a great many examples nicely illustrate the described phenomena.

As the author states in the conclusion, the results of her dissertation can be applied both in native-language teaching and the teaching of German and French as foreign languages. The empirical findings are also supported by statements and comments made by journalists, translators and interpreters whom the author interviewed within the framework of her research project. Therefore, this interdisciplinary study should not only be useful for linguists interested in text linguistics and phraseology, but also for journalists, translators, interpreters, and teachers to whom this book can be recommended as well.

TAMÁS KISPÁL
Correspondence address: kispal@lit.u-szeged.hu

References

Burger, Harald. 2010. *Phraseologie: Eine Einführung am Beispiel des Deutschen*. 4., neu bearbeitete Auflage. Berlin: Erich Schmidt.
Gréciano, Gertrud. 1987. Idiom und Text. *Deutsche Sprache* 15. 193–208.